*MARTIN NOTH*

# LEVITICUS

old
Test
ament
lib
Rary

*MARTIN NOTH*

# LEVITICUS

## A COMMENTARY

Revised Edition

The Westminster Press
Philadelphia

Translated by J. E. Anderson from the German
*Das dritte Buch Mose, Leviticus*
(Das Alte Testament Deutsch 6)
published 1962 by Vandenhoeck & Ruprecht,
Göttingen

PUBLISHED BY THE WESTMINSTER PRESS ®
Philadelphia, Pennsylvania

Printed in the United States of America


9  8  7  6  5  4  3  2  1

Library of Congress Cataloging in Publication Data

Noth, Martin, 1902-1968.
    Leviticus: a commentary.

    (The Old Testament library)
    Rev. translation of Das dritte Buch Mose, Leviticus.
    1. Bible. O.T. Leviticus — Commentaries. I. Bible.
O.T. Leviticus. English. Revised standard. 1977.
II. Title. III. Series.
BS1255.3.N613 1977      222'.13'077      77-7654
ISBN 0-664-20774-X

# CONTENTS

# PREFACE

THE BOOK OF Leviticus is one of the little-read books of the Old Testament. This is understandable, for it deals predominantly with cultic matters in a way which seems very monotonous. Closer examination, however, shows that this book is one that particularly reveals something of the living variety and historical development of the whole system of worship in Ancient Israel, a cultic worship which was a central element in her life. The present commentary attempts by means of the text to make clear the actual life and the historical changes in the cultus of Ancient Israel.

I should like to thank Dr Rudolf Smend for his steady and patient help in correcting the proofs.

*Bonn, September 1962*                                      M. NOTH

# TRANSLATOR'S NOTE

T HE ORIGINAL COMMENTARY was based on the author's own translation of Leviticus. The English edition prints the Revised Standard Version, though in a few cases where it has seemed most convenient small modifications have been made to conform to the text presupposed by the author in his commentary. Footnotes indicate all such deviations. The paragraphing of the RSV has also been modified where necessary to correspond to the subdivisions used by the author. The English chapter and verse enumeration has been followed throughout. This deviates from the Hebrew text in chs. 5 and 6. A paragraph mark (¶) against a biblical reference indicates that the text at this point has undergone later revision and that reference is made to what the author regards as the more original form of the text.

An English original would almost certainly have been written in shorter sentences; but it has often not proved possible to break up the material without displacing or destroying the long parentheses and elaborate cross-references which are such a valuable element in the commentary.

Kittel's *Biblia Hebraica* (3rd edition and later) is referred to as 'BH'.


# PUBLISHER'S NOTE

For the second impression the translation has been carefully scrutin-ized and a number of inaccuracies have been rectified.

# I

## INTRODUCTION

### 1. THE NAME AND STRUCTURE OF THE BOOK

THE 'THIRD BOOK of Moses' is named in the traditional syna-
gogue text after the first word *wayyiqrā'* (= 'and he called'). This
follows a widespread custom of the ancient Near East (cf. Noth,
*Exodus*, p. 9). In the Septuagint, the oldest translation of the Old
Testament into Greek, it has the title *Leuitikon*, and hence in the Latin
Vulgate 'Liber Leviticus', 'the Levitical (Book)'; and on this rests the
name that has become customary in English usage—'Leviticus'
(abbrev. Lev.). In this connection the term 'levitical' has a broad
sense covering all that relates to ritual worship, for the Levites occupied an important position in post-exilic times as a minor order
within the priestly body and the priests themselves claimed descent
from 'Levi'. However, the Book of Leviticus is not 'levitical' in the
strict sense, for it deals hardly at all with Levi and the Levites; less, in
fact, than any other book of the Pentateuch. Only in one passage,
25.32–34, are the Levites named, and there not with reference to their
ritual functions, but with regard to the special conditions governing
their land-tenure. With ritual worship, however, the Book of Leviticus
is much concerned: it forms, with its frequent religious celebrations
and its requirements for the priestly body and for the Israelites, the
main subject-matter of the book. In this respect the book is in large
measure a unity.

Leviticus forms part of the whole complex of the Pentateuch, the
'five Books of Moses', and in particular of its great theme—'the
appearance of God at Sinai'. The whole Pentateuch is a narrative
work; and Leviticus has accordingly a narrative framework, here
extremely simple, Israel being envisaged throughout the book in the
same situation, namely sojourning at Sinai. The narrative framework

therefore only predominates in the quite short stereotyped introductory and concluding formulae, which say that 'Yahweh spoke to Moses at Sinai'. In these, Moses is given the task of mediator (cf. Ex. 20.18–21), appointing him to receive divine instructions which he is constantly and expressly commanded to pass on to the group to which the instructions are directed, Aaron (and his sons) as priests, or to the whole of the Israelites. By far the greater number of sections in Leviticus are introduced in this way. Thus the book consists preponderantly of a large number of divine instructions of varying scope, simply linked together by the constantly recurring introductory formula; so much so that the book, considered first solely from the point of view of arrangement, appears to have little coherence. Few passages depart from this general framework. This is especially true of the complex chs. 8–10. Chapter 8.1 also begins with the usual introductory formula; but at once in v. 2 it becomes clear that Moses, in this case, is not to hand on an instruction, but himself to do something; and in the next verse we are told what Moses, commissioned by God, then did (it is the matter of the institution of Aaron and his sons to the priestly office). To this is connected the narrative in ch. 9 of the presentation of Israel's first great sacrifices accomplished by Aaron with the assistance of his sons. Finally in ch. 10 we have the narrative of a ritual incident connected with these first sacrifices, which then provides occasion for some special directions, given partly by Moses and partly by Yahweh himself. Beyond this point the pattern of instruction is only once interrupted by a piece of narrative, namely in 24.10–23. Here, however, the narrative only provides the occasion and the frame for divine instructions generally valid, beyond the particular concrete issue. In any case, 24.10–23 forms a special and peculiar section (cf. below p. 179), not important for the structure of the book. In practice, then, we have only to reckon with the complex chs. 8–10 as a narrative division within the book.

## 2. LITERARY CRITICISM AND TRADITION HISTORY

Passing from an examination of the formal structure to an analysis of the content of the book, one quickly notices within the apparently monotonous framework a clear inner articulation of the whole. The first seven chapters form a unity in so far as they deal specially with the instructions for sacrifice, which go into considerable detail. Instructions for sacrifice may be given from different points of view; and different points of view are indeed represented in Lev. 1–7. On the one hand chs. 1–6.7 put together all that the 'layman' bringing an offering needs to know; on the other hand chs. 6.8–7.38 formulate the professional knowledge required for the priest presenting the sacrifice. Again, chs. 1–3 merely lay down the ritual of sacrificial procedure; chs. 4–6.7 raise the question of occasions for particular offerings. A certain subordinate interconnection is thus clearly recognizable in Lev. 1–7; yet these chapters form a whole relatively separate from the general theme.

There follows in chs. 8–10 the narrative portion mentioned above, which not only forms a section in itself as narrative, but also revolves round a definite subject—the first sacrifices offered at Sinai in the grand manner (for previous to this the combined Pentateuchal narrative has only related the covenant sacrifice of Ex. 24.5–8 and the fatal sacrifice to the 'golden calf' in Ex. 32.6). The theme of sacrifice links together this section with what has gone before: except that chs. 1–7 give more comprehensive precepts, of general and lasting validity, whereas chs. 8–10 relate a single occasion of solemn sacrifice, to which the narrative of the priests' institution to office belonged, because without this action the priests (Aaron and his sons) would not have been able to fulfil their role in the sacrificial procedure. The episode of ch. 10 was added to this in order to illustrate the necessity of exact obedience to divine sacrificial instructions by reference to an historical example.

A stronger coherence is displayed by chs. 11–15. They deal with the subject of cultic 'cleanness' (or 'uncleanness' as the case may be). This subject, too, has different aspects. It may be a matter of a man's 'cleanness' and so capacity to take part in worship, which may have been endangered or lost through particular bodily conditions or through contact with something else 'unclean'; or it may concern the 'cleanness', and therefore edibility and fitness for sacrifice, of animals. In this field there unfolds a necessarily complicated case-law covering the determination of 'cleanness' or 'uncleanness' and the measures for cleansing the unclean. In the same way the section chs. 11–15 is also divided into numerous subsections, yet linked together and separated off by the general theme of the whole.

Chapter 16, which in other respects stands alone, has a certain connection with this theme of 'cleanness', in so far as it contains important directions for 'making atonement for' the holy place, for the priesthood and for the whole people, and thereby envisages the recovery of fitness to worship in the widest sense. In a striking way, v. 1 ex-

plicitly goes back beyond the 'cleanness' section, and is a link with
the narrative of ch. 10.

Chapters 17 and following do not admit of division under major
themes into sections classed according to content, as in the first half of
the book. Here in general each chapter contains in itself more or less
coherent groups of instructions relating to widely differing subjects,
such as the sacrificial cult, conditions for the priestly office, cultic
dues, the annual solemn feasts, the Sabbath and jubilee year,
behaviour in the community, sexual relations and the like, all
apparently in somewhat random order.

The great announcements of reward and punishment in ch. 26
are evidently meant to bring together and round off the divine
instructions. But it is unclear how much of the previous chapters is
under consideration, for the chapter merely poses the general alterna-
tives of obedience or disobedience to the divine command. The
concluding chapter on dedicatory gifts is an isolated appendix.

It follows from all this that Leviticus can hardly have been
written down in one draft, despite the unity of the historical situation
described and despite the strong concentration on predominantly
cultic instructions and operations. It is rather a book that has come
into existence in successive stages, so that here, too, the literary-
critical question must be raised. As the book belongs to the whole
body of the Pentateuch, which was only subsequently divided into
'books', the literary-critical question cannot be answered without
reference to this larger whole. The Pentateuch is a narrative work,
and constantly in Leviticus—even if only at the mention of Moses,
Aaron and Sinai—reference is made to a definite place within the
sequence of the narrative. Hence the book in its traditional form can
never have existed by itself outside the narrative framework of the
Pentateuch. But it is then probable from the outset that the narrative
portions of the book, that is chs. 8–10, must from the literary point of
view be judged primary. Thus it immediately becomes clear to which
of the various Pentateuchal narrative strata it belongs. This can be
none other than the 'priestly document' (P). For Lev. 8–10 is—
directly or indirectly—a pure and simple 'priestly' composition, as
language and content equally testify. There exists not the slightest
trace of the 'old sources', the 'Jahwistic' (J) or the 'Elohistic' (E),
either in these chapters or anywhere else in the entire book. Looked at
within the larger context, Leviticus is seen to be embedded in the big
P-narrative of Israel's sojourn at Sinai; for both the last chapters of

the preceding book, Exodus, and the first chapters of the following book, Numbers, belong exclusively to P. Now P is certainly not a unity, but composite, enlarged by secondary additions from its original basic form. This is also true of Lev. 8–10, as is especially evident from the relationship of this section to Ex. 25–31, 35–40. Only the story of the first great sacrifices in ch. 9 belongs to the original P-narrative, whilst the account of the carrying out of the priests' institution to office in ch. 8 is clearly secondary P material, both as such, and as an appendix to the instructions—themselves added as a later supplement—for this particular institution in Ex. 29. The same is true for ch. 10, obviously linked on to the secondary last verse of the previous chapter. If Lev. 8–10 are to be regarded as the literary kernel of the whole book, then it must be stated that this kernel is formed by a portion of the P-narrative already amplified by later additions.

The remaining content of the book clearly did not belong to the original or expanded P-narrative. The whole book is indeed governed by a predominantly cultic interest, prevailing likewise in the Sinai section of the P-narrative. But, as the exegesis shows, there are such striking departures in numerous details from P's views, especially with regard to the composition of the cultic personnel, and such notable differences in language, that one is led to this conclusion: the non-narrative parts of the book have been fitted into the narrative framework as a later addition and have their own independent history. It must remain an open question whether this interpolation took place into the already expanded but still independent P-narrative; or whether the document in question was already a combination of P with the 'ancient sources'. This question cannot be answered—or rather, not completely answered—for of the 'Pentateuchal sources' between Ex. 35 and Num. 10 only is P extant.

From chs. 8–10 onwards the literary growth of the book can to a certain extent be reconstructed with some measure of probability. The only literary cross-connection in the whole book is the linking, expressed in 16.1, of the great purification ritual of ch. 16 with the narrative of 10.1ff. and hence with the narrative sections of chs. 8–10. Thus this ritual might well have been once appended to the account of the first great sacrifices, and properly so, inasmuch as the ritual, if it was to be brought within the framework of the Pentateuch, fitted on best to the inception of the holy place and its arrangements. This would ensure the continuity of worship through the instructions for the great 'sanctification' of the holy place and its furnishings. But for accommodating the wide collection of sacrificial instructions (chs. 1–7) a suitable place suggested itself immediately before the narrative of the first great sacrifices, because these very sacrifices required a knowledge of the regulations governing their presentation. Thus the account of the priests' institution (ch. 8) remained linked with the sacrifice narrative (ch. 9) because closely allied to it in subject-matter, especially as the institution itself was already accompanied by sacrifices and by similar actions. However, the collection of 'cleanness' and 'uncleanness' precepts (chs. 11–15) was worked in before the great cleansing ritual of ch. 16 because it provided, in its aspect of 'cleansing', a bridge from the precepts bearing on individuals to the great general atonement. The chapters next appearing (17–25), standing side by side in a loose connection, together with the great 'reward-and-punishment' declaration of ch. 26, had already formed an independent law-book, the so-called 'Law of Holiness', before their insertion into the narrative sequence (cf. below pp. 127f.). Containing as it did ritual as well as more general ordinances, it was not ill placed here, after all the arrangements for the holy place and the beginning of ritual worship and the provisions for its continuance. Naturally, it is no longer certain in what order the above-mentioned portions were arranged in the narrative framework of the Pentateuch. For the appended chapter on dedicatory gifts (ch. 27), one can only surmise that the Pentateuch's division into 'Books' was already achieved and that it was simply placed as an isolated fragment at the end of a 'Book'.

For the non-narrative portions of Leviticus, there is therefore a plausible hypothesis about how they came to be incorporated in the P-narrative or Pentateuch-narrative, as the case may be. Yet they were none of them composed or written down in the first place with a view to this arrangement, but existed previously in their own right. They have, moreover, no connection with the 'ancient sources'. But they look so independent over against P, both in language and by a variety of differences in their ideas, that we are forbidden to assume them to have been planned and formulated as an expansion of P. This raises the question how they were handed down, both with regard to the explanation and circumstances of their composition, and to the time and place of origin. And this question must be raised for each of the portions under review. This remains true when one bears in mind that a certain similarity of the ritual situation is recognizable in all of them—except perhaps the 'Law of Holiness'—in which respect they stand particularly apart from P. Now in texts consisting primarily of instructions and precepts for cult and ritual the question of origin is always difficult to answer, there being as a rule no concrete points of attachment. Cultic and ritual regulations usually remain fairly constant; they are relatively independent of the ups and downs of political and historical events. Besides, at the back of such compositions there lies most probably a form that was first oral, handing on the relevant rules from one generation to another; and in the course of this oral 'tradition' new material must certainly have been added to old. Even in the stage of fixity represented by writing down, there was always the possibility of expansions and fresh additions. Thus any attempt to date the finally derived forms must be approximate, and with the proviso that they may contain both the more ancient and the most ancient material. To fix the place of origin is at least as important as to arrive at a date. For traditional cultic and ritual material does not live in a vacuum, nor is it theoretically formulated to be practised here and there, but grows out of the worshipping life of a particular holy place.

As far as the last point is concerned, some details dealt with in the point-by-point commentary go to show that the sacrificial instructions in chs. 1–7, and probably, too, the purification regulations in chs. 11–15, belong to the Jerusalem tradition (cf., e.g., 'the anointed priest' of 4.3ff.). It can no longer be said for certain whether this is also true of the ritual in ch. 16. Yet in the 'Law of Holiness' some details again speak for an origin in Jerusalem (viz. the reference to local cults in the Jerusalem territory in 17.7; 20.2ff., and the many points of contact with the Book of Ezekiel, the background to which is the Jerusalem priestly tradition). In point of time the final form of the non-narrative portions of Leviticus, as far as there is any possibility of dating them, belong fairly clearly to the period around the end of the Jewish state and the beginning of the so-called exile. This means, however, that these non-narrative portions, in their present state (apart naturally from the stereotyped introductory and concluding formulae and from all redactional alterations and additions), were in all essentials already complete before the narrative framework of P came into being—into which they were subsequently fitted.

All this is subject to considerable reservations, for the unyielding nature of the material scarcely allows of any more certain conclusions about the growth of Leviticus and its separate components.

## 3. THE CONTENTS OF THE BOOK

Leviticus deals almost exclusively with cultic and ritual matters. Only ch. 19, in the framework of the 'Law of Holiness', extends in some of its very varied elements beyond this field into the province of general human relationships and connects with the behaviour required by God in community law the sentence about 'love of neighbour' (19.18) and the single injunction of the sentence about 'rising up before the hoary head' (19.32). Here in the Old Testament—as shown specifically by the juxtaposition in Lev. 19—there is no question of different categories of commandment, but only of the Will of God binding on Israel, revealed in a great variety of concrete requirements. This Divine Will covers the whole of cult and ritual, so prominent in Leviticus.

For large parts of the Old Testament the cultic worship of God, with all its sacrifices, festivals and rites was a form of reverence required by God. This was as true in ancient Israel as in the surrounding religions and in the whole wide field of religious history; and there is no question that not only cultic worship in itself, but also its detailed practice in Israel, are derived from the cultic tradition of the ancient Near East, and even taken over by Israel and understood as something enjoined by her God. But in Israel's reverence for God there is a demand for the strictest exclusiveness: the whole apparatus of worship existed solely for the one God, Yahweh; and it is often enough expressly stated that Israel must offer her sacrifices 'to Yahweh'. This means that many cultic procedures and customs were taboo in Israel, being regarded as specially belonging to foreign cults. Here, it was indeed difficult to establish a systematic distinction between the commanded and the forbidden; rather, it may be supposed, what existed as an offensive foreign cult in the immediate surroundings of ancient Israel, and might therefore become a temptation to 'fall away' to 'other gods', was forbidden to Israel, along with all its special features.

About the well-pleasingness to God of cultic service no doubt is expressed in the whole of Leviticus; on the contrary, all is referred to express divine commandment, as received at Sinai—so at least in the transmitted framework of the book—through the instrumentality of Moses. There is no trace of criticism of cultic worship, as expressed by the pre-exilic prophets, although the book in its present form is later than these prophets. In this respect its matter is pre-prophetic; and it decisively contradicts the prophetic denials that God ever required of Israel sacrifice and the like (cf. esp. Jer. 7.22; also Amos 5.25).

Where, however, cultic worship is understood as a legitimate way of honouring God, it becomes important that everything should be carried out correctly and in accordance with the divine requirements. If the cultic actions are to be 'well pleasing'—and that is their intention—then they must be subject to all the rules and regulations that guarantee this. And for the numerous cultic festivals and for the various occasions giving rise to cultic acts there was necessarily an abundance of such rules and regulations, obliged to descend to detail if everything was to be duly and properly performed. The obedience required included then not only all the cultic actions in themselves, but also conscientious attention to all the details. Hence it must be understood that Leviticus, setting out from the unquestioned assumption of the divine demands in the matter of cultic activity, can yet regulate both great and small in what seems at first so strange a fashion.

# II

## INSTRUCTIONS FOR SACRIFICE

### Lev. 1.1–7.38

AFTER THE FULFILMENT of the divine ordinances for making ready the holy place, with the ritual inventory (Ex. 35–39) and the setting up of the holy place (Ex. 40), and before mention of the institution to office of the priests and the completion of the first sacrifices (Lev. 8, 9), detailed sacrificial regulations are given in the form of instructions to Moses. The section Lev. 1–7 stands then, in the broad framework of the Priestly narrative, in an appropriate place, though it certainly does not belong to its original constituents. It divides Lev. 8, 9 (dealing with the execution of divine ordinances given in Ex. 25–31) from the cognate accounts in Ex. 35–39, and would seem to be a literary addition, a conclusion supported both by the secondary literary character of these extensive accounts and by details in its contents. By its subject-matter it forms a self-contained whole with its own previous history, as will be made clear by the detailed commentary. Although self-contained, it is composite; this can be seen not only from its content and structure, but also from the introductory formulae appearing in different places and marking the beginning of subsections or special sections. The chief introductory formula (1.1, 2aα), according to which Moses receives instructions 'for the Israelites', stands alongside the introductory formula in 6.8, 9a, according to which Moses is to pass on instructions to 'Aaron and his sons', thus clearly showing the most important subdivision, further specified in the extensive and varied introductory formulae in 4.1; 5.14; 6.1; 6.19; 6.24; 7.22; 7.28.

(*a*) THE BURNT OFFERING: 1.1–17

1 ¹The LORD called Moses, and spoke to him from the tent of

meeting, saying, 2'Speak to the people of Israel, and say to them, When any man [of you] brings an offering to the LORD, [you shall bring your offering of cattle from the herd or from the flock] 3If his offering is a burnt offering from the herd, he shall offer a male without blemish; [he shall offer it at the door of the tent of meeting, that he may be accepted] before the LORD; 4he shall lay his hand upon the head of the burnt offering [and it shall be accepted for him to make atonement for him]. 5Then he shall kill the bull before the LORD; and Aaron's sons the priests shall present the blood, and throw the blood round about against the altar that is at the door of the tent of meeting. 6And he shall flay the burnt offering and cut it into pieces; 7and the sons of Aaron the priest shall put fire on the altar, and lay wood in order upon the fire; 8and Aaron's sons the priests shall lay the pieces, the head, and the fat, in order upon the wood that is on the fire upon the altar; 9but its entrails and its legs he shall wash with water. And the priest shall burn the whole on the altar, as a burnt offering, an offering by fire, a pleasing odour to the LORD.

10 'If his gift [for a burnt offering] is from the flock, from the sheep or goats, he shall offer a male without blemish; 11and he shall kill it on the north side of the altar before the LORD, and Aaron's sons the priests shall throw its blood against the altar round about. 12And he shall cut it into pieces, with its head and its fat, and the priest shall lay them in order upon the wood that is on the fire upon the altar; 13but the entrails and the legs he shall wash with water. And the priest shall offer the whole, and burn it on the altar; it is a burnt offering, an offering by fire, a pleasing odour to the LORD.

14 'If his offering to the LORD is [a burnt offering] of birds, then he shall bring his offering of turtledoves or of young pigeons. 15And the priest shall bring it to the altar and wring off its head, and burn it on the altar; and its blood shall be drained out on the side of the altar; 16and he shall take away its crop with the feathers, and cast it beside the altar on the east side, in the place for ashes; 17he shall tear it by its wings, but shall not divide it asunder. And the priest shall burn it on the altar, upon the wood that is on the fire; it is a burnt offering, an offering by fire, a pleasing odour to the LORD.'

The instructions about the burnt offering are clearly related in layout, formulation and content with those for the peace offering sacrifice in ch. 3. They give, in a simple, almost monotonous sequence of directions the information considered requisite for carrying out sacrifices, without imparting anything substantial about the special character, meaning and purpose, or the possible occasions, of sacrifice. The style is objective: where suitable, the passive form of the verb is chosen; elsewhere, however, the offerer appears constantly as subject in the third person (the second person plural address in v. 2 belongs to secondary additions). Only the simple case is considered:

an individual, no matter what the occasion, desires to present a burnt offering; nothing is said of any offering on the part of a group, or more or less official person, or community. It must be supposed that these were subject to a corresponding procedure. The whole instructions then apply to the single offerer, who must learn what he has to do himself and what sacrificial actions must be left to the priest. What we have before us is thus a sacrificial ritual: how are we to suppose it to have assumed written form? As in ancient Israel, thanks to the invention of an alphabetical script, reading and writing were no longer a limited and learned art confined to experts, it does not seem impossible that such a ritual existed in written form at the holy place and could be consulted by those wishing to present an offering. Another possibility is that, perhaps on occasions when people assembled in large numbers at the holy place, a priest customarily announced the ritual by word of mouth for general instruction of the would-be offerers, before it assumed written shape.

The age of the ritual is hard to determine, for cultic ordinances remain customarily very constant and unaltered over long periods of time; they are only bound to a particular moment in this or that special feature. In its present form the burnt-offering ritual of Lev. 1 belongs to an accretion to the Priestly document (P), secondary from the literary point of view. This is evident both from the introductory formula (cf. v. 1), and from the redaction, clearly present but not continuously carried out, in the direction of P, introducing especially 'sons of Aaron' instead of the original simple and general term 'the priest', and probably, too, the 'tent of meeting'. In ch. 1 the 'sons of Aaron' never appear independently, but always with the superfluous addition 'the priests' (vv. 5, 8, 11)—a plural which obviously conceals the original singular 'the priest', who in v. 7 has remained alongside the 'sons of Aaron' and, moreover, in vv. 9, 12, 13, 15, 17 has maintained his original independence. We can hardly ascribe such an incomplete working over of an older document to P, but rather to a later redactor wishing to fit the whole, as a supplement, into P. The similarity of subject-matter shows, however, that the ritual itself, in spite of its late incorporation into the literary framework of P (or even P and JE), is without doubt older than P. Supporting this is the fact that, according to Ezek. 44.11, the slaughter of the burnt offering or peace offering was the task of the 'serving' Levites, who were to carry this out 'for the people', whilst in the ritual of Lev. 1 the offering 'layman' himself performs the slaughter (v. 5). This tendency is even stronger in the Book of Chronicles: single sacrificial acts have passed over to the priestly body, acts which in Lev. 1 still belonged to the 'layman' (e.g. the skinning of the animals for the burnt offering, according to II Chron. 29.34 really the business of the priests or—taking their place exceptionally—the Levites; cf. on the other hand Lev. 1.6). Consequently the ritual of Lev. 1 (before the P redaction) must be considered pre-exilic. It cannot, however, be claimed as primitive, for it probably shows traces of different kinds of sacrifice worked in one on top of the other (cf. v. 4a). It cannot be earlier than the later pre-exilic times. Its home must be assumed to be a particular holy place, for it would be difficult to posit identical binding rituals for all the holy places at a time when there were still numerous legitimate holy places in Israel. The later incorporation into the Pentateuch indicates that the Temple in Jerusalem, from Josiah's time onwards the only lawful shrine, was the cultic home of the ritual in Lev. 1 ff., and remained as such beyond the exile, on into post-exilic times.

[1] The remarkable position of the subject in the introductory formula (v. 1) shows that this formula is not of uniform composition. In v. 1b we have the stereotyped introduction to divine precepts, constantly repeated from Ex. 25.1 onwards, as they are given first on Sinai, and then in Ex. 40.1 at the foot of Sinai, to Moses. The address to Moses in v. 1a looks, in view of this, like a secondary literary addition, intended to give a connection back beyond Ex. 40.36–38 to Ex. 40.34, 35. [2] In v. 2a the directions that follow are appropriately characterized as intended for all Israelites ('laymen'). The real ritual text begins at v. 2b, at which point the word *qorbān* comes in as a key-word for each and every 'presentation', a word frequently used in Lev. 1–7 and also farther on in Leviticus and Numbers, but probably foreign to the original text of P (cf. κορβᾶν in Mark 7.11, also Matt. 27.6). In a major subordinate clause with *kī* the inclusive case is next put forward of anyone (the word is the perfectly general 'man', though certainly to be restricted to Israel) who has an offering to 'present'. This inclusive case is then made specific in short, rather formal subordinate clauses with *'im* (on this sequence of *kī* and *'im* cf. Noth, *Exodus*, p. 177). [3] First there is a survey of the many possible kinds of sacrifice ([2.1aα]; 3.1a correspond to the first words of v. 3); then further, within the respective kinds, it distinguishes the different materials for sacrifice. In v. 3aα the heaping up of main clauses at this point necessitates a rather shorter formulation. The meaning is: 'In case he should offer a burnt offering; in case it should

be an offering of cattle'; and the following conditional clause is parallel to the introductions in vv. 10, 14. In Leviticus the burnt offering (Heb. *'ōlā*) is the first category of oblation to be dealt with (really 'the [in fire and/or smoke] ascending [sacrifice]'). This, as the accompanying ritual shows, is an animal sacrifice to be completely consumed by fire, and as such probably refers to a primitive type of sacrificial 'gift' by the owner of a herd (Gen. 4.4a). In Lev. 1 cattle certainly hold the first place among sacrificial animals, testifying obviously to civilized and settled conditions of living. For the burnt offering male animals were required (contrast Lev. 3), no doubt the more worthy in a general framework of preference for the male. That an animal must be 'without blemish', i.e. without any bodily abnormality, is in accordance with the serious nature of sacrificial actions (cf., however, Mal. 1.6–8). The animal is brought 'before Yahweh', i.e. simply to the holy place. The mention of the 'tent of meeting' in v. 3 belongs, like the introductory formula in v. 1, in which it has already occurred, to the literary and secondary redaction in accordance with P; this is also shown by the absence of the passage in question in the ritual constructed on parallel lines in Lev. 3. The same is true of the announcement of its purpose—that the sacrifice shall make him 'well pleasing' to God. [4] The 'laying' of the hand on the animal brought to the holy place for sacrifice is hard to explain. It may have its origin in special sacrificial rites, as in Lev. 16.31, in the sense of the transference of the offerer's own person to the animal, thus making the latter his substitute. Subsequently, this rite may have extended to all animals, to mark animal sacrifice in general as a giving of oneself, intended (as the addition in v. 4b explains) to effect the 'atonement' needed to make it 'well pleasing' to God. [5] The 'slaying' of the animal 'before Yahweh', i.e. in the holy place, is only briefly noted (v. 5a), obviously because everyone may be presumed to know how that is done. In what follows it is laid down that the blood shed in the slaughtering had to be caught in a vessel in order to prepare for the subsequent blood-rite. To carry this out was the business of the priest (v. 5b was doubtless originally in the singular, with 'the priest' as subject); he had to catch the blood in a vessel, take it to the altar and then sprinkle it round about towards the sides of the altar. This blood-rite originates from the notion that the life of the sacrificial animal resides in its blood (cf. 17.11), and that the life as such belongs to God and can therefore form no part of the human gift presented for sacrifice. It is therefore, before the offering of the sacrifice, applied to the altar, the place belonging to God and devoted to God (the superfluous placing of the altar in v. 5b$\beta$ is again a redactor's addition). [6] With the skinning of the sacrificial animal (v. 6a) the preparation of the real presentation begins. What is to be done with the discarded skin is not here stated; according to 7.8 it belonged to the sacrificing priest. This, though not mentioned here, may well be understood; if not, the skin would certainly have to be destroyed, for the giving over of a part of a sacrificial animal for profane use hardly entered into consideration. The skinning, and likewise the disposition of the offering in its 'portions', was the business of the sacrificing 'layman'; for the latter is everywhere understood as the agent wherever the priest is not expressly mentioned as subject. The 'division' of the skinned animal into 'parts' is again thus briefly mentioned because obviously the sacrificer is assumed to be conversant with its details. [7] In what follows there are named as special 'parts' of the animal the head and the fat, the entrails and the legs. Now it is once more the priest's turn (that vv. 7, 8 were originally in the singular, with 'the priest' as subject, is shown most clearly by v. 7a, where the singular 'the priest' has remained alongside of 'the sons of Aaron'); for now the action lies at the altar itself, reserved, according to the present ritual, for the priest. The priest has to kindle 'fire' on the altar (the probably later regulation in 6.12, 13 requires a continually burning fire on the altar). There is no more precise indication how and with what materials this is to be done; but on this fire he had to pile up pieces of wood that could be formed into a fire hot enough to consume a complete animal sacrifice. [8] Finally the priest must 'heap up' on it the 'parts' of the animal for burning. The special naming of 'head and fat' as an appendage to the general term 'parts' is out of keeping and makes one suspect a later addition, especially as the pair of words crops up again in v. 12 in a syntactically very strange position and, moreover, in a different place in the ritual structure. Does this mean that the later introduction of 'head and fat' would indicate a subsequent usage by which 'head and fat' were only placed on the altar after the other portions? [9] From the start at all events special treatment was prescribed (v. 9a) for 'entrails and legs'; these, needing special cleansing, had to be first washed in water by the offerer before they were finally consigned to the altar fire. The burning of 'the whole', expressly noted in the concluding formula (v. 9b), was essential for the burnt offering, with the single exception mentioned above—the skin. Moreover, the burnt offering finally becomes known as the 'fire offering' (the usual, though by no means certain translation of the technical expression *'iššā* by derivation from the word *'ēš* = 'fire'), a 'fire offering of pleasing odour (*rēaḥ nīḥōaḥ*) to Yahweh'. This extremely massive pronouncement on the intended effect of the sacrifice consumed on the altar has kept its place with remarkable tenacity as a firmly imprinted formula, right on into the cultic terminology of exilic and post-exilic times. The phrase 'smell (of the) pleasing odour' first meets us in J, Gen. 8.21. It seems to stem from the cultic speech and thought-forms belonging to the land of the two rivers. According to the flood narrative in the Gilgamesh Epic XI 160 'the gods smelt the sweet savour' of the sacrifice offered after the flood (cf. also I Sam. 26.19; Amos 5.21; Lev. 26.31). On the other hand, the cultic calendar of the land of the two rivers recognizes 'a day of heart's ease' (*nūḥ libbi*) for the gods (Akk. *nūḥ* and Heb. *nīḥōaḥ*, a 'soothing', go back to the same stem). By this is meant the appeasement through sacrifice of the divine anger, actual or possible. The rituals of Leviticus, otherwise silent on the purpose and intention of sacrifice, seem automatically to have taken up this ancient formula traditionally bound up with the technical terms for different kinds of sacrifice.

[10–13] The next section (vv. 10–13) has to do with the burnt offering of a smaller animal. It is shorter and confines itself to enumerating the most important actions in sacrifice, for there is no need to repeat all the identical procedure. It remains questionable whether the few deviations are of material importance, or merely due to chance: notably the absence of the 'laying' of the hand on the animal's head. Did this fall out of use in the case of less valuable smaller animals, or was it to be understood without special mention? The same question must be raised about the absence of any reference to the skinning of the animal. The direction that the slaughter shall take place on the north side of the altar is an addition to the text. Perhaps this is merely a regulation prescribing a special place for the slaughter of smaller animals, whilst for cattle-slaughter a place was envisaged (not mentioned because so obvious) in front of the altar, that is at the east side of the altar.

[14–17] Least costly, and therefore specially suitable for poorer folk (cf. 5.7), yet recognized as fully valid and bearing the same concluding formula, was the burnt offering of a bird. Here, it was a question of the two kinds of dove regularly mentioned in the Old Testament as suitable for sacrifice. In this case the procedure must necessarily be

different from that used with the larger animals. The blood-rite
which the priest must fulfil consisted here of squeezing the bird's
body against the altar wall (v. 15b)—for it would not have been
possible to catch the small quantity of blood in a vessel, the bird's
head having been previously wrung, i.e. nipped off with the fingers
(contrast, as there expressly stated, 5.8), and consigned to the altar
fire (v. 15a). The offerer had then to remove the bird's crop and its
contents and throw them on the refuse-heap (v. 16), located to the
east of the altar and designated 'the place of fat', because intended
for the fatty ashes and other remains of the burnt offering after
removal from the altar. Instead of the 'dividing' into 'portions', the
bird's body was torn open, without being pulled to pieces, the bird
being held by both wings, without tearing them off (thus we must
probably understand the somewhat obscure statement of v. 17aα).
The offerer having performed this, the priest then laid the bird's body,
too, upon the altar fire.

## (b) THE MEAL OFFERING: 2.1–16

2 ¹'When any one brings a cereal offering as an offering to the LORD,
his offering shall be of fine flour; he shall pour oil upon it, and put
frankincense on it, ²and bring it to Aaron's sons the priests. And he shall
take from it a handful of the fine flour and oil, with all of its frankincense; and the priest shall burn this as its memorial portion upon the
altar, an offering by fire, a pleasing odour to the LORD. ³And what is
left of the cereal offering shall be for Aaron and his sons; it is a most
holy part of the offerings by fire to the LORD.

4 'When you bring a cereal offering baked in the oven as an offering,
it shall be unleavened cakes of fine flour mixed with oil, or unleavened
wafers spread with oil. ⁵And if your offering is a cereal offering baked
on a griddle, it shall be of fine flour unleavened, mixed with oil; ⁶you
shall break it in pieces, and pour oil on it; it is a cereal offering. ⁷And
if your offering is a cereal offering cooked in a pan, it shall be made of
fine flour with oil. ⁸And you shall bring the cereal offering that is made
of these things to the LORD; and when it is presented to the priest, he
shall bring it to the altar. ⁹And the priest shall take from the cereal
offering its memorial portion and burn this on the altar, an offering by
fire, a pleasing odour to the LORD. ¹⁰And what is left of the cereal
offering shall be for Aaron and his sons; it is a most holy part of the
offerings by fire to the LORD.

11 'No cereal offering which you bring to the LORD shall be made with
leaven; for you shall burn no leaven nor any honey as an offering by
fire to the LORD. ¹²As an offering of first fruits you may bring them to
the LORD, but they shall not be offered on the altar for a pleasing odour.
¹³You shall season all your cereal offerings with salt; you shall not let

the salt of the covenant with your God be lacking from your cereal offering; with all your offerings you shall offer salt.

14 'If you offer a cereal offering of first fruits to the Lord, you shall offer for the cereal offering of your first fruits crushed new grain from fresh ears, parched with fire. [15]And you shall put oil upon it, and lay frankincense on it; it is a cereal offering. [16]And the priest shall burn as its memorial portion part of the crushed grain and of the oil with all of its frankincense; it is an offering by fire to the Lord.'

Chapter 2 has been fitted in between chs. 1 and 3, which belong closely together and correspond exactly. Whilst 3.1a depends on the principal subordinate clause 1.2b and in parallel with 1.3aα introduces a further particular case, ch. 2 begins in v. 1a with an independent main clause. From this it might be deduced that ch. 2 originally followed chs. 1 and 3, as ch. 2 is harmonious with the whole body of chs. 1–3. Yet the special features of ch. 2 in details of formulation and arrangement would rather favour the hypothesis that this was a later addition inserted between 1 and 3, forming, however, with chs. 1 and 3 a relatively compact unity within the larger whole of sacrificial instructions in Lev. 1–7. For ch. 2 also deals with a ritual intended for the 'layman'. However, this ritual is not nearly as unified as those of chs. 1–3. The formulation alone shows this. Verses 1–3, a section in strict ritual form, is followed by vv. 4–10, a section using the second person singular,* passing over in v. 11 to the second plural, only to return to the singular in v. 13. The third-named section is not at all homogeneous in content, which points to its having taken shape gradually, from start to finish, leaving open the question whether the process of growth was already at an end when the insertion between chs. 1 and 3 took place, or was carried farther in stages that cannot be more precisely specified. The basic form of ch. 2 points to the same origins as ch. 1 (cf. above pp. 20ff.), and for the same reasons.

Chapter 2 deals with the 'meal offering', Hebrew *minḥā*; the word *minḥā* has the quite general root-meaning 'gift', 'present' (cf., e.g., I Sam. 10.27), and in the cultic field it first denoted any (sacrificial) 'gift' (cf., e.g., Gen. 4.3b–5a). In the later usage—under consideration in this chapter—it became a technical term for non-animal or vegetable 'gifts'. The usual translation 'meal offering' (so Luther) is incorrect† inasmuch as the burnt offering, too, had no less the

*[Not distinguishable in RSV; see older versions. Ed.]

†[In German this is true; in English the phrase is ambiguous. RSV translates, 'cereal offering'. Ed.]

character of an offered repast. This translation must then be understood in a special sense, like the Hebrew *minḥā*. In Lev. 2 the meal
offering is dealt with as an independent kind of sacrifice, which is
doubtless true of earlier times; in post-exilic sacrificial practice (cf.
Num. 15.1–16) it appears as a supplement to the burnt offering (and
peace offering).

[1–3] Even the beginning of the meal-offering ritual is not quite
smoothly expressed, for in the main clause there is a feminine subject
('one' = Heb. *nepeš* [fem.]; contrast 1.2aβ), yet farther on occurs a
masculine subject. The staple material for the meal offering is here
and in the sequel coarsely ground flour ('groats')—presumably of one
of the principal grains of the country, wheat or barley—to which is
added (olive) oil (v. 1b), in general use for baking. The addition of
incense (v. 1b) could hardly have been an original part of the meal
offering, but must be derived from the perfume offering, which could
lend additional solemnity to the meal-offering procedure. [2] The
offering 'layman' had to prepare the meal offering, consisting in this
case only of the raw materials for baking (apart from the incense),
outside the holy place, and then 'bring it in' to the priest (so originally
in v. 2a); then give a handful of the prepared ingredients to the
priest, for whom the actions at the altar were reserved, and who thus
had to consign it to the altar fire (v. 2). The heavy style in v. 2aβ is
probably due to the fact that a closer definition of 'handful' was only
added later, with the intention of stressing that only a part of the
meal and oil was to be taken, but the whole of the incense. The
technical term *'azkārā*, appearing only in conjunction with the meal
offering in the Old Testament, and designating that part of the
offering finally consumed on the altar, can no longer be explained
with any probability. None of the suggested translations (Luther: 'as
a memorial'; the Zurich Bible: 'as a sweet savour') is convincing.
[3] The original ritual did not state what was to be done with the
remains of the prepared raw material not consumed by fire; the
remark in v. 3 that the remains belonged to 'Aaron and his sons' is a
later addition, but quite possibly based on an earlier usage by which
the remains were handed over to the priest; for as making it available
for secular consumption is unlikely, some kind of ritual destruction
seems most probable.

[4–10] The section vv. 4–7, with its address in the style of the
priestly *tōrā* directed to giving information in answer to questions,
adds to the ritual of vv. 1–3, dealing only with the presentation of raw

material, further possibilities of presenting food prepared for eating. This section is not very strictly phrased: v. 4 begins with *kī*, vv. 5 and 6, however, with *'im*, although both are parallel main clauses. All three of the cases foreseen run to a common conclusion in vv. 8–10. The material is in each case wheat or barley groats and olive oil; only the manner of preparation is constantly varied. Probably we are dealing with the usual way of preparing human food: the presence of some rather uncertain technical terms prevents us from giving a clear detailed explanation. [4] Verse 4 speaks first of baking, as it was wont to be carried out from ancient times and still is today amongst the inhabitants of civilized lands in the customary baker's oven (Heb. and Arab. *tannūr*). The dough was stuck against the inner side of a clay cylinder, previously heated by a fire lit inside it. This forms the oven. (For details, see G. Dalman, *Arbeit und Sitte in Palastina* IV [1935], pp. 88–126.) In this way you can bake thicker 'cakes' (Heb. *ḥallā*—but it must remain uncertain whether, as a possible derivation of the word might indicate, this means a 'ring-cake' with a 'hole' in the middle) or thinner 'flat-cakes' (Heb. *rāqīq*) which must in any case for the meal offering be unleavened—*maṣṣōt* in fact.* [5–6] Later, we come on to (vv. 5, 6) dough baked on an iron dish, probably the primitive customary method with settled tent-dwellers, later used in settled conditions and still surviving in today's round and slightly convex *ṣādš*. (See *Illustrated World of the Bible Library*, vol. 1 [1959], p. 180.) The finished product was to be 'broken' and thus assume the form in which it was presumably used for ordinary consumption.

[7] Finally (v. 7) we have a quite short description of the preparation of the meal offering in a—no doubt earthenware—pan; the text tells us nothing about its special form or shape.

[8–9] The manner of presentation (vv. 8, 9) corresponds essentially with that described in v. 2. We are not told how, in these cases involving already prepared cakes (in contrast to v. 2), the 'bringing' of the *'azkārā* to be burnt on the altar was carried out by the priest. [10] The same is true for v. 10, as for the similar v. 3.

[11–12] In vv. 11–16 there follow, loosely interconnected with the foregoing, some further detailed directives—secondary material, no doubt. First in vv. 11, 12 (with plural address) there is the command implicit in vv. 1–3, explicit in vv. 4–10 (*maṣṣōt*), not to bring any meal offering in a 'leavened' state, which would injure the original and intact condition of the offering. The apparently striking conjunction

*[The word matzoth is used by Jews to describe such unleavened bread. Ed.]

of leavened dough and honey possibly rests on the fermentive action which honey, too, possesses (Heb. *debaš* = Arab. *dibs* probably means fruit-honey). Leavened dough and honey, i.e. cakes prepared with leavened dough and honey, may only be offered as 'first fruits', i.e. as a gift to the holy place or priests, and not as a sacrifice. **[13]** In v. 13, reverting to the singular, the salting of all meal offerings, not previously mentioned but perhaps to be understood in the foregoing, is expressly required. Salting was probably part of the general preparations for baking, but here it is given a symbolic interpretation by reference to the salt-covenant between God and people, in which the people are to join when salting the offering. In the Old Testament there are references, though infrequently, to the otherwise well-known idea of the 'salt-covenant' (Num. 18.19; II Chron. 13.5), going back to the idea still prevalent among the Arabs that eating salt together establishes a mutual community bond. **[14–16]** Finally vv. 14–16 deal with a meal offering of first fruits, meaning the tender young corn-shoots. The fresh young ears are to be roasted and dried at a fire and then rubbed into coarse meal. This is then offered in the same manner as the ingredients for the meal offering in v. 2. We have here a closely related type of offering; only here the special case of the young corn has been added at a later stage.

## (c) THE PEACE OFFERING: 3.1–17

3   1'If a man's offering is a sacrifice of peace offering, if he offers an animal from the herd, male or female, he shall offer it without blemish before the LORD. 2And he shall lay his hand upon the head of his offering and kill it at the door of the tent of meeting; and Aaron's sons the priests shall throw the blood against the altar round about. 3And from the sacrifice of the peace offering, as an offering by fire to the LORD, he shall offer the fat covering the entrails and all the fat that is on the entrails, 4and the two kidneys with the fat that is on them at the loins, and the appendage of the liver which he shall take away with the kidneys. 5Then Aaron's sons shall burn it on the altar upon the burnt offering, which is upon the wood on the fire; it is an offering by fire, a pleasing odour to the LORD.

6 'If his offering for a sacrifice of peace offering to the LORD is an animal from the flock, male or female, he shall offer it without blemish. 7If he offers a lamb for his offering, then he shall offer it before the LORD, 8laying his hand upon the head of his offering and killing it before the tent of meeting; and Aaron's sons shall throw its blood against the altar round about. 9Then from the sacrifice of the peace offering as an offering by fire to the LORD he shall offer its fat, the fat tail entire, taking it away close by the backbone, and the fat that covers the entrails, and

all the fat that is on the entrails, [10]and the two kidneys with the fat that is on them at the loins, and the appendage of the liver which he shall take away with the kidneys. [11]And the priest shall burn it on the altar as food offered by fire to the LORD.

[12] 'If his offering is a goat, then he shall offer it before the LORD, [13]and lay his hand upon its head, and kill it before the tent of meeting; and the sons of Aaron shall throw its blood against the altar round about. [14]Then he shall offer from it, as his offering for an offering by fire to the LORD, the fat covering the entrails, and all the fat that is on the entrails, [15]and the two kidneys with the fat that is on them at the loins, and the appendage of the liver which he shall take away with the kidneys. [16]And the priest shall burn them on the altar as food offered by fire [for a pleasing odour]. [All fat is] for the LORD. [17]It shall be a perpetual statute throughout your generations, in all your dwelling places, that you eat neither fat nor blood.'

The instructions for the peace offering are presented in Lev. 3 in the strict and consistent formulation of a ritual, parallel to the burnt-offering ritual of Lev. 1 and originally joined on directly to it; for the first protasis in v. 1a presupposes the principal dependent clause in 1.2a$\beta$ and stands parallel to 1.3a$\alpha$. The peace-offering ritual has a clearly visible structure, for it presents two cases, namely offerings from the herd (v. 1b$\alpha$) or from the flock (v. 6a), the latter case sub-divided into sheep (v. 7a) and goats (v. 12a). This falls into three convenient subsections, largely corresponding in language. In Lev. 3, too, the later redaction towards P is easily recognized, because not consistently carried through. In place of the original subject 'the priest' (with singular construction) v. 2b introduces 'the sons of Aaron, the priests', and vv. 5a, 8b, 13b, the 'sons of Aaron' (with plural construction). Yet in vv. 11a and 16a, exactly corresponding in construction to v. 5a, the original singular and simple expression 'the priest' has remained. Similarly with the 'tent of meeting': the expression crops up in constructions where, in the exactly corresponding places in the burnt-offering ritual (1.5a, 11a), the phrase 'before Yahweh' occurs, which is certainly to be regarded as original. As for the history of the peace-offering ritual contained in Lev. 3, the same holds good as for the burnt-offering ritual in Lev. 1.

The technical term for the peace offering is in Hebrew *zebaḥ*. It is derived from the stem *zbḥ* = 'to slaughter ritually', and is allied to the Hebrew stem *šḥṭ*, denoting quite generally and neutrally the slaughter of an animal as such and also used regularly in Lev. 1 and 3 for the act of slaughter of a sacrificial animal. For cultic slaughter the first requirement was the setting up of an altar; whence it comes about that in pre-Israelite Syria and Palestine (cf. the Ugaritic) and more still in the Old Testament the word in general use for altar (Heb. *mizbēaḥ*) really and originally means 'the place of slaughter for (the) sacrifice', although the slaughter no longer takes place on the altar (cf., however, Gen. 22.9, 10 for the obviously primitive use). In Lev. 3, as frequently elsewhere in the Old Testament, the idea of *zebaḥ* is more closely defined by the dependent genitive *šelāmīm*. This word, nearly always plural in the Old Testament (only in Amos 5.22 do we find in the received text the singular *šelem*), and probably to be taken as an abstract plural, occurs only in conjunction with the idea of *zebaḥ*, or in its stead. It goes back to the stem *šlm* = 'to be intact, unconsumed'. Its specific meaning in ritual language (even in the Ugaritic cultic terminology) can no longer be fixed with any certainty. The addition of the word 'peace' refers to the 'intactness' of the relationship between God and the worshippers and fastens on the special manner and meaning of the peace offering—that only definite parts of the animal were burnt on the altar, the rest being eaten by the participants in a sacrificial meal. This constituted, in the original understanding, a meal shared by God and the worshippers, and formed the basis of the community and its constant reinvigoration and renewal. The ritual in Lev. 3 says not a word about the sacrificial meal: it concerns solely the preparation of the victim and its offering at the altar. There is only negative evidence of the sacrificial meal inasmuch as the text leaves open the question as to what was done with the portions of the animal not burnt on the altar. This gap is filled by the sacrificial meal, tacitly presupposed as belonging to the 'peace offering'. However, we are not to suppose that the sacrificial meal did not have its own very important and definite cultic regulations, demanding exact compliance; but the rituals in Lev. 3 are only interested in what the 'layman' needed to know about sacrificial procedure in the narrower sense.

[1–16] The three subdivisions (vv. 1b–5; vv. 6–11; vv. 12–16) are almost alike, even in wording, and corresponded even more closely in the unedited original than in the text before us. The sole factual difference is that when a sheep was slain for sacrifice the fat tail belonged to what was burnt on the altar. This single peculiarity made it basically necessary to separate herd from flock, and in the flock sheep from goats, treating each in separate sections, and to distinguish the two classes in the flock otherwise than in the burnt-offering section (1.10–13). The action is precisely the same as that of the burnt offering, including the blood-rite carried out by the priest (cf. above pp. 21f.), with the one difference that in the peace offering both male and female animals were always allowed, instead of only males, as in the burnt offering. It is further to be noted that in the case of the flock the 'laying' of the hand on the sacrifice is required (vv. 8aα, 13aα), a requirement lacking in the flock section of the burnt-offering ritual. After the blood-rite the offering 'layman' had to cut out from the slaughtered animal those parts which the ritual required to be handed over to the priest for burning on the altar as Yahweh's appointed portion of the sacrificed animal. These portions, to which belonged especially certain fat parts (apart from the kidneys), are enumerated in a stereotyped and fairly detailed manner (vv. 3b, 4; vv. 9aβb, 10; vv. 14b, 15). In the case of the sheep (Heb. *keśeb*, here, as in 1.10, understood from the context as a generic term), the fat tail, as mentioned above, came to be added to the sacrificial parts required from all slaughtered animals (v. 9), indicating that where this ritual was in use fat-tailed sheep were normally available.

[5] A few further details are worth notice. With peace offerings of cattle, v. 5 presupposes that a burnt offering has first been presented. There is no corresponding condition for sheep or goats; but it would be hard to say whether this is a factual difference, or whether an analogous requirement is to be tacitly understood. This might indicate a regular morning burnt offering (according to the probably later ordinances in 6.12) which had first to be presented before any peace-offering portions might be sacrificed; but it could also mean that whoever wished to present a peace offering—at any rate from the herd—must first offer a burnt offering. [11–16] For the flock, the concluding formula (vv. 11b, 16b) has, instead of the familiar expression used with the burnt offering—'a fire offering of pleasing odour to Yahweh' (repeated, though probably not in the original version, for the cattle, v. 5b)—'food offered by fire to Yahweh'. (Verse 16's comment, 'as a pleasing odour' might well be a later addition.) And this can scarcely be accidental: rather it expresses the primitive thought more tenaciously and persistently than with the burnt offering that the peace offering was bound up with a meal. This was shared not only by the participants in the sacrificial meal, but also by the divine Partner. [17] In v. 17 we have a secondary addition forbidding in quite general terms the consumption by the offerer of the blood and the fat in the peace offering. (The word *kol-ḥēleb*, 'all the fat', has crept in by mistake from v. 17 after v. 16.)

## (d) OCCASIONS FOR ATONING SACRIFICES: 4.1–6.7*

4 ¹And the LORD said to Moses, ²'Say to the people of Israel, If any one sins unwittingly in any of the things which the LORD has commanded not to be done, and does any one of them, ³if it is the anointed priest who sins, thus bringing guilt on the people, then let him offer for the sin which he has committed a young bull without blemish to the LORD for a sin offering. ⁴He shall bring the bull [to the door of the tent of meeting] before the LORD, and lay his hand on the head of the bull, and kill the bull before the LORD. ⁵And the anointed priest shall take some of the blood of the bull [and bring it to the tent of meeting;] ⁶and the priest shall dip his finger in the blood and sprinkle part of the blood seven times before the LORD [in front of the veil of the sanctuary]. ⁷And the priest shall put some of the blood on the horns of the altar [of fragrant incense] before the LORD [which is in the tent of meeting], and the rest of the blood of the bull he shall pour out at the base of the altar [of burnt offering which is at the door of the tent of meeting]. ⁸And all the fat of the bull of the sin offering he shall take from it, the fat that covers the entrails and all the fat that is on the entrails, ⁹and the two kidneys with the fat that is on them at the loins, and the appendage of the liver which he shall take away with the kidneys ¹⁰(just as these are taken from the ox of the sacrifice of the peace offerings), and the priest shall burn them upon the altar of burnt offering. ¹¹But the skin of the bull and all its flesh, with its head, its legs, its entrails, and its dung, ¹²the whole bull he shall carry forth [outside the camp] to a clean place, where the ashes are poured out, and shall burn it on a fire of wood; where the ashes are poured out it shall be burned.

13 'If the whole congregation of Israel commits a sin unwittingly and the thing is hidden from the eyes of the assembly, and they do any one of the things which the LORD has commanded not to be done and are guilty; ¹⁴when the sin which they have committed becomes known, the assembly shall offer a young bull for a sin offering and bring it before the tent of meeting; ¹⁵and the elders of the congregation shall lay their hands upon the head of the bull before the LORD, and the bull shall be killed before the LORD. ¹⁶Then the anointed priest shall bring some of the blood of the bull to the tent of meeting, ¹⁷and the priest shall dip his finger in the blood and sprinkle it seven times before the LORD in front of the veil. ¹⁸And he shall put some of the blood on the horns of the altar which is in the tent of meeting before the LORD; and the rest of the blood he shall pour out at the base of the altar of burnt offering which is at the door of the tent of meeting. ¹⁹And all its fat he shall take from it and burn upon the altar. ²⁰Thus shall he do with the bull; as he did with the bull of the sin offering, so shall he do with this; and the priest shall make atonement for them, and they shall be forgiven. ²¹And he shall carry forth the bull outside the camp, and burn it as he burned the first bull; it is the sin offering for the assembly.

22 'When a ruler sins, doing unwittingly any one of all the things

*Hebrew: 5.26.

L.–C

which the LORD his God has commanded not to be done, and is guilty, [23]if the sin which he has committed is made known to him, he shall bring as his offering a goat, a male without blemish, [24]and shall lay his hand upon the head of the goat, and kill it in the place where they kill the burnt offering before the LORD; it is a sin offering. [25]Then the priest shall take some of the blood of the sin offering with his finger and put it on the horns of the altar of burnt offering, and pour out the rest of its blood at the base of the altar of burnt offering. [26]And all its fat he shall burn on the altar, like the fat of the sacrifice of peace offerings; so the priest shall make atonement for him for his sin, and he shall be forgiven.

27 'If any one of the common people sins unwittingly in doing any one of the things which the LORD has commanded not to be done, and is guilty, [28]when the sin which he has committed is made known to him he shall bring for his offering a goat, a female without blemish, for his sin which he has committed. [29]And he shall lay his hand on the head of the sin offering, and kill the sin offering in the place of burnt offering. [30]And the priest shall take some of its blood with his finger and put it on the horns of the altar of burnt offering, and pour out the rest of its blood at the base of the altar. [31]And all its fat he shall remove, as the fat is removed from the peace offerings, and the priest shall burn it upon the altar for a pleasing odour to the LORD; and the priest shall make atonement for him, and he shall be forgiven.

32 'If he brings a lamb as his offering for a sin offering, he shall bring a female without blemish, [33]and lay his hand upon the head of the sin offering, and kill it for a sin offering in the place where they kill the burnt offering. [34]Then the priest shall take some of the blood of the sin offering with his finger and put it on the horns of the altar of burnt offering, and pour out the rest of its blood at the base of the altar. [35]And all its fat he shall remove as the fat of the lamb is removed from the sacrifice of peace offerings, and the priest shall burn it on the altar, upon the offerings by fire to the LORD; and the priest shall make atonement for him for the sin which he has committed, and he shall be forgiven.

5 [1]'If any one sins in that he hears a public adjuration to testify and though he is a witness, whether he has seen or come to know the matter, yet does not speak, he shall bear his iniquity. [2]Or if any one touches an unclean thing, whether the carcass of an unclean beast or a carcass of unclean cattle or a carcass of unclean swarming things, and it is hidden from him, if someone comes to know it,* he shall be guilty. [3]Or if he touches human uncleanness, of whatever sort the uncleanness may be with which one becomes unclean, and it is hidden from him, if someone comes to know it he shall be guilty. [4]Or if any one utters with his lips a rash oath to do evil or to do good, any sort of rash oath that men swear, and it is hidden from him, if someone comes to know it he shall [in any

*Reading *yāda'* for the obviously accidental error of *ṭāmē'* (cf. vv. 3, 4). [RSV renders the Hebrew text as it stands: 'and he has become unclean', and in vv. 3, 4: 'when he comes to know it'. Ed.]

of these] be guilty. ⁵When a man is guilty in any of these, he shall confess the sin he has committed, ⁶and he shall bring his guilt offering to the LORD for the sin which he has committed, a female from the flock, a lamb or a goat, for a sin offering; and the priest shall make atonement for him for his sin.

7 'But if he cannot afford a lamb, then he shall bring, as his guilt offering to the LORD for the sin which he has committed, two turtledoves or two young pigeons, one for a sin offering and the other for a burnt offering. ⁸He shall bring them to the priest, who shall offer first the one for the sin offering; he shall wring its head from its neck, but shall not sever it, ⁹and he shall sprinkle some of the blood of the sin offering on the side of the altar, while the rest of the blood shall be drained out at the base of the altar; it is a sin offering. ¹⁰Then he shall offer the second for a burnt offering according to the ordinance; and the priest shall make atonement for him for the sin which he has committed, and he shall be forgiven.

11 'But if he cannot afford two turtledoves or two young pigeons, then he shall bring, as his offering for the sin which he has committed, a tenth of an ephah of fine flour for a sin offering; he shall put no oil upon it, and shall put no frankincense on it, for it is a sin offering. ¹²And he shall bring it to the priest, and the priest shall take a handful of it as its memorial portion and burn this on the altar, upon the offerings by fire to the LORD; it is a sin offering. ¹³Thus the priest shall make atonement for him for the sin which he has committed in any one of these things, and he shall be forgiven. [And the remainder shall be for the priest, as in the cereal offering.]'

14 The LORD said to Moses, ¹⁵'If any one commits a breach of faith and sins unwittingly in any of the holy things of the LORD, he shall bring, as his guilt offering to the LORD, a ram without blemish out of the flock, valued by you in shekels of silver, according to the shekel of the sanctuary; it is a guilt offering. ¹⁶He shall also make restitution for what he has done amiss in the holy thing, and shall add a fifth to it and give it to the priest; and the priest shall make atonement for him with the ram of the guilt offering, and he shall be forgiven.

17 'If any one sins, doing any of the things which the LORD has commanded not to be done, though he does not know it, yet he is guilty and shall bear his iniquity. ¹⁸He shall bring to the priest a ram without blemish out of the flock, valued by you at the price for a guilt offering, and the priest shall make atonement for him for the error which he committed unwittingly, and he shall be forgiven. ¹⁹It is a guilt offering; he is guilty before the LORD.'

6 ¹*The LORD said to Moses, ²'If any one sins and commits a breach of faith against the LORD by deceiving his neighbour in a matter of deposit [or security,] or through robbery, or if he has oppressed his neighbour ³or has found what was lost and lied about it, swearing falsely —in any of all the things which men do and sin therein, ⁴when one has

---

*Ch. 5.20 in Hebrew.

sinned and become guilty, he shall restore what he took by robbery, or what he got by oppression, or the deposit which was committed to him, or the lost thing which he found, ⁵[or anything about which he has sworn falsely;] he shall restore it in full, and shall add a fifth to it, and give it to him to whom it belongs, on the day of his guilt offering. ⁶And he shall bring to the priest his guilt offering to the LORD, a ram without blemish out of the flock, valued by you at the price for a guilt offering; ⁷and the priest shall make atonement for him before the LORD, and he shall be forgiven for any of the things which one may do and thereby become guilty.'

It is not by chance that 4.1, 2aα begins with a new introductory formula; for in 4.1–6.7 (6.8, 9aα has, like 4.1, 2aα a more detailed introductory formula) we again have before us in essence directions for sacrifice, and the style throughout is once more ritualistic. The point of departure and the conclusion are, however, in each of the sections different from Lev. 1–3. Each starts with a main clause standing first, setting out a definite occasion for sacrifice, and concludes with a statement of the effect of the particular sacrifice. The occasion is always a trespass committed by someone, and the conclusion always an expiation of this trespass. We are dealing then with sacrificial procedure having expiatory effects. This chapter is distinguished from the rituals in Lev. 1–3 by a style in places very complicated and bombastic, especially in the linked main clauses. The chapter is thus shown to be later as a whole and added on subsequently to the actual rituals. These chapters, as will be shown in detail, are thus not from one mould, but have grown gradually into their present state. Yet at least in their basic form they could be earlier than P; they have undergone a subsequent not very thorough working over in the direction of P. In many points—e.g. the role of the priest, in contradistinction to the offering 'layman'—they show relationship with the rituals in Lev. 1–3, make specific references to them at suitable points, and presuppose their existence. Their ultimate point of origin might therefore be sought in the cultic practices of the Temple at Jerusalem. Their lack of unity makes closer dating impossible; one can only attempt a relative chronology, that is, distinguish between older, more recent, and most recent material. Although the oldest portions may go back to pre-exilic times, we are dealing in the main— as definite details later referred to will show—with exilic and post-exilic times, when cultic procedure was still taking place on the site of the destroyed Temple of Solomon, forms of worship were being sketched for a new holy place which was to be built, and the regular orderly cult took on a new beginning in the so-called Temple of Zerubbabel. The literary growth of this chapter was probably not yet complete when the corpus of sacrificial instructions in Lev. 1–7 was fitted in to the narrative framework of P.

Chapter 4 deals with cases in which someone has trespassed unwittingly and unintentionally against some divine commandment. We are not told specifically what kind of trespass is envisaged, but we gather from the construction of the main clauses that it is a question not of failure to observe the prescribed procedure, but rather the carrying out of forbidden procedure. Provision for the possibility of a cultic atonement always applies to something done 'unwittingly' (Heb. technical term *bišgāgā* from the stem *šgg*, probably with the root-meaning 'to err'); for deliberate infringement of divine commands or prohibitions there was no such possibility. For atonement a sacrifice had to be presented, here characterized as *ḥaṭṭā't*; this term, usually rendered 'sin offering', is not a genuine sacrificial term like 'burnt offering' and 'peace offering', but the word for 'transgression' (both uses run parallel in the chapters under consideration), and denoted first of all not a particular kind of sacrifice, but the purpose of the sacrifice ('offered for "transgression" '), and became only secondarily a special sacrificial designation. By type, the 'sin offering' belongs to the category of peace offerings, to which repeated reference is made (vv. 10, 26, 31, 35); but the special purpose of the 'sin offering' excludes the sacrificial meal belonging to the peace offering, thus constituting a deviation from the peace-offering ritual. Chapter 4 is divided into four subsections from the point of view of a person who has on different occasions committed a 'trespass' and must therefore bring a 'sin offering' (vv. 3–12; 13–21; 22–26; 27–35); the animals to be offered differ in each case. In general, the cultic procedure is the same in all four cases; yet there are differences of detail pointing to a very complicated relationship of the four sections to one another. On the one hand, the two last sections bear the marks of greater primitiveness (e.g. in the provision of only *one* altar in the holy place); on the other hand, the first two sections seem to be more complete, containing as they do elements whose original kinship with the ritual seems at least very probable (e.g. the 'sprinkling' of part of the sacrificial blood). This suggests as the earliest stage general and unified 'sin offering' directions; as time went on these were frequently split up into subsections and edited from the point of view of different people needing atonement. In the process the original directions seem to have survived in completest form in the first section, which on the other hand has been particularly subject to later working over.

[4.1–2] The introductory formula (vv. 1, 2aα) and the main clause immediately after, contained in every section but repeated in varying forms (v. 2aβb), is followed by the special section about 'the anointed priest' (vv. 3–12). [3] The expression 'the anointed priest' only occurs in the Old Testament here and once more in v. 16, and additionally in the secondary distorted phrasing of 6.23; otherwise we only hear of the 'anointing' of the High Priest (Aaron) or of the priests (the sons of Aaron). The expression is most noteworthy, for on one side it signifies with great probability the end of the Davidic Kingdom. Only when it ended did the 'anointing' pass to the chief priest in Jerusalem as the remaining representative of the still existing community. On the other side, it is no longer customary in post-exilic times (Haggai and Zechariah already use the title 'High Priest', literally 'Great Priest'; cf. Hag. 1.1; Zech. 3.1, etc.). This would suggest that the section vv. 3–12 might have taken its present form in the time of the exile, or in any case soon after. Certainly there lies underneath an older form, not referring to 'the anointed priest'; for 'the anointed priest' appears in v. 3 as the person to be atoned and again in v. 5a as the one who initiates the special act of 'sprinkling' the sacrificial blood, whereas in the sequel this act (v. 6) and the further cultic procedure (vv. 7, 10) are carried out merely by the priest, not in any way characterized as a member of a priestly hierarchy. The simple expression 'the priest' is appropriate only if it is contrasted with a 'layman', which supports the conclusion that the older form of this section, for the most part preserved, referred to the 'sin offering' of any 'layman': only through a secondary remodelling of the opening sentence was the whole orientated to the special case of 'the anointed priest'. An unwitting transgression by the 'anointed priest' must, as v. 3 expressly states, lead to the 'guilt of the whole people', for he, as head, represents the whole. An atonement was therefore in this case particularly important, and the offering—a young bull—specially valuable. For the same reason this case was put first in the sequence of sections. [4] The person to be atoned had to bring the animal into the holy place 'before Yahweh' (the expression 'before Yahweh' clashes with the adjacent expression 'to the door of the tent of meeting', thus showing an element of working over in the direction of P); then he had to complete the act of 'laying on the hand', which in the sin offering doubtless preserved its original and special meaning, the transference to the animal of guilt, conceived in some quite crude sense. Finally, he had to slay the animal 'before Yahweh' (v. 4). [5–7] Here followed the action with the blood to be carried out by the priest, and appearing here (vv. 5–7) as a peculiarity of the sin offering. From the blood caught in the vessel some was sprinkled seven times with the priest's finger 'before Yahweh', i.e. presumably sprinkled in the air. What this action meant or effected is nowhere explained. Presumably it signified a consecration of the blood by the sprinkling of a part in the consecrated precincts according to the sacred number seven. Thus the ensuing action, the smearing of the blood by the priest on the horns of the altar, would have the expiatory effect essential for the sin offering; for this, not only the blood, but the blood dedicated to Yahweh by 'sprinkling', was requisite. The pouring out of the remaining blood at the base of the altar signified the return of the rest not used for the special blood-rite to Yahweh, to whom as the seat of the animal's life it belonged. In the passage vv. 5–7 there are again traces of secondary working-over by P. This comes out in the very unsyntactical interpolation of the 'veil of the sanctuary', which does not properly fit on to the preceding expression 'before Yahweh'. Moreover, the altar whose horns were to be smeared with blood is described as the 'altar of fragrant incense' (following the mention of the altar of incense which is even secondary in P: cf. Ex. 30.1–10 and *Exodus*, pp. 234f.)—but in the corresponding sentences of the third and fourth sections (vv. 25a, 30a) the altar of burnt offering is named—and this altar is distinguished from the altar of burnt offering at the base of which the blood left over is to be poured out. Clearly there was only one altar, the altar of sacrifice pure and simple (*hammizbēaḥ*), i.e. the 'altar of burnt offering' (thus v. 5b is also secondary); and it is not even certain whether the additions mentioned reflect later cultic practice after the exile, since a blood-rite at the altar of incense in the 'holy place' of the Temple is surely out. Probably these additions represent theoretical instructions for the special case of 'the anointed priest', no longer existing in post-exilic times, for which the blood-rite at the altar of incense in the Temple seemed suitable. [8–10] In vv. 8–10 the act of sacrifice follows, corresponding precisely to that of the peace offering (cf. above pp. 30f.) expressly referred to in v. 10a. If the peace offering was meant to establish or strengthen the community between God and the participants, the sin offering was intended to reconstitute it. At all events there was no question of the man who had incurred guilt taking part

in a common sacrificial meal until the sacrificial procedures were fulfilled and atonement effected. [11-12] In this case therefore the parts
of the animal not burnt on the altar, normally serving for the sacrificial meal, must be ritually destroyed by burning in a special place
'outside' (vv. 11, 12). The particular mention of the skin, heading the
list of parts to be thus burnt, indicates that in peace offering as in
burnt offering (cf. 1.6a) skinning took place before removal of the
parts to be sacrificed. The massing of place details in v. 12 suggests
secondary expansion: such might be the superfluous mention of 'the
camp', coming in from redaction in the direction of P, following P's
conception of the camp. The mention of a 'clean place' 'outside'
(supply 'the sanctuary') must surely be original, as even the remains
of the sacrificial animal were not allowed to return to profane
ground; so, too, must the concluding sentence that deals with the
burning on the refuse-heap for sacrificial remains (v. 12b), located in
the 'clean place'. The full technical term *šepek had-dešen* = '(place
for) the disposal of the fat(-ashes)' occurs only at this place in the Old
Testament (cf. also above p. 25 on 1.16). It remains uncertain who
the subject is in v. 12a: probably the offerer needing expiation, for
the priest is not expressly mentioned.

[13-21] The second section (vv. 13-21) follows the form of the
first, is dependent on it, and secondary to it. To avoid having to
repeat all the details, it uses shorthand phrasing (e.g. the short mention of 'all its fat' instead of the lengthy details of vv. 8-10a), or
replaces more exact description by expressly referring back to the
first section (vv. 20a, 21a). The interconnection is so extensive that the
'anointed priest' crops up once more, though here quite out of place
(v. 16) at the beginning of the blood-ritual; here, too, the further
performance of the blood-rite is handed over to 'the priest'.

[13] The case foreseen in this section concerns transgressions of
divine commandments or prohibitions by an unknown person who
does not recognize his trespass and so is neither able nor willing to
present the requisite sin offering (as far as the passage is dealing with
an 'unwitting' and therefore expiable offence). The whole community
is thereby involved in trespass and must accept the burden of its expiation, which it is able to do, seeing that the trespass is for the
community at any rate an 'unwitting' trespass. The beginning of this
section has lost its unity through secondary alterations. The confused
juxtaposition of 'congregation' ('*ēdā*) and 'assembly' (*qāhāl*) can hardly
be original: we must suppose *qāhāl* primary, and '*ēdā* introduced by

redaction towards P. Thus the first sentence, v. 13aα, might originally have run otherwise and only pointed to the occurrence of some trespass which, because unexpiated, and through the idea of collective guilt, operated as though the whole 'assembly' had done something forbidden and so incurred guilt (thus the wording of v. 13b). [14] In this case, the whole community being concerned, a valuable young bull was the required sin offering (v. 14). [15] In the procedure that follows, so far as it did not belong to 'the priest', some individual obviously represented the 'assembly', as the singular verb in v. 15b shows.* The text no longer indicates who he may have been, for his name has given way to the secondary introduction of the 'elders of the congregation' in v. 15a. [16–19] The sacrificial procedure exactly follows that of the first section. [20–21] Verses 20b and 21b contain two concluding phrases; this can hardly have been original. If one assumes the readiest explanation, that the sentences in vv. 20, 21 have gradually come in in the traditional order, then v. 20b would be the original concluding sentence (it recurs in the same words in 26b, 31b, 35b). Moreover, the complete dependence of the second section on the first suggests that the final sentence once stood at the end of the first section, and in the end disappeared from it only by mistake. It expresses the intended atoning effect of the sin offering; and it is to be noted that 'the priest' appears as the subject of the atoning action and that God is not expressly named. He only appears indirectly as the logical subject of the concluding passive expression, which one can only surmise to be the reflection of a concluding declaration by the priest. The subject-matter suggests that in the sin offering, at least in its formulation, the notion of an effect *ex opere operato* is fairly deeply embedded. If v. 20b represents the original concluding sentence, then v. 21a was added later by one who wished to make clearer the reference to the first section. This led to the need for a further concluding formula (v. 21b), inserted before the redaction in line with P and therefore containing the key-word *qāhāl* (not *'ēdā*).

[22–26] The third section (vv. 22–26) considers the case of a *nāśi'* who has trespassed. It remains uncertain who is meant by the title *nāśi'*. The title appears without article, in a general sense. This does not suggest 'the prince' as a future substitute for the Davidic Kingdom in Ezekiel's sketch of the future (Ezek. 44.3, etc.); or the 'prince of Judah' in the Chronicler's narrative about the beginnings of post-exilic times (Ezra 1.8); especially as the *nāśi'* in Lev. 4 seems

*[Noth renders v. 15b, 'and he shall kill . . .'. Ed.]

to be quite subordinate to the 'anointed priest', both by the position of the section and by the sin offering provided for him. Rather, it suggests one of those tribal 'spokesmen' existing in ancient times (cf. Ex. 22.27 and Noth, *Exodus*, pp. 187ff.) and appearing again in the P narrative (Ex. 16.22, etc.). The question is whether anything of the kind still survived or had been revived at the time covered by Lev. 4; or whether we are dealing only theoretically with an ideal tribal constitution, to be reconstituted perhaps, in which a *nāśī'* would have his place. The section vv. 22–26 is introduced by an unusual conjunction. By means of the generally underlying directions for the sin offering, it has been accommodated to the case of the *nāśī'*. It has one peculiarity, that in this case a he-goat is prescribed for the sin offering; for the rest, its details are very close to the following section. [22–23] In the linked conditional clauses the phrase *weʾāśēm ʾō hōdaʿ ʾēlāw* (vv. 22–23) presents difficulties recurring word for word in vv. 27–28 and therefore scarcely capable of being 'emended' by a critical 'easing' of the text in the direction of vv. 13–14. Rather this phrase should be attributed to the ancient common substratum. It has been simplified in the very secondary second section and in the first section it has subsequently fallen out after v. 3a. The phrasing, with its use of *ʾō* (= 'or') sets out two possible ways in which the 'unwittingly' committed trespass may become conscious. The second way is that 'someone' should make the offender aware of his trespass. (In spite of a change of subject the new indefinite subject is not expressed, but this is admissible in Hebrew). The word *weʾāśēm* will then cover the sense of the objective incurring of guilt and the subsequent becoming conscious of guilt. [24] In what follows (v. 24, 'in the place where they kill the burnt offering before Yahweh') the indication of the place for slaughter is noteworthy. This phrasing sounds original and reminds one strikingly of the passage where Cyrus gives permission for return from exile. It describes the place for rebuilding the Temple on the site of Solomon's former Temple in the words 'the place where sacrifices are offered and burnt offerings are brought' (Ezra 6.3). Did the basic form of the sin-offering directions, like the Cyrus passage, presuppose the situation between the destruction of the old and the building of the new Temple? [25–26] In vv. 25, 26 there is, in contrast to the first two sections, mention of only one altar; and this, after a previous mention of two altars, is characterized in v. 25 as 'the altar of burnt offering', though we know that it was originally called simply 'the altar' (so v. 26). In v. 25 the action

of 'sprinkling' the sacrificial blood is lacking (cf. above p. 39, v. 6).
Was this action not suitable for the offering of animals from the
flock? That is improbable. Is it lacking because what is in any case a
rather succinct section cannot repeat everything previously said in the
first section? That, too, is unlikely, seeing how special the action was.
Or did the compiler perhaps wish through these omissions to show
the cases dealt with in the last two sections as less important than the
first two? At all events this action may have belonged to the ancient
basic form of the sin-offering instructions and not have been added
subsequently to the first two sections. The lack of reference to any
procedure for dealing with the remains of the animal, as found in
vv. 11, 12, and (with reference back to them) in vv. 20a, (21a), is
easily explained by the tendency to avoid apparently superfluous
repetition in the interests of brevity.

[27–35] Verses 27–35 deal with the basic case of an unwitting
trespass by an 'ordinary layman'. The previous sections show that a
'single' person is meant, in contradistinction to the community of
vv. 13–21, one from 'the people of the land' (an expression marking
the difference from office-bearers or other prominent persons) [RSV:
'common people']. In this case a female animal from the flock sufficed
for sacrifice, either sheep or goat, as set out in two parallel passages
(vv. 28–31 and vv. 32–35), probably because we are here considering
people of small means. In both parts again only one altar is mentioned; the act of 'sprinkling' the sacrificial blood is missing; so is the
destruction of the remains (cf. the details of the third section above,
p. 41). Moreover, there is again a variable tendency towards
brevity. Nothing materially new is added. In the conditional clause
structure (vv. 27–28) there is the same formula as in vv. 22–23 (see
above). The place of slaughter is designated in v. 29b in shortened
form 'in the place of burnt offering'; v. 33b, on the other hand, has
the full dependent clause as in v. 24. The one altar is again in vv. 30a,
34a 'the altar of burnt offering'; but in vv. 30b, 34b merely 'the altar'.
In v. 31a there appears in connection with the sacrificial procedure,
and quite isolated, the expression 'for a pleasing odour to Yahweh'
(cf. above p. 24). Verse 35 describes the sin offering as presented
'upon the offerings by fire to Yahweh', i.e. after other previously
offered sacrifices—again a quite isolated observation.

[5.1–13] Chapter 5.1–13—clearly a kind of appendix to ch. 4—
presents a special case of trespass, the failure to divulge a known
offence. This case, joined on to the general introductory sentence

(vv. 1aβb–4) in an unusually complicated, obscure and clumsy sequence of conditional clauses, capable of several meanings, finally coming to rest in v. 5a, and may be variously interpreted. However, the nature of this case is clearly indicated. [1] First (v. 1aβb) we learn that someone unlawfully utters a curse. Someone else (with $w^eh\bar{u}$' the feminine $nepe\check{s}$ = 'one' is carried on as a masculine—cf. 2.1; 4.2), being present ($r\bar{a}$'$\bar{a}$), or hearing of this ($y\bar{a}da$'), fails to report the matter, and in so doing incriminates himself. (The $w^en\bar{a}\acute{s}\bar{a}$' $^{'a}w\bar{o}n\bar{o}$ at the end of v. 1 is the equivalent of the $w^{e'}\bar{a}\check{s}\bar{e}m$ at the end of vv. 2, 3, 4; the variation points, however, to a lack of literary unity in the conditional-clause sequence.) [2–3] Verses 2 and 3 concern the cultic uncleanness of a person who, through accidental contact with something unclean, animal or human, occasioned the trespass ($nepe\check{s}$ here, in contrast to v. 1aα, is the person who only gave occasion for the trespass). Someone else notices this (with $w^eh\bar{u}$' in v. 2bβ and v. 3bβ there is an imperceptible change of subject, and this $w^eh\bar{u}$' has the same relationship as the $w^eh\bar{u}$' in v. 1), without bringing it to the notice of the tainted person (this last point is not expressly stated, but is implied), thus becoming guilty himself. [4] Finally in v. 4 the case is posed of someone ($nepe\check{s}$ again, as in v. 2) involuntarily and unsuspectingly uttering a curse, a word of power working 'good or evil' without the will of the utterer, and another hearing the unintentional oath or learning of it and then failing to make it known. Thus all these cases involve not the person who gave the first occasion for guilt, but only the person who knew and who failed, for any reason at all—most likely through negligence—to inform the culprit or make the matter public. By this failure he prevents the curser being brought to punishment or the polluted man taking the requisite initiative for ritual cleansing or any measures to counter the effects of the accidental curse. This trespass, not exactly 'unwitting', but all the same an oversight, could be cultically expiated by a sin offering. [5–13] Verses 5b–13 deal accordingly with the required sin offering; they fall into three parts, corresponding to the material to be brought for the offering. The people concerned are of small means or even poor; but they may have been incriminated by their failure to report a trespass and must now appear with an offering. The kind and worth of the offering are graded to suit their means, though the sacrificial procedure retains the same fully effective atoning quality, as the stereotyped phrasing, familiar from ch. 4, constantly affirms (vv. 6b, 10b, 13a). [5–6] The list begins with a female from the flock, already represented in ch. 4 as the lowest grade of possible animals for sacrifice (v. 6). After the guilty man has confessed his offence, which in general was not a notorious and definable matter of fact, and has freely admitted his trespass, the sin offering was presented. Its completion by the sacrifice of a female animal from the flock, already described in ch. 4, needs no additional detail. This at once makes it clear that ch. 4 is presupposed in the present section: thus v. 6 only consists of an introductory sentence and an incomplete concluding formula. In v. 6 we note the first appearance of the word 'āšām, really meaning 'guilt', but here bearing the sense of 'atonement for guilt', 'penance'. It is not here a sacrificial term for 'guilt offering', for the sacrifices in 5.1–13 are always expressly characterized as 'sin offerings' (ḥaṭṭā't). [7–10] According to vv. 7–10 poorer folk could be content with a sacrifice of two of the customary doves (cf. 1.14–17). This needed a little more precise detail, ch. 4 not having envisaged a sin offering of doves. It is noticeable that only one dove was to be presented as a sin offering: the other was to be a burnt offering. (Did the burnt offering still belong to the sin offering, and this—as a regular matter of course—not need to be expressly stated?) Whilst the dove for the burnt offering must be presented (v. 10a) according to the burnt-offering ritual (1.14–17), the dove for the sin offering required a somewhat different procedure. The difference was this: for the sin-offering dove the head was not wrung off, but only the neck slit and with the blood which came out was performed the act of 'sprinkling' peculiar to the sin offering (cf. 4.6 and above p. 39). This blood was to be sprinkled 'against the side of the altar' (the section mentions only one altar), whilst the rest of the blood was to be pressed out at the base of the altar (slightly different from the burnt-offering ritual of 1.15b). The body of the bird is not further mentioned, but was probably dealt with according to the procedure of 4.11, 12. [11–13] A man so poor that he could not even offer a dove might satisfy the sin-offering requirements by making a vegetable offering (vv. 11–13) with the tenth (part) of an ephah of wheat—or barley-meal. The ephah frequently occurs in the Old Testament as a dry measure, especially for grain. Its size can no longer be determined; estimates vary from about 23 to about 40 litres. In any case the tenth of an ephah represented a very modest amount. The offering of grain recalls the meal offering (ch. 2), and this section, too, contains some technical terms from the meal offering. Yet we are not here dealing with a meal offering, but a sin offering, though of vegetable material (this is expressly stated in vv. 11bβ, 12b). Verse 11bα shows that in this case the preparation of a cake by adding oil, and its consecration with incense, have disappeared, leaving only the offering of simple flour. The latter, however, followed the rules for the meal-offering ritual, the priest taking a 'handful' and burning it on the altar as 'azkārā (cf. above p. 27). The question of what was to be done with the rest of the meal receives the answer that it shall belong 'to the priest' 'as in the meal offering' (cf. 2.3, 10). This is given in a statement coming after the concluding phrase, and therefore probably a secondary addition.

[5.14–6.7] The rest of the section (5.14–6.7) is shown by the very short introductory formula (v. 14) to be a further supplement to what precedes. It is shown not to be a unity both by the contents of the subsections (vv. 14–16; vv. 17–19; 6.1–7) and also by the occurrence of a further short introductory formula in 6.1. It has thus been added to in stages; yet it presents a relatively coherent whole, for in all the cases covered the manner of carrying out the expiation is the same. This is supported by the regular recurrence of certain forms of expression. To discover what the act of expiation consisted of is the real problem in this section. At any rate we may note that the whole section says nothing and hints at nothing about a real sacrificial procedure. [15–16] Verse 15 starts—like 6.1, the introduction to the third section—from a 'falsification' (Heb. ma'al) as the matter of the trespass, against the 'holy things of Yahweh', i.e. against property belonging to Yahweh or specifically to his sanctuary or its priests. In practice, this 'falsification' points first and foremost to sacrificial gifts (for an example in a special case cf. Josh. 7.1), gifts which might be either of inferior value or possibly not used in accordance with the ritual, or even withheld. In any case the possibility of atonement depended on this happening 'unwittingly' (bišgāgā): an intentional action of this kind was punishable by death (cf. Num. 15.30). The expiation of such a trespass, again affirmed in v. 16b of the concluding formula by the usual phrasing (cf. 4.20b and elsewhere), required (v. 16a) not only compensation to the priest for the defective goods, with a fifth superadded, no doubt by way of punishment—in money value, as this regulation implies—but also a cultic gift in the narrower sense, described in v. 15 as 'āšām (cf. v. 6 and above p. 45) consisting of a 'ram without blemish'. But now most strikingly in connection with the ram the passage speaks not of any sacrificing but of assessing the money value of the ram. There comes in here, and also in v. 18a and 6.6b, the scarcely translatable set phrase $b^e$'$erk^ek\bar{a}$, perhaps meaning 'according to the measure of your comparison'. Here, as in some other Hebrew set phrases, the possessive pronoun has the sense of 'one'—'if one compares it'. The objects to be compared are obviously the thing itself and its money value. But what is the point of ascertaining the money value of the ram? The money compensation for the defective goods was a separate matter, and the phrasing of the passage could not allow it to mean that the money value of the ram had been calculated for this purpose. Nor can we assume from the text that the ram to be offered preserved (after official valuation) a certain minimum money value. Here, the mention of the 'shekel of silver' (literally 'silver in units of weight') is in opposition to the 'ram', and must be literally translated 'a ram without blemish from the flock, that is, in comparison, shekel silver based on the holy shekel'. That can only mean that the ram's value in money, and not the ram itself, was to be 'brought in'; and that in making payment the standard for the shekel should be the shekel-weight valid for a sacrifice. This would suppose varying standards of value for the shekel, the average being about 12–15 grams. Coin can hardly be meant, for this can scarcely come into consideration at the time of this section, even if it were of fairly late literary composition. Silver or other metal by weight must be meant, for which the number of units of weight ($\check{s}eqel$) must be determined. In these circumstances we can easily see that this and the following section are not discussing a sacrifice at all and so the word '$\bar{a}\check{s}\bar{a}m$ does not denote a particular kind of sacrifice ('guilt offering') but means 'compensation', 'making amends'. Why, then, is the sentence in v. 15b phrased as though a ram were to be 'brought in'? Certainly the older custom was actually to bring in an animal. When later on the reckoning of a money equivalent took the place of this bringing, the instructions were still worded as though the sum of money *were* the ram.

More difficult to answer is the question why in the cases dealt with in 5.14–6.7, but not in the trespasses previously reviewed in chs. 4 and 5, a money substitute for the sacrificial animal is provided. Perhaps this merely goes back to the fact that the section 5.14–6.7 is materially later, and so testifies to a progressive simplification and secularization of the cultic material that has taken place in the course of time.

[17–19] This explanation is particularly apposite to the next section (vv. 17–19). This is probably still later than its two neighbours; for in 6.1–7 we return to the theme of 'misdoing', already treated in vv. 14–16 (but not in vv. 17–19). Probably the two 'misdoing' sections were once together, and only became separated by the subsequent secondary insertion of vv. 17–19, so that in 6.1 a new short introductory formula, corresponding to v. 14, seemed fitting. Verses 17–19 would then contain probably the latest portion, from the literary point of view, within the complex of Lev. 4–6.7. From another point of view—the subject-matter—it was put in precisely at this point because we are dealing here again with a 'ram in money value', as in vv. 14–16, and the comparatively complicated details in 6.1–7 had to be left in place at the end. The occasion for the directions in vv. 17–19 is exactly the same as in the cases contained in ch. 4. This is shown by the almost word-for-word correspondence of the conditional clauses 4.2abβ, 13, 22, 27. Here again we are dealing with a no more precisely defined 'unwitting' trespass against a divine commandment or veto (the key-word $\check{s}^e g\bar{a}g\bar{a}$ does not appear in the conditional clause but reappears in the concluding formula, v. 18b). New material is introduced which does not appear in ch. 4: a ram was to be brought (the nearest to the ram is the he-goat of the $n\bar{a}\acute{s}\bar{\imath}$' in 4.22–26—cf. the free choice in 4.27–35 between goat and sheep); and this ram is to be paid for in money value as an 'atonement'. (The more detailed definition of v. 15bβ is reduced to the short formula $be^cerk^ek\bar{a}\ le^{\,\flat}\bar{a}\check{s}\bar{a}m$.) The introduction of the ram perhaps only means that when the sin offering was commuted to a money 'atonement' it had become customary to reckon in terms of a ram. The new rules for the cases in ch. 4 now given in 5.17–19 can only be explained by assuming that 5.17–19 represent modifications of a later date which might, or were bound to, replace the older instructions.

[6.1–7] Chapter 6.1–7 deals once again with cases of 'misdoing', not this time (as in 5.14–16) in connection with the 'holy things of Yahweh', but with the possessions of other people. True, v. 2a speaks of a 'misdoing towards Yahweh', but apparently only inasmuch as Yahweh protects and guarantees safe possession of a man's property. For in vv. 2b, 3, with their concrete details, we have, not an addition to, but a more exact definition of, the 'misdoing towards Yahweh' in v. 2a. The eventualities mentioned exclude by their subject-matter any thought of 'unwitting' actions; yet the trespasses in question rank as atonable, since they concern the mishandling, not of 'holy' things, but of human property. The injured party is styled $\check{}\bar{a}m\bar{\imath}t$. This term, which recurs frequently in the Holiness Code, can no longer be precisely determined in this special sense, particularly as even its etymology is obscure. It appears from its occurrence to be near in sense to the idea of 'fellow man', 'neighbour' (*rēaʿ*) and to designate the man living in one's circle, to whom therefore in practice it is one's duty to behave in the humane fashion required by God. (The rendering 'companion' can only be regarded as an attempt to escape from an awkward difficulty.) The trespass, as the beginning of v. 2b shows, is a 'lying' or 'concealing' (Heb. *kḥš*), not theft or robbery. This is made clear by the 'entrusted property' (*piqqādōn*). The expression alongside, *tᵉśūmet yād*, only occurring here and meaning literally 'that which is in the hand', is perhaps synonymous, and probably a literary addition, as may be gathered from its absence from the enumeration of trespasses in v. 4. These goods, then, if entrusted without witnesses or documentary proof, could by a 'lie' be given out as one's own property; this is also the case with an object found (v. 3aα), which in the absence of witnesses could be claimed as one's own. Less clear is the case of 'misappropriation' (Heb. *gāzel* or *gᵉzēlā* from the stem *gzl* = 'to take away, rob'); the context scarcely suggests a forcible robbery or a regular theft, but rather some deceptive way of appropriating someone else's property. This is also the case with 'extortion' (Heb. *ʿšq*), which might have consisted of a false representation of facts or some kind of threat. For cases of contention about rights of ownership, not susceptible of decision in the absence of grounds of proof and witnesses, there was already provision in the Book of the Covenant of 'an oath before Yahweh' (cf. Ex. 22.7–11 and Noth, *Exodus*, p. 184). There is also mention in v. 3aβb of an oath, related to all the above possibilities—a false oath constituting the climax of 'lying' and 'concealing'. It is remarkable that in the sequel this false oath does not apparently meet with any special reprobation: an 'atonement' is required only for the misappropriation of the property as such. The further mention of the false oath in v. 5aα is obviously an addition, for in comparison with v. 3 it adds the false oath as a further item in the list of property offences; which suggests the question whether even in v. 3 the mention of false swearing was not subsequently added. The instructions for expiating the offence of vv. 5aβb, 6, assume that the matter has meanwhile become known, raising the question how that could have happened: perhaps through a confession or by some betrayal of the delinquent. The latter had to restore the wrongfully appropriated goods to their rightful owner, adding a fifth of their value (cf. above 5.16a), implying that—normally at least—payment in money value took place. This accounts for the form of the cultic atonement 'a ram valued in money', as in vv. 15b, 18a, and again expressed in the shortened phrasing of v. 18a. The explanation of the completed atonement rounds off the whole with a somewhat prolix sentence in v. 7.

(e) INSTRUCTIONS FOR THE PRIESTS AND VARIOUS MATTERS:
6.8–7.38

6 8*The LORD said to Moses, 9'Command Aaron and his sons, saying, This is the law of the burnt offering. The burnt offering shall be on its† hearth upon the altar all night until the morning, and the fire of the altar shall be kept burning on it. 10And the priest shall put on his linen garment, and put his linen breeches upon his body, and he shall take up the ashes to which the fire has consumed the burnt offering on the altar, and put them beside the altar. 11Then he shall put off his garments, and put on other garments, and carry forth the ashes outside the camp to a clean place. 12The fire on the altar shall be kept burning on it, it shall not go out; the priest shall burn wood on it every morning, and he shall lay the burnt offering in order upon it, and shall burn on it the fat of the peace offerings. 13Fire shall be kept burning upon the altar continually; it shall not go out.

14 'And this is the law of the cereal offering. The sons of Aaron shall offer it before the LORD, in front of the altar. 15And one shall take from it a handful of the fine flour of the cereal offering with its oil and all the frankincense which is on the cereal offering, and burn this as its memorial portion on the altar, a pleasing odour to the LORD. 16And the rest of it Aaron and his sons shall eat; it shall be eaten unleavened in a holy place; [in the court of the tent of meeting they shall eat it]. 17It shall not be baked with leaven. [I have given it as their portion of my offerings by fire; it is a thing most holy, like the sin offering and the guilt offering.] 18Every male among the children of Aaron may eat of it, [as decreed for ever throughout your generations, from the LORD's offerings by fire; whoever touches them shall become holy].'

19 The LORD said to Moses, 20'This is the offering which Aaron and his sons shall offer to the LORD [on the day when he is anointed]: a tenth of an ephah of fine flour as a regular cereal offering, half of it in the morning and half in the evening. 21It shall be made with oil on a griddle; [you shall bring it well mixed, thou shalt break it‡ like a cereal offering, and offer it for a pleasing odour to the LORD.] 22The priest [from among his§ sons,] who is anointed [to succeed him,] shall offer it to the LORD as decreed for ever; the whole of it shall be burned. 23Every cereal offering of a priest shall be wholly burned; it shall not be eaten.'

*Ch. 6.1 in Hebrew.
†[So Noth, following BH. RSV has 'the'. Ed.]
‡[So Noth (cf. BH), reading t⁰puttenā for the unintelligible tupīnē, rendered 'in baked pieces' by RSV. Ed.]
§[See commentary. RSV has 'Aaron's'. Ed.]

24 The LORD said to Moses, 25'Say to Aaron and his sons, This is the law of the sin offering. In the place where the burnt offering is killed shall the sin offering be killed before the LORD; it is most holy. 26The priest who offers it for sin shall eat it; in a holy place it shall be eaten, in the court of the tent of meeting. 27Whatever* touches its flesh shall be holy; and when any of its blood is sprinkled on a garment, you shall wash that on which it was sprinkled in a holy place. 28And the earthen vessel in which it is boiled shall be broken; but if it is boiled in a bronze vessel, that shall be scoured, and rinsed in water. 29Every male among the priests may eat of it; it is most holy. 30But no sin offering shall be eaten from which any blood is brought into the tent of meeting to make atonement in the holy place; it shall be burned with fire.

7 1'This is the law of the guilt offering. It is most holy; 2in the place where they kill the burnt offering they shall kill the guilt offering, and its blood shall be thrown on the altar round about. 3And all its fat shall be offered, the fat tail, the fat that covers the entrails, 4the two kidneys with the fat that is on them at the loins, and the appendage of the liver which he shall take away with the kidneys; 5the priest shall burn them on the altar as an offering by fire to the LORD; it is a guilt offering. 6Every male among the priests may eat of it; it shall be eaten in a holy place; it is most holy. 7The guilt offering is like the sin offering, there is one law for them; the priest who makes atonement with it shall have it. 8And the priest who offers any man's burnt offering shall have for himself the skin of the burnt offering which he has offered. 9And every cereal offering baked in the oven and all that is prepared on a pan or a griddle shall belong to the priest who offers it. 10And every cereal offering, mixed with oil or dry, shall be for all the sons of Aaron, one as well as another.

11 'And this is the law of the sacrifice of peace offerings which one may offer to the LORD. 12If he offers it for a thanksgiving, then he shall offer with the thank offering unleavened cakes mixed with oil, un-leavened wafers spread with oil, and cakes of fine flour well mixed with oil. 13With the sacrifice of his peace offerings for thanksgiving he shall bring his offering with cakes of leavened bread. 14And of such he shall offer one cake from each offering, as an offering to the LORD; it shall belong to the priest who throws the blood of the peace offerings. 15And the flesh of the sacrifice of his peace offerings for thanksgiving shall be eaten on the day of his offering; he shall not leave any of it until the morning. 16But if the sacrifice of his offering is a votive offering or a free-will offering, it shall be eaten on the day that he offers his sacrifice, and on the morrow [what remains of it shall be eaten], 17but what remains of the flesh of the sacrifice on the third day shall be burned with fire. 18If any of the flesh of the sacrifice of his peace offering is eaten on the third day, he who offers it shall not be accepted, neither shall it be credited to him; it shall be an abomination, and he who eats of it shall bear his iniquity.

*Or 'Whoever'.

19 'Flesh that touches any unclean thing shall not be eaten; it shall be burned with fire. All who are clean may eat flesh, 20but the person who eats of the flesh of the sacrifice of the LORD's peace offerings while an uncleanness is on him, that person shall be cut off from his people. 21And if any one touches an unclean thing, whether the uncleanness of man or an unclean beast or any unclean abomination, and then eats of the flesh of the sacrifice of the LORD's peace offerings, that person shall be cut off from his people.'

22 The LORD said to Moses, 23'Say to the people of Israel, You shall eat no fat, of ox, or sheep, or goat. 24[The fat of an animal that dies of itself, and the fat of one that is torn by beasts, may be put to any other use, but on no account shall you eat it.] 25For every person who eats of the fat of an animal of which an offering by fire is made to the LORD shall be cut off from his people. 26Moreover you shall eat no blood whatever, whether of fowl or of animal, in any of your dwellings. 27Whoever eats any blood, that person shall be cut off from his people.'

28 The LORD said to Moses, 29'Say to the people of Israel, He that offers the sacrifice of his peace offerings to the LORD shall bring his offering to the LORD; from the sacrifice of his peace offerings 30he shall bring with his own hands the offerings by fire to the LORD; he shall bring the fat with the breast, that the breast may be waved as a wave offering before the LORD. 31The priest shall burn the fat on the altar, but the breast shall be for Aaron and his sons. 32And the right thigh you shall give to the priest as an offering from the sacrifice of your peace offerings; 33he among the sons of Aaron who offers the blood of the peace offerings and the fat shall have the right thigh for a portion. 34For the breast that is waved and the thigh that is offered I have taken from the people of Israel, out of the sacrifices of their peace offerings, and have given them to Aaron the priest and to his sons, as a perpetual due from the people of Israel. 35This is the portion of Aaron and of his sons from the offerings made by fire to the LORD, consecrated to them on the day they were presented to serve as priests of the LORD; 36the LORD commanded this to be given them by the people of Israel, on the day that they were anointed; it is a perpetual due throughout their generations.'

37 This is the law of the burnt offering, of the cereal offering, of the sin offering, of the guilt offering, [of the consecration,] and of the peace offerings, 38which the LORD commanded Moses on Mount Sinai, on the day that he commanded the people of Israel to bring their offerings to the LORD, in the wilderness of Sinai.

According to the introductory sentence (6.8, 9aα) the directions in this piece were for the priests ('Aaron and his sons'), and the contents bear this out. It deals preponderantly with the priestly role in the sacrificial procedure and the knowledge required for it. It assumes in general the rituals and instructions intended for the 'layman' in Lev. 1–6.7, and might well, like the latter, have the cultic practice of the Jerusalem Temple as its basis. In ancient times the priests' professional knowledge must first have been passed on by word of mouth; but at least in important points it must finally have been written down. It may be that the catastrophe falling on Jerusalem and its sanctuary in 587 BC was the stimulus for committing to writing this oral tradition. This is pure supposition, but it must approximately indicate the time to which Lev. 6.8–7.38 belong in their basic form. For this complex, too, is in essentials earlier than P and has received an easily detectable redaction in the direction of P, which seems indeed to have gone rather farther here than in the preceding chapters. The question of dating is no longer easy to determine in detail, for these two chapters are anything but a literary unity. This is shown by the various new introductory formulae in 6.19; 6.24, 25aα; 7.22, 23a; 7.28, 29a, coming in after the chief introductory sentences. The last two introduce apparently secondary additions, dealing no longer with priestly professional knowledge but containing, as the formulae themselves show, instructions for the 'layman'. One would be inclined to see the basis of the whole in the sections beginning with the stereotyped sentence: 'This is the ordinance for the . . . offering' (6.9aβ, 14a, 25aβ; 7.1a, 11a). Their order, however, is not systematic in plan or execution. On the whole one is left with the impression of a collection of elements of priestly professional knowledge arranged without much plan either in the original version or in subsequent repeated expansions.

[6.8–13] The section under the key-word 'burnt offering' (6.9aβ) deals merely with the priestly task of tending the altar fire (vv. 9b–13). This covered all 'fire offerings'; but as the burnt offerings needing complete burning had first claim on the altar fire, this key-word provided the best place for everything to do with the altar fire. The theme being limited to the altar fire shows that there was no intention to enumerate systematically and completely all the obligations of the priest's office; for the burnt-offering ritual of Lev. 1, the priest had also to carry out the sprinkling of the blood (v. 12b). The priest's main duty to the altar fire was to keep it always burning, and never—even at night—let it go out (so in conclusion v. 13). This was to be observed even in the necessary cleaning of the altar to be undertaken each morning by the priest. The morning burnt offering—the wording here suggests *one* daily burnt offering as the regular rule—was always to remain all night on the altar and the fire was to be continuously maintained (if required perhaps by adding extra wood). A detailed instruction tells the priest how to clean the altar each morning (vv. 10, 11). He must put on the priestly garments (cf. the suffix of *middō*) with breeches (cf. Ex. 28.42f. and Noth, *Exodus*, p. 227) and clear away the 'fat' ['ashes']—the fat-saturated remains of the sacrifice and ashes—and deposit them alongside the altar; then change his clothes (the priestly garments being worn only inside the sanctuary) and take the sacrificial remains 'outside to a clean place'. (The mention of 'the camp' might well belong to redaction in the direction of P.) (Compare 4.11, 12, dealing with a sin offering, where the portions not to be burnt on the altar were in corresponding manner to be 'taken out' to 'a clean place', in this case by the offerer himself.) While carrying out this whole procedure the priest had to see that the fire did not go out; he then had to fan it into life again by laying on new wood (v. 12a) and thereupon arrange the (regular?) burnt offering and possibly after that offer further sacrifices.

[14–18] In the meal-offering instructions intended for the priest (vv. 14–18) the only interesting things are the priest's prescriptive part in the sacrificial procedure and then the use of the sacrificial material left over. On the first point both subject-matter and for the most part wording are in full agreement with the meal-offering ritual of Lev. 2; that is to say with the case there put first and foremost—a meal offering of raw grain for baking (2.1, 2). [14–15] Only one thing is remarkable—the construction at the beginning of v. 14b (Heb. infinitive absolute)—quite peculiar within the sacrificial instructions of Lev. 1–7; likewise the abrupt transition from the plural 'sons of Aaron' in v. 14b to the singular subject in v. 15—a sure sign of secondary remodelling of an original text.* It can scarcely be doubted that v. 14b originally read simply 'the priest' instead of 'the sons of Aaron' (as in the whole preceding section vv. 8–13). Next to this, going beyond 2.2, something more is said about the manner of 'presenting' the meal offering brought by any 'layman', before the necessary information is given about the removal of the *'azkārā* (cf. above p. 27) and its burning on the 'altar'. [16–18] The remainder of the grain is made over to the priests (vv. 16–18) in the context of the regulations governing the priests, thus giving it a place suited to the subject-matter (in 2.3, 10 it was dealt with in secondary additions); yet this passage is obviously not a literary unity—witness the

---

* Even the suffix of *mimmennu* in v. 15aα, now apparently unrelated, yet not to be changed by critical emendation to the text, presupposes a different original text in v. 14b, with an appropriate masculine singular (perhaps *qorban hamminḥā*, following 2.1).

occurrence of the first person for Yahweh in v. 17aβ and the form of address in v. 18aβ. Besides this, 'the priests' in this passage have been secondarily replaced by 'the sons of Aaron'; the sentence v. 18aα is repeated in 6.29a and 7.6a, in both of which places in the transmitted text the original phrasing 'the priests' instead of 'the sons of Aaron' has remained. In the same way v. 16bβ, with its mention of 'the court before the tent of meeting', which in any case overcrowds the text and is quite superfluous after the immediately preceding indication of place, might well owe its presence to redaction in the direction of P. The priests are now told how to deal with the remaining baking material which belongs to them—2.1, 2 makes clear that this is the meaning. They were to eat it, and bound to put it to this use; but first it must be baked. Three points in all this had to be observed: first, only 'unleavened bread' might be baked—i.e. cakes without yeast, as v. 17aα again stresses. Then these cakes might only be eaten in the holy precincts ('in a holy place'); for a sacrificial gift, once brought in, might not again be brought into contact with profane surroundings, in order to avoid the dangerous effects of a contagious 'holiness'. This is stressed in v. 18 [aβ]b, a probably secondary addition, referring to all 'fire offerings'. Finally (v. 18aα) only the male members of the priestly families might eat of them: it remains an open question whether the two last-named regulations do not, in fact, coincide, for the female members would scarcely be allowed to frequent the holy precincts. The reference to 'sin offering' and 'guilt offering', stressing (v. 17b) the 'most holy' character of the sacrificial remains belonging to the priests, shows that these two kinds of sacrifice (cf. with what follows 6.24–7.10) were particularly important to the author of this observation. It is also relevant, inasmuch as meal offering, sin offering and guilt offering are all kinds of offering in which edible remains were left over for the priests. For the rest, 'the priests' in the plural are for the first time mentioned in this context, belonging to the basic form of the directions in Lev. 1–7 (before the redaction towards P); for a share in the meal offering belonged to the whole college of priests serving the sanctuary, who are assumed to be at hand, not only to the priest on duty for the particular sacrifice (v. 18aα). The remark extending this regulation for all time to all 'fire offerings to Yahweh' (v. 18aβ) is probably an addition arising from a later usage, which did not yet hold good generally for the basic form of the directions in Lev. 6.7–7.38 (cf. 6.26).

[19–23] Verses 19–23 add to these priestly meal-offering regulations an instruction about a meal offering to be managed by the priests themselves. By the new short introduction in v. 19 this paragraph is shown to be a later addition which then attracted to itself the main introductory sentence in the adjacent section, from 6.8, 9aα and vv. 24, 25aα; and furthermore by the fact that this special section interrupts the sequence of sections beginning with 'this is the ordinance for the . . . offering'. Besides this, two different accounts of the priestly meal offering are strangely intermingled in this section. On the one hand, the account of an offering to be presented regularly day by day (especially v. 20b); on the other, the account of an extraordinary offering 'on the day of anointing'. This last is easily seen to be secondary. Its occurrence is probably to be explained by a natural misunderstanding of the initial words in v. 22 (see below). 'The priests' (so originally v. 20, instead of 'Aaron and his sons'; see below v. 22) had themselves—not merely to officiate for the offerings of others—but to 'offer' an 'offering' in the form of a meal offering, and that daily. Apart from v. 20b, this is indicated primarily by the *tāmīd* at the end of v. 20aβ. It was certainly modest in amount (for the 'tenth of an ephah of meal' cf. 5.11 and above p. 45), and in two halves, one in the morning and one in the evening (v. 20b). It was to be baked (v. 21aα) in two ways laid down as possible in 2.5, on a metal dish, probably according to a method handed on from a not yet settled way of life (cf. above p. 27). The singular address in the sentences of v. 21aβb is certainly an addition, partly connected in content with 2.6. Then it was to be completely burnt (as a 'whole offering', Heb. *kālīl*), for in an offering by the priests themselves the usual share of the material 'brought in for sacrifice' was not applicable: they had to make the whole over to Yahweh through the fire, as a sacrificial gift. Verse 22a lays it down that the head priest was the one to perform all this, preparing the offering for the college of priests and then no doubt 'presenting' it on the altar. The present wording of v. 22a means the High Priest newly installed in office, but describes him in a most singular manner as 'the priest anointed to his place from amongst his sons', referring back to the rather remote mention of Aaron's name in v. 20a. This remarkable connection is most easily explained by the assumption that the original wording was simply 'the anointed priest', who, as the head priest, had in this case to carry out the actual priestly functions (on the title 'the anointed priest', belonging to a particular time, as applied to the chief priest of the sanctuary at Jerusalem, cf. 4.3, 5 and above p. 38).

A misunderstanding of this title, no longer current in post-exilic times, turned the thoughts of a later reviser to the act of anointing the priest. Thus he made out of the 'anointed priest' the High Priestly successor of Aaron who had just been admitted by anointing to his office and so related the whole section, by an inserted reference, to the act of priestly anointing (v. 20) and the special and rare cases of a change of High Priest.

[24–30] The sections that now follow, on the 'sin offering' (6.24–30) and 'guilt offering' (7.1–7 and the supplement, 7.8–10), introduced by the stereotyped heading 6.25aβ; 7.1a, were probably the latest components in the series characterized by these headings. If, as may be readily assumed, the priestly regulations had originally been arranged in the same order as the sacrificial rituals in chs. 1–3, then after the burnt offering and meal offering the peace offering would have followed immediately; but it does not, in fact, follow until 7.11–21, the sin offering and guilt offering having thrust their way in between. Thus it comes about that, quite apart from the special case of the guilt offering (cf. below pp. 58f.), the sin-offering section clearly assumes the regulations of ch. 4, and that not only in what is assumed to be the primary material, but in the transmitted form that has already undergone secondary development. Chapter 6.24–7.7 (10) must therefore be ascribed to a comparatively late period, probably soon after the exile. At all events the redaction towards P—here only slight—is later still and came in as a later addition to an earlier form.

[25] The sin-offering section (6.24–30) deals merely with the priest's share of the meat offering—after a general sentence about the slaughter of the sacrificial animal, going back to the phrasing of 4.24aβ, but now passive in construction, because the slaughter was not the priest's business (v. 25bα), and after the stereotyped reference to the 'most holy' nature of the sacrifice (v. 25bβ). The other functions of the priest in the sin offering, according to ch. 4, such as the 'blood-sprinkling' and 'blood-smearing', are here ignored. [30] In the process, after v. 30 the sin offering dealt with in 4.3–12 and 4.13–21 disappears altogether, the sin offering in which some of the sacrificial blood was brought in to be 'sprinkled' in the 'tent of meeting' (4.5, 6 and 4.17, 18) and in which the parts not burnt on the altar (4.11, 12 and 4.20a [21a]) had to be destroyed 'without'. There remained only the sacrifices of 4.22–26 and 4.27–35, which do not mention either the sprinkling or the destruction of the remains; in these the later regulations of 6.26–29 assigned the remains of the

sacrificial animal 'to the priest', and specially to the particular priest on duty at that sacrifice (v. 26), so that the sin offering (and with it the guilt offering; see below) became the chief source of priestly income. Thus the essential content of this section is the command to the priest to be specially circumspect in his dealings with this 'most holy' material. Not only must it—naturally—be consumed only in a 'holy place' (v. 26bα, v. 26bβ are probably, like v. 17bβ, an addition), but the contagious 'holiness' must above all be kept in mind. [27–28] This is immediately expressed in general terms and then (vv. 27b, 28) set out in detail. Any spot of blood from the meat belonging to the priest on any clothing must be removed by cultic washing (v. 27b)—the blood of the sin-offering animal had to be 'sprinkled' or 'scattered' as part of the ritual. The vessel in which the meat had been boiled for eating (note that here it is boiling, not roasting) must, if earthenware, be broken in pieces, or, if a valuable bronze vessel, at least be thoroughly cleansed (v. 28). The incongruous singular address in v. 27b probably rests on a wrong vocalization: without altering the consonants it can be taken that a passive phrasing (corresponding to v. 28) was originally intended, as can be seen from the Septuagint. [29] The instruction in v. 29, allowing all male members of the priests' families to participate in the share of the sin offering, contradicts the express direction in v. 26a and was probably added later on the grounds of actual practice, for the priest on duty could hardly eat by himself all the share of the sin offering that was his by right.

[7.1–7] In 7.1–7 the word 'āšām appears in the special sense of 'guilt offering' (the sense is different in 5.14–26; cf. above p. 46); thus 'guilt offering' appears alongside of 'sin offering' without its being clear what really was the difference between them, especially as v. 7a expressly states that the same directions are valid for sin offering and guilt offering. Now this remark refers indeed specially and in the first instance to the priestly share in the sacrificial animal and only indirectly to the treatment of the animal as a whole; but this was in fact, as shown by the preceding directions, essentially the same for guilt offering and sin offering. No information is to be expected in this context about the occasion and purpose of the guilt offering as distinct from the sin offering: that question is generally not raised at all in the instructions for the priests' actions in the different sacrifices, as set out in Lev. 6.8–7.38, and only comes up for special reasons in the peace offering in 7.11ff. Leviticus 14 provides the best source for gathering something of the meaning of the 'guilt offering'. There it occurs in the ritual for the cleansing of the lepers.

If we have here a genuine example of the original part played by the 'guilt offering', it must be assumed that just as the sin offering of Lev. 4 served to atone for an 'unwitting' trespass, so the aim of the guilt offering was to do away with the cultic uncleanness incurred in all innocence. Then the word *'āšām*, really meaning 'incurring of guilt', must have become specialized as a cultic technical term in two different and independent senses: one meaning 'atonement' for the 'false dealing' (so 5.14–26; cf. above p. 46); the other meaning 'guilt offering' for the purpose of ritual cleansing. In the latter case the usual rendering 'guilt offering' is not quite exact. In 7.1–7 the course followed by the guilt offering appears to be assimilated to that of the sin offering. The only unusual feature is that vv. 2–5 give detailed instructions for carrying out the sacrificial procedure, not usual elsewhere in Lev. 6.8–7.38, for the rituals themselves are assumed to be well known. This shows once again the dependence of this sin- and guilt-offering section on Lev. 4 and 5; that is to say, because both these chapters gave the necessary information about the sin offering, but nothing about the guilt offering, the collection of priestly professional knowledge—or it may be a later supplement to this collection at the place where the guilt offering was discussed—added some information about the manner of carrying it out.

[1] The section 7.1–7 contains no essentially new detail. The guilt offering, like the sin offering, ranks as 'a most holy matter' (v. 1b and again v. 6bβ; cf. 6.17b). [2] Verse 2 is in abbreviated form, the acting subject not being expressly named, since the essentials could be gathered from the analogous sin-offering procedure. The slaughtering (plural form) was the duty of the offerer; the 'throwing' of the blood (singular) the duty of the priest. The place of slaughter is described much as in 6.25bα, following 4.24aβ. [3–4] The portions of the sacrificial animal to be burnt on the altar (vv. 3, 4) are the same as in the sin offering (4.8, 9), which here follows the peace-offering ritual (3.4, 5 and elsewhere). The mention of the 'fat tail' in the enumeration of these parts shows that for the guilt offering a sheep was the usual animal (cf. 3.9). The section clearly intends to enlarge again on the definition of the priest's share in the sacrificial animal. [6–7] First (v. 6) this portion is appointed for all the male members of the priestly families; and then—after a concluding formula (v. 7a)—follows the contradictory regulation that the share

should belong specifically to the priest who has presided over the 'atoning' sacrifice. A similar discrepancy, but in reverse order, appears in the sin offering (6.26, 29a). Probably v. 6 of the guilt-offering section presupposes the sin-offering directions, already supplemented by secondary material; and later on, by v. 7b—an obvious addition—a formal assimilation is effected with the sin-offering directions, in which the sentence 6.26a once stood. Thus in the already secondary complex 6.24ff. the guilt-offering section would seem to be even later than the sin-offering section.

[8–10] To the last sentences of the guilt-offering section there have been added in vv. 8–10, very loosely and probably rather late, some further regulations about the priest's part in various sacrifices (burnt offering and meal offering). This subject was understandably important for the priestly tradition; and it is probable that the priestly claims increased with time and sought fixed written form by all sorts of additions to the existing collections of priestly professional technique. This section raises the question whether there were not in general lists compiled of the priests' share in the offerings and of the priestly dues. This question is suggested by the Carthaginian 'sacrificial tariffs', the best-known example of which is the so-called 'Sacrificial Tariff of Marseilles'.* Here, such compilations appear even as inscriptions on stone, doubtless erected in the respective holy places. It is true that the examples known hitherto come from not earlier than the third century BC; but some historical connection between these lists and the Old Testament is not far to seek, since Carthage was founded as a Tyrian colony, and its cultic institutions go back to the old 'Canaanite' heritage. This is shown by the fact that all kinds of cultic technical terms in these 'tariffs' show relationship with the cultic language of the Old Testament. Today, the regulations about the priestly share in the offerings only appear in Lev. 6 and 7 in dispersed form (cf. apart from the present passage, especially 6.16–18⁋ and 7.30–34); but they might well go back to comparable older collections. [8] In v. 8 the animal's skin is allotted to the priest on duty at the burnt offering. [9–10] There follows in vv. 9, 10 an additional clause to the regulations about the sacrificial share in the case of the meal offering, as given in 6.16–18⁋ (cf. above pp. 54f.). According to the latter, the remains of baking-meal brought

*German trans. H. Gressmann, *Altorientalische Texte zum Alten Testament* (2nd ed., 1955), pp. 448–50; Eng. trans. J. B. Pritchard, *Ancient Near East Texts Relating to the Old Testament* (2nd ed., 1955), pp. 502f.

for the meal offering was to belong to all the male members of the priestly families. This regulation is here expressly confirmed and specially stressed by the last words of the verse ('to one and all'); it is, moreover, related to the meal offering 'mingled with oil' (2.1b) and 'dry', i.e. merely raw meal (cf. 5.11). Chapter 6.16–18¶ took no account of the cases handled in 2.4–7—meal offerings consisting of cakes baked ready for eating. Verse 9 provides that in these cases, briefly designated by the technical terms of 2.4–7, the portions of the sacrificial gift that are not burnt shall belong to the priest on duty for that particular sacrifice.

[11–21] The section dealing with the peace offering (vv. 11–21) differs in various respects from the preceding sections. Firstly, a distinction is here drawn between different occasions for sacrifice, because with varying occasions went varying details, not indeed in the sacrificial action itself, but in the procedures connected with it. Secondly, special regulations—not relevant to other kinds of sacrifice—were needed to deal with the special category of peace offerings, which was followed by a sacrificial meal shared by the participants in the sacrifice. [11] In this case, then, and most unusually, the sacrificer is first introduced (v. 11b), for on him depended both the occasion and the purpose of the sacrifice. [12] Then vv. 12aα and 16aα give two parallel cases: the first, where an offerer wishes to present his peace offering as a 'thank offering' for some benefit received from God. In that case, as now laid down in v. 12aβb, he was to add vegetable garnishings to the animal offering, corresponding in part to the meal offerings; of these the priest on duty was also to have his share. These garnishings were to consist of flat cakes and wafers, unleavened, as prescribed in 2.4 and in addition—so v. 12b would seem to mean—dough mixed into cake-form, but unbaked.

[13] Finally, there is brought as a supplementary 'offering' 'cakes' made of leavened dough (v. 13); that is quite unusual, for in general 'leavened' dough or cakes were forbidden in the cultic precincts (cf. 6.17aα); yet Amos (4.5) in an admittedly not very clear passage, seems to recognize the kinship of 'that which is leavened' with the 'thank offering' (cf. also the regulations in the Law of Holiness, on the offering of first fruits, 23.10). Perhaps we are here dealing with an ancient 'thank-offering' practice which still survived. [14] From these supplementary gifts one of each kind—a wafer, a flat cake, a portion of dough—was to be dedicated to Yahweh by 'heaving' (Heb. *terūmā*), i.e. by being raised on high before the altar; they were to be

handed over to Yahweh by this symbolic action, but not burnt on the altar. In the end, they were to belong to the priest who had carried out the rite of sprinkling the blood, that is, fulfilled the priestly functions for that particular peace offering (v. 14b). This is the point to which the whole of the regulations about the supplements to the 'thank offering' are obviously directed. The remainder of these gifts then presumably served as a supplementary dish in the sacrificial meal. The priest's share in the meat from the peace offering, the main substance of the sacrificial meal, is not here mentioned.

[15] There follows in v. 15 one additional regulation about the sacrificial meal: the flesh of the sacrifice must be consumed at the sacrificial meal that same day, or at all events during the ensuing night—in any case before the next morning—a regulation deriving ultimately perhaps from the nocturnal Passover sacrifice. [16] The next case (v. 16aα) concerns a peace offering in fulfilment of a vow, or a freewill offering—i.e. one presented without any special occasion. It is no doubt specially mentioned because the procedure for it was somewhat different from that of the 'thank offering'. The difference would appear to be this: there is here no reference to vegetable gifts and so none at all to any priestly share in them. But it is questionable whether this negative element could be responsible for the special treatment of the vow and freewill offerings. We shall then see the peculiarity of the freewill gift in eating meat at the sacrificial meal on the day following the sacrifice (v. 16aβb), although the remark 'and on the next day' in the previous pronouncement appears to be a lame extension of the eating of the flesh on the day of sacrifice only. This pronouncement and the details following in vv. 17, 18 must therefore be held original; only the clumsily added concluding sentence in v. 16, in which the 'rest was to be eaten' on the following day, may be reckoned a secondary addition: obviously the vow and freewill offerings ranked as less important, making it possible for the strict order for consumption on the day of the sacrifice to be somewhat relaxed for them, at any rate by granting *one* more day. [17] Anything then left over must be destroyed by burning (v. 17). [18] Verse 18 puts the responsibility for this on the offerer and the individuals sharing in the sacrificial meal, no longer on the officiating priest or the priests in general. For the priests had nothing more to do directly with the sacrificial meal; so nothing is said here of any priestly share in the peace-offering meat or sacrificial meal. The regulations for eating the meat from the peace offering have simply

been taken up, as further details belonging to the peace-offering theme, into the collections of priestly professional knowledge, for they must naturally have been known by the priests and in given cases the priests might have to supply information about them. The infringement of the rule governing the time allowed for eating the meat from the peace offering had consequences both for the initiator of the sacrifice (v. 18a) and for the infringer (v. 18b). The offerer had reason to take care that the rule was observed by those whom he had invited to take part in the sacrificial meal. If broken, it would render his sacrifice unacceptable to God, and not, as was its intention, 'well pleasing' and 'reckoned' to him as a cultic observance: in other words, it would be in vain. The 'vanity' of his efforts is expressed by a professional technical term no longer clear in its meaning—*piggūl*.* It occurs, apart from this passage and a similarly worded one in the Law of Holiness (19.7), only in Isa. 65.4 and Ezek. 4.14; apparently it means specifically, not the flesh no longer allowed to be freely eaten, but rather the sacrificial transaction itself, now rendered null and void. The infringer himself, however, had to bear this guilt in person, though it is not exactly explained precisely what this means. In the case of the 'unwitting trespass' it was probably a question of atonement by a sin offering; in the case of a deliberate deed, there would be some kind of punishment. **[19–21]** Finally vv. 19–21 give some further general 'cleanness' regulations to be observed by those taking part in the sacrificial meal. The meat from the sacrifice must not come into contact with anything cultically unclean (v. 19a), nor may any portion of it be eaten by anyone in a state of cultic unclean-ness (vv. 19b–21). Meat that had become unclean had to be de-stroyed by burning; and a cultically unclean person who neverthe-less presumed to eat of the peace-offering meat was to be—in a frequently recurring set phrase—'cut off from his people' (20b, 21b), i.e. be excluded from the cultic community and punished by death. These regulations assume that the sacrificial meal took place or at least might take place outside the holy precincts; perhaps they even assume that the participants were allowed to 'take home' with them some of their share of the sacrificial meat. For within the precincts there was nothing 'unclean' which might have been dangerous to the sacrificial meat; and 'unclean persons', whether they had become temporarily unclean through contact with some unclean object (v. 21aα), or whether they were in a state of uncleanness (v. 20aβ), were not allowed in the sanctuary.

*[RSV: 'abomination'. Ed.]

[22–27] As an appendix to the complex of Lev. 6 and 7 there have been added later two further sections, marked off from what precedes by new headings (vv. 22, 23a and 28, 29a) and characterized by these as 'for the Israelites'. They do not contain special priestly professional knowledge, but regulations that concerned everyone. In the first of these sections (vv. 22–27) the veto against eating fat or blood is emphatically sharpened and its infringement threatened with 'cutting off from his people'. The fat portions, as the specially valuable parts of every sacrificial animal—unless these were from a burnt offering, and had to be completely burnt—belonged, as God's share, to the altar. The blood, however, as the seat of the 'life' of the animal (cf. above pp. 22f.) was God's property outright and had to be given back to God before the sacrifice was offered. All this refers to the larger animals for sacrifice, enumerated in v. 23b: the blood reference also covers the birds (v. 26b). The immediate and obviously original connection of v. 25 with v. 23 shows v. 24 to be a later addition, appending an observation about the use of the fat from animals of the flock or domestic animals, either dead or torn by wild beasts. The fat might not be eaten; but not being consecrated to God, it might be put to any practical use, such as the greasing of equipment or instruments.

[28–36] The section vv. 28–36 preserves a regulation about the priestly share in the peace offering not mentioned in the peace-offering instructions of vv. 11–21. We are probably dealing here with a regulation not provided in the first place but introduced later on. Even so, the redaction towards P in this section only took place as a secondary addition; for v. 31a and v. 32a still retain the general term 'the priest'. Only in v. 31b and onwards has 'the priests' been generally replaced by 'the sons of Aaron'. [29–30] At first (vv. 29b, 30) it is prescribed as a duty for anyone wishing to present a peace offering that he himself must 'bring in' the portions of the sacrificial animal to be surrendered. The verb 'bring in' is here used in an unaccustomed fashion with special reference to the presentation of the surrendered portions. The technical terms 'offering' (qorbān) and 'fire offering to Yahweh' have the same limited reference. Clearly, the expressions from cultic language in this section have already in transmission lost their original and exact meaning. The only new feature is that according to v. 30b, as well as the fat (cf. 3.3b, 4 and elsewhere), the breast of the sacrificial animal was also to be surrendered and offered to Yahweh as a wave offering by the ritual act of 'waving', i.e. swinging to and fro in the hands. The technical term 'waving' (Heb. *tenūpā*) occurs here for the first and only time in Lev. 1–7. It is known to P (cf. Ex. 29.24, 26, 27 and Noth, *Exodus*, p. 232), but its occurrence here shows it to be earlier than P; it is also represented in the Law of Holiness (23.15ff.). The offering to Yahweh symbolized by 'waving' had the practical significance that the breast belonged to the priest's share in the sacrifice; [31] whilst the fat was according to the ancient ritual to be burnt by the priest on the altar, the breast was to belong 'to the priests' (so originally v. 31b). [32–33] The progressive expansion of the priestly claims is shown by the supplementary vv. 32, 33 (seen to be secondary by the transition to the second person plural). This adds to the animal portions to be surrendered the 'right thigh' (presumably the hinder thigh) and assigns this, not like v. 31b to all the priests, but specially to the officiating priest who performed the blood-rite in the particular sacrifice and who had completed the presentation of the fat. In this case the gesture of 'heaving' (cf. v. 14 and above pp. 61f.) was required as a symbolic action of offering to Yahweh; in this case, too, the presentation has the practical purpose of assigning it to the priest. [34] In specially solemn fashion (Yahweh speaking in the first person) the handing over of breast and right thigh to the priestly body are referred to an explicit and permanently valid expression of the will of Yahweh. [35–36] And vv. 35, 36 assign the gifts from the 'fire offerings' exclusively to 'Aaron and his sons'—perhaps not only the last-named, but all mentioned in Lev. 6 and 7—by a divine promise given on the day of their anointing, i.e. institution to office, and irrevocable. This leads on to the narrative following in ch. 8 of the institution of Aaron and his sons, which is, however, a literary supplement.

[37–38] For in vv. 37, 38 we have probably a later concluding formula to chs. 6.8–7.38. The kinds of sacrifice mentioned in the stereotyped introductory formulae (6.9aβ, 14a, 25aβ; 7.1a, 11a) are enumerated in the same order; only the '(hand)-filling' has been added secondarily, with references to ch. 8. All these directions are referred back to commands received by Moses on Sinai—without regard for the introductory sentences in 1.1 uttered by Yahweh from the tent of meeting—and dated from the day on which the sacrificial cult in the wilderness of Sinai was to begin.

# III

## THE BEGINNING OF CULTIC WORSHIP
## AT SINAI

### Lev. 8.1–10.20

#### (a) THE INSTITUTION TO OFFICE OF AARON
#### AND HIS SONS: 8.1–36

8 ¹The LORD said to Moses, ²'Take Aaron and his sons with him, and the garments, and the anointing oil, and the bull of the sin offering, and the two rams, and the basket of unleavened bread; ³and assemble all the congregation at the door of the tent of meeting.' ⁴And Moses did as the LORD commanded him; and the congregation was assembled at the door of the tent of meeting.

5 And Moses said to the congregation, 'This is the thing which the LORD has commanded to be done.' ⁶And Moses brought Aaron and his sons, and washed them with water. ⁷And he put on him the coat, and girded him with the girdle, and clothed him with the robe, and put the ephod upon him, and girded him with the skilfully woven band of the ephod, binding it to him therewith. ⁸And he placed the breastpiece on him, and in the breastpiece he put the Urim and the Thummim. ⁹And he set the turban upon his head, and on the turban, in front, he set the golden plate, the holy crown, as the LORD commanded Moses.

10 Then Moses took the anointing oil, [and anointed the tabernacle and all that was in it, and consecrated them. ¹¹And he sprinkled some of it on the altar seven times, and anointed the altar and all its utensils, and the laver and its base, to consecrate them.] ¹²And he poured some of the anointing oil on Aaron's head, and anointed him, to consecrate him. ¹³And Moses brought Aaron's sons, and clothed them with coats, and girded them with girdles, and bound caps on them, as the LORD commanded Moses.

14 Then he brought the bull of the sin offering; and Aaron and his sons laid their hands upon the head of the bull of the sin offering. ¹⁵And Moses killed it, and took the blood, and with his finger put it on the horns of the altar round about, and purified the altar, and poured out the blood at the base of the altar, and consecrated it, to make atonement

for it. [16]And he took all the fat that was on the entrails, and the appendage of the liver, and the two kidneys with their fat, and Moses burned them on the altar. [17]But the bull, and its skin, and its flesh, and its dung, he burned with fire outside the camp, as the LORD commanded Moses.

18 Then he presented the ram of the burnt offering; and Aaron and his sons laid their hands on the head of the ram. [19]And Moses killed it, and threw the blood upon the altar round about. [20]And when the ram was cut into pieces, Moses burned the head and the pieces and the fat. [21]And when the entrails and the legs were washed with water, Moses burned the whole ram on the altar, as a burnt offering, a pleasing odour, an offering by fire to the LORD, as the LORD commanded Moses.

22 Then he presented the other ram, the ram of ordination; and Aaron and his sons laid their hands on the head of the ram. [23]And Moses killed it, and took some of its blood and put it on the tip of Aaron's right ear and on the thumb of his right hand and on the great toe of his right foot. [24]And Aaron's sons were brought, and Moses put some of the blood on the tips of their right ears and on the thumbs of their right hands and on the great toes of their right feet; and Moses threw the blood upon the altar round about. [25]Then he took the fat, and the fat tail, and all the fat that was on the entrails, and the appendage of the liver, and the two kidneys with their fat, and the right thigh; [26]and out of the basket of unleavened bread which was before the LORD he took one unleavened cake, and one cake of bread with oil, and one wafer, and placed them on the fat and on the right thigh; [27]and he put all these in the hands of Aaron and in the hands of his sons, and waved them as a wave offering before the LORD. [28]Then Moses took them from their hands, and burned them on the altar with the burnt offering, as an ordination offering, a pleasing odour, an offering by fire to the LORD. [29]And Moses took the breast, and waved it for a wave offering before the LORD; it was Moses' portion of the ram of ordination, as the LORD commanded Moses.

30 Then Moses took some of the anointing oil and of the blood which was on the altar, and sprinkled it upon Aaron and his garments, and also upon his sons and his sons' garments; so he consecrated Aaron and his garments, and his sons and his sons' garments with him.

31 And Moses said to Aaron and his sons, 'Boil the flesh at the door of the tent of meeting, and there eat it and the bread, that is in the basket of ordination offerings, as I was commanded,* saying, "Aaron and his sons shall eat it"; [32]and what remains of the flesh and the bread you shall burn with fire. [33]And you shall not go out from the door of the tent of meeting for seven days, until the days of your ordination are completed, [for it will take seven days to ordain you. [34]As has been done today, the LORD has commanded to be done to make atonement for you. [35]At the door of the tent of meeting you shall remain day and night for seven days, performing what the LORD has charged, lest you die; for so I am commanded.'] [36]And Aaron and his sons did all the things which the LORD commanded by Moses.

*[So Noth (cf. BH). RSV: 'I commanded.' Ed.]

FOR THE FIRST time we meet in ch. 8 a detailed narrative—the first in Leviticus. Its subject-matter is the execution of the instructions given by Yahweh to Moses in Ex. 29 for the institution of Aaron and his sons to their priestly office. This is, then, an account of the very institution presupposed for the beginning of cultic sacrifice narrated in the following chapter. However, the institution itself was already a complicated act in which Moses was the first to carry out the priestly functions. Looked at in a wider context, Lev. 8 is seen to be a continuation of Ex. 35–39. This describes how the instructions given in Ex. 25–31 were carried out, but lacks the counterpart to Ex. 29, because the subject order required first an account of the setting up of the cultic arrangements, and only then an account of the cultic activities practically initiated by the priests' institution to office. Before the insertion of the end of Exodus and the complex of the cultic instructions in Lev. 1–7, Lev. 8 followed on Ex. 35–39. It was, of course, marked off from what went before, because 8.1–5 begins with a new command of Yahweh; so the account of the fulfilment of the instructions simply carried on in the previous manner. Closer inspection shows that the literary relationships are very complicated, both within the instructions complex and between it and the complex describing their execution. As far as the theme of the priests' institution is concerned it must be borne in mind that, because it had to deal with the priests' investiture, it also had connections with the theme of preparing the priestly robes for Aaron and his sons (instructions, Ex. 28; execution, Ex. 39.1–31). On the whole the narrative in Lev. 8 follows the wording of Ex. 29; but there are detailed divergences which do not allow us to ascribe both chapters to the same hand. The relationship of Lev. 8 to Ex. 29 corresponds here to that between the accounts of the carrying out of instructions in Ex. 35–39 and their one-time form in Ex. 25–31 (cf. Noth, *Exodus*, pp. 274–80). Now, Ex. 29 is shown to be probably secondary compared to Ex. 28 (cf. Noth, *Exodus*, p. 229) and a later addition to P. Any direct assignment of Lev. 8 to the original P-form is thus ruled out. On the other hand, it is clear that the accounts of the carrying out of instructions in Ex. 35–39 no longer presuppose the pure P-narrative in Ex. 25–31, but the P-narrative enlarged by later additions. The same is true of Lev. 8; and there is nothing against placing Lev. 8 and Ex. 35–39 in the same succession and assuming that Lev. 8 has undergone the same redactionary process as Ex. 35–39 and represents the original continuation of the last section. A single instance may clarify this relationship. In the directions for the high-priestly robes appears the apotropaic 'plate of pure gold' on the front of the High Priest's special head-band (Ex. 38.36, 37). In the instructions for Aaron's institution the same 'apotropaion' is called 'the holy crown' (Ex. 29.6). In the account of the carrying out of these directions, however, in Ex. 28 these two different designations appear simply joined in the expression, 'the plate, the holy crown of pure gold' (Ex. 39.30); and corresponding to this in Lev. 8.9 we have 'the golden plate, the holy crown'.

It was appropriate that later on the complex of the cultic instructions in Lev. 1–7, in addition to the secondary conclusion of Exodus, should be inserted between Ex. 39 and Lev. 8, inasmuch as the chapter Lev. 8 pointed directly to the beginning of the sacrificial cult described in Lev. 9. This had already been suggested by the fact that Lev. 8 had been provided with a new introduction in view of this connection (vv. 1–5).

[1–5] The introduction to Lev. 8 brings together the directions in Ex. 29.1b–3, 5aα, 7a and tells Moses to call together 'all the congregation' in front of the tent of meeting. He is told to announce the ensuing priestly institution with special solemnity as the carrying to completion, in their presence and before their eyes, of a divine command (vv. 1–5). [6] Verses 6, 7, though shortening the phrasing of Ex. 29.4, 5, introduce a certain unevenness. Verse 6 deals both with Aaron and his sons and with the ablutions required for their cultic cleansing (cf. Noth, *Exodus*, p. 230), whereas v. 7 passes on immediately to Aaron alone and his investiture. [7–9] This investiture (vv. 7–9) takes its description from Ex. 29.5aβb, 6, with variations in expression and with a somewhat different order, more suitable to the context, in enumerating the separate parts of the priestly robes. But it follows Ex. 28.4, 39 in adding the girding about with a girdle (lacking in Ex. 29) and the mention (following Ex. 28.30) of the 'Urim and Thummim', to be placed in the breastpiece, which do not appear in Ex. 29 and 39—in 39 perhaps only because they did not have to be prepared, but are assumed to be already to hand (but cf. also Noth, *Exodus*, pp. 279f.). [10–12] The act of anointing (vv. 10–12) certainly referred originally as in Ex. 29.7 specially to Aaron and to him alone, solely on the grounds that this vital act had passed down from the Davidic king to the chief priest of the Jerusalem Temple (cf. above p. 38). Again, vv. 10aβb, 11, speak of an anointing of the 'dwelling' ['tabernacle'] and its contents, as well as the altar and the laver with its base—quite unexpectedly in this context; this obviously rests on secondary additions based on Ex. 40.9–11. There, in a rather late passage, the anticipated anointing of Aaron *and* his sons (so here) is preceded by the anointing of the holy place and its furniture, in a wording corresponding extensively with that of Lev. 8.10, 11. Incidentally, v. 11a freely adds the sevenfold 'sprinkling' of oil (cf. 14.16, 27). [13] The clothing and anointing of Aaron were followed by the much simpler clothing of Aaron's sons (v. 13) based on Ex. 29.8, 9. Now the scene was set for the cultic actions (in the narrower sense) concerned with the priests' institution to office, carried out in the same manner, and therefore together, for Aaron and his sons. From now on, then, no distinction was to be made between Aaron and his sons. [14–17] First, the presentation of the sin offering had to be accomplished: the account of it in vv. 14–17 is in almost complete agreement with Ex. 29.10–14, with quite minor variations in the wording. This sin offering was a precautionary cleansing of the priests about to be instituted from any 'unwitting trespass'. Moses carried out the functions reserved for the priest officiating at the usual sin offering; as the great plenipotentiary of Yahweh, he could and must do so before Aaron and his sons were instituted to office. The sin offering described in Lev. 8 in accordance with Ex. 29 followed in essentials the sin-offering ritual presupposed in ch. 4, though not exactly corresponding with one of the special cases provided for in ch. 4. The animal for sacrifice was a young bull as in 4.3–12; there was, however, no blood-'sprinkling', and thus no distinction between two altars (agreeing with 4.22–26, 27–35 against 4.3–10, 13–21). But destruction of the remaining portions of the animal took place (as in 4.11, 12, but not mentioned in 4.21–35). The enumeration of the fat parts for burning differs in small details from the stereotyped formula of ch. 4 (vv. 8, 9, and elsewhere). One must conclude from this that the sin-offering ritual in Lev. 8 follows the substance, but not the wording, of the sin-offering ritual in ch. 4. It is worth noting the significance given in Lev. 8 to smearing the blood on the altar—also not yet present in Ex. 29—namely that it would 'purify' the altar. This was scarcely the original meaning of this action, which was probably rather a 'consecration' of the sacrificial animal's blood. [18–21] In vv. 18–21, corresponding to Ex. 29.15–18, there follows the burnt offering, for which one of the two prepared rams is used. This burnt offering was the first sacrificial gift of the priests just about to be instituted, who appear as offerers whilst Moses again carries out the special priestly functions. In contrast to the somewhat shortened phrasing of Ex. 29.17 (perhaps no longer intact) the description of the actual presentation in Lev. 8.20, 21 follows to some extent, though not exactly, the burnt-offering ritual presupposed in ch. 1 (vv. 6b, 8, 9, 12, 13). **[22–32]** The list of the sacrificial acts is concluded by the offering of the 'ram of ordination', related in vv. 22–32, following Ex. 29.19ff. In this section the relationship of Lev. 8 to Ex. 29 is more complicated because the second half of the latter chapter has been much enlarged by later accessions. Its original form corresponds fairly extensively, even in the wording, with Lev. 8. The expression 'to fill the hand' had been from ancient times an Old Testament technical term for the appointment of the priest (cf. Noth, *Exodus*, pp. 230f.). From this expression has been formed the noun, always in the abstract plural, *millū'îm* = '(hand)-filling', designating the Aaronic priest's institution to office, as found in the secondary additions to P, and so here also. In the presentation of the ram of 'ordination' we are then dealing, after the preceding sin offering and burnt offering, with a sacrificial usage provided specially for the consecration of priests. This presentation is shown by its ritual to belong to the category of peace offering (cf. Lev. 3) and demonstrates all the essential elements of the peace-offering presentation—with, of course, a special addition connected with the special nature of the priestly consecration. If the meaning of the 'peace offering' was to establish or strengthen the community between God and the participants in the sacrifice, then the special 'ordination' sacrifice was there to establish the special community between God and his priests. (The expression 'peace offering' occurs neither in the original form of Ex. 29 nor in Lev. 8, but only in a later addition in Ex. 29.28; but this is clearly the thing here intended.) **[22]** There was a very special feature in the 'ordination' peace offering, where Aaron and his sons appeared as the offerers (v. 22b) and Moses again functioned as the officiating priest and in which a ram was the sacrificial animal (cf. Lev. 3.6–11). **[23, 24]** It was this: of the blood to be sprinkled according to the peace-offering ritual against the altar, a part was applied to the priests about to be consecrated—to the lobe of their right ear, to the right thumb, and to the right big toe, as vv. 23, 24a indicate, a little more lengthily but in factual agreement with Ex. 29.20aβ. The list of the parts of the body just mentioned occurs also in the cleansing ritual for lepers, where it is a question of applying blood and oil (14.14, 17, 25, 28). These parts of the body are no doubt representative of the whole as the 'extremities' on the privileged right side. The application of the blood was intended to make a specially close connection between the priests and the altar against which the rest of the blood was thrown, and so with God. **[30]** The sprinkling of the priestly garments which Ex. 29.21 at this point requires, Lev. 8 transfers in the interests of better arrangement to the end of the actual peace offering (v. 30). From the preceding verses it is clear that there would, in fact, have been none of the sacrificial blood left over. This may then be a later addition, introduced first into Ex. 29, then transferred to Lev. 8, into what looked like a better place. **[25–28]** In preparation for the offering on the altar, the parts to be burnt were 'laid upon the hands' of Aaron and his sons so that they might carry out the gesture of 'waving' (the Heb. *hiph'il* [*hēnīp*] is here used, as in Ex. 29.24b, with a 'doubled' causative meaning); only then were the parts burnt on the altar by Moses, in this case the officiating priest. In the customary peace offering this act of presentation through 'waving' was not prescribed for the offerer; it belonged to the special features of the 'ordination' sacrifice. In the 'ordination' sacrifice, in addition to the portions to be burnt there was added not only the usual fat portions belonging to the peace offering, but also a supplementary meal offering, as in the thank offering (cf. 7.12). As well as these, there was the right (hinder) thigh, which 7.32, 33 gives as the share of the officiating priest in the usual peace offering. Here, however, in a priestly sacrifice, it had to be burnt along with the rest on the altar. **[29]** With the observation in v. 29 that Moses, the sacrificial action now completed (v. 28aβb), 'took' the breast as the portion falling to him (cf. 7.31b), Lev. 8 follows the plan of Ex. 29.26. This plan, however, already showed at this point a secondary addition, to which later supplements (Ex. 29.27, 28 and 29.30) were added (cf. Noth, *Exodus*, p. 232), not presupposed in Lev. 8. (For v. 30 see above.) **[31, 32]** After the sacrifice had been completed the ritual required a sacrificial meal shared by the offerers, in this case Aaron and his sons: this accordingly is next described (vv. 31, 32), following Ex. 29.31, 32, 34 (v. 33 being an obvious later addition). The chief difference over against the original is that not Moses, but Aaron and his sons, should do the cooking in preparation for the sacrificial meal, as indeed was the usual custom in the peace offering, in which the officiating priest had nothing more to do with the participants' sacrificial meal. Moses in this case was only playing his part in giving instructions to Aaron and his sons with reference to an express divine command. The flesh to be eaten from the peace offering was to be boiled (not roasted); cf. 6.28 in reference to the priests' share in the sin offering, corresponding to the parts to be eaten in the peace offering. Then, together with the remainder of the prescribed supplementary bread offering that had not been sacrificed (v. 26a), it was to be consumed on the same day: anything left over of meat or bread had to be destroyed by burning (cf. 7.17). **[33–36]** Following the short observation in Ex. 29.35b, vv. 33–36 now lay down in summary fashion that the whole 'ordination' solemnities should last seven days. During these seven days Aaron and his sons must, on pain of death for any infringement, remain in the holy place and not leave the entrance of the tent of meeting, i.e. the neighbourhood of the altar, where the whole act of institution took place. Verse 34 adds the direction that on each of these seven days the 'filling of hands' ceremony, already described in detail, must be repeated. However, this section shows marked unevenness in its phrasing. Verse 35b makes Moses' instructions to Aaron and his sons, begun in v. 31, run on to v. 35a, and v. 36 contains—quite appositely—a statement that these instructions were carried out. But now in v. 33b there crops up a pronouncement about the 'filling of hands' in the third person singular;* and it is at first not at all clear who is the subject. This case will hardly admit of an impersonal subject ('one'); Yahweh could hardly have been merely understood; moreover, the continuation (v. 34) rules out Yahweh as subject. In Ex. 29.35b Moses appears as subject of 'laying on hands' (in the role of Yahweh's plenipotentiary); this will also be the original sense in Lev. 8.33b, 34. In that case, this passage, with its third person, will not fit into a speech by Moses, but represents a later addition which ignored the context and left it quite open who was here supposed to be speaking. All this shows the requirement for the seven days' repetition of the 'filling of hands' ceremony to be a secondary interpolation. Thus Moses' original instructions to Aaron and his sons only concerned the eating of the portions of the peace-offering 'ordination' ram, with the added bread, and the seven-day sojourn in the holy place. The concluding sentence v. 36 is in accordance with this; it shows that Moses' task for the first day was fulfilled and brought to an end with the final instruction to Aaron and his sons (vv. 31–33a); and that he now had only to follow these last instructions given to him, which he then proceeded to do.

*[This is not clear in RSV. Noth translates: 'he will fill thy hand . . .; as he has done. . . .' Ed.]

## (b) THE FIRST PUBLIC SACRIFICES IN ISRAEL: 9.1–24

9 [1]On the eighth day Moses called Aaron and his sons and the elders of Israel; [2]and he said to Aaron, 'Take a bull calf for a sin offering, and a ram for a burnt offering, both without blemish, and offer them before the LORD. [3]And say to the people of Israel, "Take a male goat for a sin offering, and a calf and a lamb, both a year old without blemish, for a burnt offering, [4]and an ox and a ram for peace offerings, to sacrifice before the LORD, and a cereal offering mixed with oil; [for today the LORD will appear* to you.]" ' [5]And they brought what Moses commanded before the tent of meeting; and all the congregation drew near and stood before the LORD. [6]And Moses said, 'This is the thing which the LORD commanded you to do; and the glory of the LORD will appear to you.' [7]Then Moses said to Aaron, 'Draw near to the altar, and offer your sin offering and your burnt offering, and make atonement for yourself and for the people; and bring the offering of the people, and make atonement for them; as the LORD has commanded.'

8 So Aaron drew near to the altar, and killed the calf of the sin offering, which was for himself. [9]And the sons of Aaron presented the blood to him, and he dipped his finger in the blood and put it on the horns of the altar, and poured out the blood at the base of the altar; [10]but the fat and the kidneys and the appendage of the liver from the sin offering he burned upon the altar, [as the LORD commanded Moses.] [11]The flesh and the skin he burned with fire outside the camp.

12 And he killed the burnt offering; and Aaron's sons delivered to him the blood, and he threw it on the altar round about. [13]And they delivered the burnt offering to him, piece by piece, and the head; and he burned them upon the altar. [14]And he washed the entrails and the legs, and burned them with the burnt offering on the altar.

15 Then he presented the people's offering, and took the goat of the sin offering which was for the people, and killed it, and offered it for sin, like the first sin offering. [16]And he presented the burnt offering, and offered it according to the ordinance. [17]And he presented the cereal offering, and filled his hand from it, and burned it upon the altar, [besides the burnt offering of the morning.]

18 He killed the ox also and the ram, the sacrifice of peace offerings for the people; and Aaron's sons delivered to him the blood, which he threw upon the altar round about, [19]and the fat of the ox and of the ram, the fat tail, and that which covers the entrails, and the kidneys, and the appendage of the liver; [20]and they put the fat upon the breasts, and he burned the fat upon the altar, [21]but the breasts [and the right thigh] Aaron waved for a wave offering before the LORD; as Moses commanded.

22 Then Aaron lifted up his hands toward the people and blessed them; and he came down from offering the sin offering and the burnt offering and the peace offerings. [23][And Moses and Aaron went into the tent of meeting; and when they came out they blessed the people,]

*[So Noth (BH), EVV, reading *nir'e* for *nir'ā*, 'has appeared'. Ed.]

and the glory of the LORD appeared to all the people. ²⁴[And fire came forth from before the LORD and consumed the burnt offering and the fat upon the altar;] and when all the people saw it, they shouted, and fell on their faces.

This chapter relates the first public sacrifices of Israel. True, in the previous chapters sacrifices have already been offered at the 'ordination' of Aaron and his sons and at these 'the whole congregation' was present (vv. 3–5). Yet they were only spectators, not in any way participants in sacrifice; and so they soon vanished from the field of the narrative. Not even the conclusion mentions them again, saying e.g. that they were sent home while Aaron and his sons had to remain seven days in the holy place (v. 33a). In the narrative of ch. 9, however, the community took part from beginning to end. Here, at least in the second half of the proceedings, they were the sacrificers. This was the beginning of their cultic service to God, which from now on could and must be continued in a way which is not at first very precisely defined.

Now it is indeed quite clear that the narrative in ch. 9 does not presuppose the preceding chapters, which have therefore not occupied this place from the start. The fact that according to ch. 9 Aaron and his sons first had to present a sin offering and a burnt offering for themselves, before they could function as priests in presenting sacrifices for Israel, obviously leaves out of account that immediately before, in the 'ordination', a sin offering and burnt offering and a special 'ordination' offering had been presented on behalf of Aaron and his sons; still less does it take account of the repetition of those sacrifices on seven successive days (so the supplementary vv. 33b, 34). But even the instructions in Lev. 1–7 are clearly not presupposed by ch. 9. It is true that the presentations of ch. 9 took place on the whole in the manner prescribed in the ritual and instructions of chs. 1–7; but the cultic terminology is strikingly different from chs. 1–7, in spite of many correspondences necessarily due to the subject-matter. This is so even in stereotyped phrasing and word-order, which crop up again and again in chs. 1–7, always in the same fixed form, in spite of all the literary diversity of this complex. Incidentally, the cultic language of ch. 9 seems to be less developed and differentiated than that of chs. 1–7. Hence it appears not only that ch. 9 was not composed on the same literary level as ch. 8 and chs. 1–7; but also that in the framework of the larger literary context ch. 9 was there before the preceding chapters. Did ch. 8 then belong to the secondary narrative supplement to P, which presupposes the basic form of the P-narrative (cf. above p. 68)? And was the complex of chs. 1–7 an originally independent whole, which was only incorporated later into an existing narrative? If so, ch. 9, which must originally have stood in a narrative framework, must obviously be ascribed to the original P-narrative, and must be linked to the original P-narrative in the concluding portion of Exodus. This is far the most probable solution of the literary-critical problem of Lev. 9. This chapter is the first (and only) piece of 'original P' in Leviticus.

[1] The last P-elements in Exodus are probably to be found in 39.32, 42, 43 and 40.17 (cf. Noth, *Exodus*, p. 282). They describe the 'tabernacle' with its complete furnishings prepared according to the divine instructions, deemed worthy by Moses and set up on the first day of the first month in the second year. It is at this point that Lev. 9.1 may have joined on. The dating in v. 10 is the first exact note of time since Ex. 40.17 and presupposes details of day and month as there given (in Ex. 40.17). There is no doubt that Lev. 9.1aα refers back to Ex. 40.17. It is then a natural suggestion to link the 'eighth day' in v. 1aα with the seven days of the 'ordination' in 8.33 (35), and so to take the naming of the 'eighth day' as presupposing at least ch. 8 and perhaps also chs. 1–7. Then the setting up of the 'tabernacle' (Ex. 40.17) would have been immediately followed by the communication of the divine cult-instructions (Lev. 1–7), and these immediately by the seven-day priestly institution (Lev. 8). This would make the 'eighth day' the first possible day for the real beginning of the cultus. This is the significance of the naming of the day, in any case in the present Pentateuchal context. Perhaps it was from the start the intended meaning of the 'eighth day'; for there was no perceptible reason for a seven days' wait after the setting up of the 'tabernacle' till the performance of the first sacrifice, unless these seven (or more accurately six) days were filled up with something. Hence we must at least question whether the dating in v. 1aα is not in itself original, but the numbers secondarily adjusted to fit the present context. The dating itself is characteristic of P (cf. Ex. 16.1b; 19.1 and elsewhere), and the presence of a dating formula at the beginning can be taken as an argument for assigning Lev. 9 to P. But we must reckon with the possibility that the original bore a different number of days; even perhaps, if Lev. 9 originally followed straight after Ex. 40.17, simply the words 'on this same day'. Verse 1 ascribes the initiative for all that follows to Moses. He gave Aaron and

his sons the requisite instructions for what they should do themselves and what they should command the Israelites to do. (The phrase 'the elders of Israel'—who do not appear again—is perhaps secondary.) [2–4] Aaron and his sons were to choose young but full-grown animals for their sin offering and burnt offering (v. 2); ('*ēgel* has the same sense as *par* in the sin-offering instructions of ch. 4—e.g. 4.3). The Israelites were to choose for their sin offering a fully grown he-goat, but for their burnt offering yearling animals (v. 3); and for their peace offering, too, fully grown animals (v. 4). The Israelites' meal offering was to be 'mingled with oil' (v. 4). Here, *minḥā* designates not only the kind of sacrifice, but also the material, which is not the case in chs. 1–7, where 'groats' (*sōlet*) are customarily named as the material for the meal offering. The announcement of the 'Lord's appearing', belongs in v. 4b to the instructions passed on by Moses to Aaron for transmission to the Israelites. It is not a very suitable anticipation of the solemn announcement of 'the appearing of the glory of Yahweh' through Moses, and is probably a secondary addition. [5–6] This announcement had its proper place in the context of the words spoken by Moses after the requisite animals for sacrifice had been brought along, and when the 'whole assembly' had appeared before Yahweh (v. 5). At this point he addressed the assembly (v. 6), explaining to them that what was about to happen was the execution of an express command of Yahweh, who would appear in his 'glory' in the newly erected holy place in the presence of the Israelites, just as he had up till then appeared in his 'glory' on Sinai (Ex. 24.16, 17).

[7] The carrying out of the appointed sacrifices is laid by Moses upon Aaron (v. 7abα), supported in the prescribed actions by his sons, acting as his ministrants. Moses here recalls a command of Yahweh (v. 7bβ), directing not only this particular commission, and not only the choice and sequence of the sacrificial animals, but also ritual regulations to be observed in the process. Now the original P, up to this point, had made no mention of sacrificial instructions said to have been given to Moses by Yahweh. It is here tacitly assumed that Moses had received such instructions on Sinai, and either that Moses had meanwhile passed them on to Aaron and his sons, or that Moses, no doubt present at the following sacrificial proceedings, from time to time gave the necessary indications. At all events the following narrative of the execution of the sacrifices intends us to understand that everything, as carried out, was in accordance with the will of

Yahweh revealed to Moses. The appearance of the 'glory of Yahweh' after the end of the sacrifices confirms this expressly; and the natural conclusion of this narrative would be that from now on the priests' offerings and Israel's offerings were to be presented in this manner. Aaron was to 'perform' the appointed sacrifices; the verb 'perform', literally 'make' (Heb. *'śh*), refers here (and likewise in vv. 16b, 22b) always to the whole body of sacrificial proceedings. In this present sense it is quite foreign to the sacrificial instructions in chs. 1–7. It is worth noting that this makes the priest the operating subject in all presentations, not only in his own, but also in the people's (contrast the rituals in 1.2aβ, 3a; 2.1a and elsewhere). That might well be characteristic of the cultic material of P. In v. 7 the sacrifices to be presented by the Aaronic priests are mentioned again separately, but the people's offerings (cf. vv. 3, 4a) only under the very comprehensively used collective 'presentation' (*qorbān*). 'Atonement' is stressed as the purpose of all these offerings (the technical term for 'atone', Heb. *kipper*, is constructed with *b'd*, a construction not found in chs. 1–7 and ch. 8, but frequently present in the ritual of ch. 16). That, too, is characteristic of the presentation in P. That the atonement of the priests was at the same time meant to have an atoning effect for the people is shown by the representative position of the priest according to the outlook of P: an unatoned guilt in the priest would have made the whole people guilty. [8–11] The summary directions of Moses to Aaron (v. 7) are followed by his solitary completion of the sacrifice, immediately before the priestly sin offering (vv. 8–11). Its carrying out, with slaughter, blood-throwing, offering of the fat and destruction of the remains, correspond materially with the sin-offering ritual forming the basis of ch. 4. When Aaron presented this offering as 'his' (v. 8bβ), he represented thereby the whole group of the Aaronic families. His sons assisted as ministers at the sacrifice, catching the blood flowing from the slaughter in a vessel and handing it to Aaron so that he could perform the customary blood-rite, the smearing on the horns and pouring out at the base of the altar—the one altar here assumed, the (burnt-offering) altar of Ex. 27.1–8 (agreeing with 4.22–35 against 4.3–21). The enumeration of the fat portions to be burnt on the altar (v. 10a) differs in detailed expression and somewhat more compressed compass from the stereotyped enumeration in ch. 4 (vv. 8b, 9, etc.), but carries the same meaning. The same is true for the enumeration of the remaining portions to be finally destroyed by burning in v. 11 (compare on the other hand 4.11). The dependent clause in v. 10b is a superfluous later addition, modelled on v. 7bβ, by an overlearned reviser. It stands at an awkward spot, in the middle of the sacrificial procedure narrative. **[12–14]** In the burnt offering (vv. 12–14) offered by Aaron for himself and his whole house his sons were again assisting. After Aaron had carried out the slaughter (v. 12a) they not only handed the blood for the blood-throwing (v. 12b), now that he was officiating at the altar, but also handed him the 'parts' of the sacrificial animal, divided presumably by them (cf. 1.6a, 12aα), together with the head for burning (v. 13). There is a departure here from the ritual in ch. 1 inasmuch as there the entrails and legs had first to be washed and then burnt together with the previously mentioned 'parts' (vv. 8, 9). Here however (vv. 13, 14 and similarly 8.20, 21) the burning of the 'parts' and the head are first mentioned, and then—separately—the burning of the entrails and legs. **[15–16]** After the priestly sacrifices have been dealt with more or less in detail, there follows an account of the first items to be 'presented' by the people—the sin offering with the he-goat and the burnt offering with the two yearling animals of v. 3bβ (a calf and a lamb), very short and with express references to the just-narrated priestly offerings or to the 'ordinances' (vv. 15, 16) valid for both. It is thus probably to be assumed—though it is unfortunately not expressly stated—that the sons of Aaron ministered at the people's sacrifices in the same way as at the priests', for in the latter they had certainly taken part as offerers. This assumption, backed by the analogy from v. 18b, is important in that it makes a significant departure from the ritual in ch. 1. There, the sacrificial actions not immediately involving the altar were still to be carried out by the 'layman', whilst in ch. 9 everything seems already to have passed into the hands of the cultic personnel. **[17–21]** The information about the meal offering and peace offering of the people (vv. 17–21) is rather more detailed, because the priests had not had to present offerings of this kind and so nothing had yet been said about them. The meal offering consisted of flour mixed with oil (cf. v. 4aβ, where nothing is said of a baked offering), a handful of which was to be taken by Aaron for burning on the altar. This shows a deviation worth noting from the ritual in ch. 2: there is no mention here of any addition of incense; and the 'taking of a handful' does not imply the stereotyped technical expression of 2.2; 5.12; 6.15, but is a more general turn of speech. The strange allusion to the 'morning burnt offering' in v. 17b is an obvious gloss, intended to make a distinction between the present meal offering and the meal-offering supplement to the regular morning burnt offering (cf. Num. 28.4, 5), which is certainly not under discussion in this passage. Last in order comes the peace offering of the people (vv. 18–21) in which an ox and a ram were presented (cf. v. 4aα). Aaron's sons again performed the services corresponding to those in the previous sacrifices (vv. 18b–20), again in contrast to the ritual of ch. 3, where the offering 'layman' had to perform all the preparatory actions. Apart from the blood for the blood-throwing (v. 18b), the sons of Aaron had in this case to prepare especially the fat parts destined for burning (here, in the plural ḥᵃlābīm; but in chs. 1–7 the singular is usual). These are enumerated in v. 19 in a shorter form varying in detailed order from the stereotyped ritual instructions (3.3, 4, etc.). The sons of Aaron had to lay these parts ready—including the fat tail (only applicable to one of the animals, the ram). They were to be laid on the 'breast-parts' of the sacrificial animals (the plural ḥāzōt occurs only here in the Old Testament; the sacrificial instructions in 7.30, 31 use the singular ḥāze). These breast-parts served a special purpose: first, Aaron was to burn the upper fat parts in the usual fashion on the altar (v. 20), and then dedicate the underlying breast-parts with the symbolical gesture of presentation, the 'waving'. (The 'right thigh' which crops up abruptly in v. 21, though not mentioned in v. 20, would be an addition based on 7.32, 33, 34.) Then—this is not expressly stated, but is no doubt intended—he was to keep these portions for himself; for the breast-parts are only specially mentioned because they formed the priest's share of the peace offering (cf. 7.30, 31). We are finally left with an open question—as in the short account of the meal offering in v. 17a: what happened to the remaining portions of the sacrificial material? They might have served for a following sacrificial meal. But the narrative is silent here, as in the sacrificial rituals of ch. 3. From this we may perhaps conclude that the real purpose of the whole narrative is to introduce the kinds of sacrifice to be practised from now on, and the manner of their presentation. No further information seemed to be needed about the use of the remains of the meal offering, and particularly the parts of the peace-offering animals not to be burnt on the altar, in an ensuing sacrificial meal. Hence it receives no further mention, not even in an illustrative example (cf. also below pp. 87f. and 10.12ff.).

[22] The presentation of the people's offering (in the retrospective enumeration of v. 22b the meal offering is not mentioned, presumably

being considered as closely allied to the peace offering) followed the priestly blessing by Aaron (cf. Num. 6.22–27), probably customary down the ages and certainly so in the later cult. It was given from the altar, before the priest 'came down', turning towards the people and with hands upraised 'toward the people' (v. 22). [23] The sequel in vv. 23, 24 is clearly expanded through later additions. Verse 23a shows this by the repeated blessing of the people, this time by Moses and Aaron, after they have both gone into and then come out of the tent of meeting. There is no reason for this second blessing. The blessing given by Aaron to the people in v. 22a had been a fully valid blessing, hardly needing any confirmation or amplification. The entry of Moses with Aaron into the tent of meeting also seems point-less: nothing is added by way of explanation and it can only be sup-posed that a later hand wished to see Aaron led in by Moses, the great plenipotentiary of Yahweh, into the real holy place and thus authorized to frequent it. On the other hand the news of the appear-ance of 'the glory of Yahweh' before 'all the people' (v. 23b), which Moses had already announced (v. 6b), must be reckoned as part of the original P-narrative in ch. 9. This was certainly, according to P, the first appearance of the glory of Yahweh in the newly erected holy place. In it Yahweh had accepted the holy place itself and the first sacrifices offered in its precincts as 'well pleasing' (from this, too, Ex. 40.34, 35 are seen to be a secondary anticipation). Nothing at all is said about the form in which this glory appeared, and could be 'seen' by the people: it certainly suggests the cloud with the devouring fire in which, according to P, the glory of Yahweh had first appeared 'before the eyes of the Israelites' (Ex. 24.15b–17). Now, this glory had begun to appear in the midst of Israel in the legitimate sanctuary erected at Yahweh's command and dedicated by the first sacrifices to his purposes. It would accompany the Israelites farther on their way by its periodic appearances. The interior of the 'tent of meeting', with the ark in the farthermost room (Ex. 25.10–22) and with the table for the 'bread of the Presence' (Ex. 25.23–30) and the candle-stick (Ex. 25.31–40) in the large front room, plays most noticeably hardly any part in P. According to the Jerusalem Temple model, these interior arrangements once belonged to the form of the sanctu-ary; P, however, considered it only as the place of particular appear-ances and where the offerings were presented 'before Yahweh'. [24] The account given in v. 24a of fire from Yahweh going out from the Presence and consuming the sacrifice and its parts on the altar must be a later addition. It must derive from the fire element in the appearance of Yahweh (cf. Ex. 24.17a) and aims at depicting the acceptance of the sacrifice by Yahweh in particularly vivid and wonderful terms—perhaps also by an analogy from parallel religious stories. It disregards the fact that Israel must first continue her wanderings with the tabernacle in its purpose of crudely establishing the heavenly origin of the altar fire that from now on would burn (cf. 6.9–13) upon the altar. In any case the statement in 24a cannot be reconciled with the preceding narrative, according to which the sacrifice, inclusive of the burning, was completely offered on the altar; not even with the expedient that the offerings had only been prepared beforehand for burning on the altar (cf. on the other hand vv. 10a, 13b, 14b, 17aβ, 20b); or by assuming that the divine fire only hastened and completed a burning that was already in progress, which would have been far too modest a role for the divine fire. The narrative must have run otherwise if it was originally working up to the conclusion of v. 24a. Only the amplifier of v. 24a, with the preceding narrative in front of him, and unwilling and unable to alter it, may have had recourse to one or other of these expedients. Verse 24b, belonging to the original narrative, referred in the first place not to the divine fire, but to the appearing of the glory of Yahweh; and this reference makes good sense.

### (c) A PRIESTLY ERROR AND APPENDED WARNINGS TO THE PRIESTS: 10.1–20

10 ¹Now Nadab and Abihu, the sons of Aaron, each took his censer, and put fire in it, and laid incense on it, and offered unholy fire* before the LORD, such as he had not commanded them. ²And fire came forth from the presence of the LORD and devoured them, and they died before the LORD. ³Then Moses said to Aaron, 'This is what the LORD has said, "I will show myself holy among those who are near me, and before all the people I will be glorified." ' And Aaron held his peace. ⁴And Moses called Mishael and Elzaphan, the sons of Uzziel the uncle of Aaron, and said to them, 'Draw near, carry your brethren from before the sanctuary out of the camp.' ⁵So they drew near, and carried them in their coats out of the camp, as Moses had said. ⁶And Moses said to Aaron and to Eleazar and Ithamar, his sons, 'Do not let the hair of your heads hang loose, and do not rend your clothes, lest you die, and lest wrath come upon all the congregation; but your brethren, the whole house of Israel, may bewail the burning which the LORD has kindled. ⁷And do not go out from the door of the tent of meeting, lest you die; for the anointing oil

*[Noth renders 'strange fire', i.e. foreign: see commentary. Ed.]

of the LORD is upon you.' And they did according to the word of Moses.

8 And the LORD spoke to Aaron, saying, 9'Drink no wine nor strong drink, you nor your sons with you, when you go into the tent of meeting, lest you die; it shall be a statute for ever throughout your generations. 10You are to distinguish between the holy and the common, and between the unclean and the clean; 11and you are to teach the people of Israel all the statutes which the LORD has spoken to them by Moses.'

12 And Moses said to Aaron and to Eleazar and Ithamar, his sons who were left, 'Take the cereal offering that remains of the offerings by fire to the LORD, and eat it unleavened beside the altar, for it is most holy; 13you shall eat it in a holy place, because it is your due and your sons' due, from the offerings by fire to the LORD; for so I am commanded. 14But the breast that is waved and the thigh that is offered you shall eat in any clean place, you and your sons and your daughters with you; for they are given as your due and your sons' due, from the sacrifices of the peace offerings of the people of Israel. 15The thigh that is offered and the breast that is waved they shall bring with the offerings by fire of the fat,.to wave for a wave offering before the LORD, and it shall be yours, and your sons' with you, as a due for ever; as the LORD has commanded.'

16 Now Moses diligently inquired about the goat of the sin offering, and behold, it was burned! And he was angry with Eleazar and Ithamar, the sons of Aaron who were left, saying, 17'Why have you not eaten the sin offering in the place of the sanctuary, since it is a thing most holy and has been given to you that you may bear the iniquity of the congregation, to make atonement for them before the LORD? 18Behold, its blood was not brought into the inner part of the sanctuary. You certainly ought to have eaten it in the sanctuary, as I commanded.' 19And Aaron said to Moses, 'Behold, today they have offered their sin offering and their burnt offering before the LORD; and yet such things as these have befallen me! If I had eaten the sin offering today, would it have been acceptable in the sight of the LORD?' 20And when Moses heard that, he was content.

The chapter first relates (vv. 1–7) a cultic incident which, in the author's opinion, follows directly upon the sacrificial actions in ch. 9 and on the appearance of the divine 'glory' which conclusively confirmed these actions. To it are joined a number of instructions to the priests (vv. 8–20) relating in part—either correcting or supplementing —to the sacrificial actions of ch. 9. In the second part it is quite obvious that we are dealing with detailed later additions to ch. 9; but even the first part, to which the second is loosely joined, could hardly have been an original part of the P-narrative, especially as it is clearly linked on to the mention of the fire which came out (cf. above pp. 81f.) from the divine glory and which is already secondary in ch. 9.

[1–7] Behind the narrative of the first part there stood in the far background internal disputes between different priestly groups, about which we have no further knowledge. The group of Nadab and Abihu (v. 1) stand over against the group of Mishael and Elzaphan (vv. 4, 5). In the late standardized form of the Levitical genealogies Nadab and Abihu appear as the two oldest sons of Aaron (Ex. 6.23; 28.1; I Chron. 6.3; and with reference to the present narrative, Num. 3.2–4; 26.60f.; I Chron. 24.1f.); Mishael and Elzaphan as the cousins of Aaron (Ex. 6.22), that is, sons of the youngest brother of his father, Uzziel (Ex. 6.18). Whilst nothing else at all is known about the two last-named, and we know only from the present narrative that they represented a priestly group or played a part some time or other in priestly disputes, the names Nadab and Abihu do crop up again in Ex. 24.1, 9, in connection with a very early tradition about the covenant at Sinai. They appear alongside of Aaron, but without being brought into any definite relation of kinship with him; and it seems as if they belonged to a rather early stage of the tradition (cf. Noth, *Exodus*, pp. 194ff.). Their mention by name does not seem to have any still discoverable point. As their image in Ex. 24 has completely faded, no further information can be gleaned about the historical position of the group they represented. Only this much is clear: the tradition which associated them with events at Sinai can have known nothing of the defamation lying at the back of Lev. 10.1–7, so that Nadab and Abihu had once played a positive part in relation to the Israelite priesthood—for it seems to have been a question all through of priests, or representatives of a particular priestly group or groups. There is, of course, no longer any possibility of determining even approximately, in point of time or place, the part they played or the circumstances of the later scandal; so, too, the real motive for the later elimination of Nadab and Abihu can no longer be grasped with any certainty. Only this emerges from Lev. 10.1–7: that the group represented by Nadab and Abihu were once present, but in the judgment of the later priesthood failed; and perhaps this, too—that they had been replaced or suppressed by the Mishael-Elzaphan group.

[1] It is not very clear from v. 1 where the guilt of Nadab and Abihu lay, the guilt which called down upon them such fearful divine punishment. They had acted of their own accord (v. 1bβ), which in any case was not permissible in the cultic field. They had done so in offering 'strange fire' before Yahweh (v. 1ba). They had thus pre-

sumably taken the fire for their censers 'from somewhere', but not from the altar fire, which was alone legitimate; the secondary addition in 9.24a is probably to be understood in the sense of a heavenly origin for the altar fire. We may further ask whether over and above this the very burning of incense was not accounted a part of their unjustifiable presumptions. The original P knew nothing of an altar of incense, and perhaps would not recognize the possibility of using incense in censers, without an altar, as Nadab and Abihu did (cf. Noth, *Exodus*, pp. 234f.), although the burning of incense was and remained an old cultic custom, even in Israel. Possibly—we might at any rate so construe the story—the lawfulness of 'censing' in the Israelite cult was from time to time contested and stigmatized by the opponents of its use as presumptuous offering of 'strange fire'. The susceptibility of incense-offerings to 'foreign' influences—although the use of incense was in itself basically recognized—is made clear in the express warning against 'strange incense' in Ex. 30.9, a later addition to the P-narrative. [2] Their joint offence was immediately followed by divine punishment on the spot (v. 2); and this at once removed them from the Sinai scene in which they had according to tradition played a positive part (see above). [3] Their father Aaron, however, who had the chief oversight of the whole sacrificial procedure, could only take in shamed silence (v. 3) Moses' reproachful indication that Yahweh deals specially severely with those 'who are near to him'. The word of Yahweh, quoted here by Moses, must be understood to mean by 'those who are near' the priests, specially distinguished and therefore specially responsible. It had presumably become a traditional and proverbial expression, in which the 'holiness' and 'glory' of Yahweh were not first to be taken in the sense of punishing zeal, but rather the conjunction of a 'holy glory'. For the parallelism in this poetically phrased saying indicates that 'those who are near', in whose 'midst' (so probably in the original; cf. e.g. Ezek. 20.41) Yahweh will show himself holy, should really be in keeping with 'all the people', before whose eyes he will show himself glorious. [4] The two brothers Mishael and Elzaphan, about whom the Old Testament has nothing else specific to tell us, were charged with the task of carrying out the dead bodies of the two men judged by God (v. 4). This can only be explained by supposing that they were representatives of a group who had appeared as opponents of Nadab and Abihu in the earlier form of the narrative in 10.1–7, now completely lost to us. [5] The remark in v. 5, that the burnt corpses were carried out 'in their shirts'* presupposes, somewhat unrealistically, that these 'shirts', the official garb of the ordinary priests (cf. Ex. 28.40aα), had remained unburnt in the judgment by fire. Perhaps it is meant to stress the removal of their garb from the holy place, in order that it should never again be used. 'Out of the camp' certainly suggests the place of incineration for the sacrificial remains (cf. 4.12); in this case the burning was already complete. [6–7] Appended in vv. 6, 7 is another instruction of Moses to Aaron and the two remaining younger sons of Aaron (following the Levitical genealogy in Ex. 6.23, etc.)—that is, to the only adult priests still surviving—to observe the directions in 21.10. In the interests of cultic cleanness they were to abstain from the usual customs of mourning, which could be left to the non-priestly Israelites (v. 6b). Dependence on the Law of Holiness requirement in 21.10 is shown by correspondence in phrasing. (These two passages are the only places in the Old Testament where letting the hair hang loose and rending the clothes as customary signs of mourning are described with the same expression.) There is also a parallel in the basis of the requirement for the 'anointing oil of the Lord' upon the priests (v. 7aβ). The secondary character of 10.6, 7 as compared with 21.10 is shown by the fact that in 21.10 the anointing is reserved for the 'High Priest'; but in 10.6, 7, on the other hand, it seems to have already extended to all priests. Any infringement by the priests would incur not only their own death, but also the divine anger upon the whole community (v. 6aβ). (The logical subject of the impersonal verb, literally 'there is anger', is naturally Yahweh.) Furthermore, during the removal of the burnt bodies the priests were not to leave the holy place (v. 7aα). It is worth noting that vv. 6 and 7 assume, in the directions covering mourning, that a death brought about by fearful divine judgment is to be dealt with no differently from a 'natural' death, in which the priests would have had to behave in the same manner.

[8–11] Under a new heading, in which most unusually Yahweh addresses Aaron directly, without Moses as an intermediary (v. 8), there is added a prohibition—quite unrelated to this context—of all consumption of intoxicating drinks by the priests when entering the holy place to carry out cultic duties. This addition seems to rest on Ezek. 44.20, 21, where some regulations concerning the priests' hair (cf. here v. 6) are followed immediately by a veto against drinking of wine by the priests 'when they enter into the inner court'. This

*[So Noth's translation; RSV renders 'coats'. Ed.]

dependence on Ezek. 44 goes further; for the strange general reason for the veto in vv. 10, 11 might rest on Ezek. 44.23, where teaching about the difference between holy and secular and between clean and unclean (in the same order here as in v. 10) is assigned to the priests as one of their tasks. What Ezek. 44 enumerates in a sequence, Lev. 10 puts together in such a context and manner that the veto in v. 9a is understood by the priests as a practical confirmation of the careful distinctions made between the cultic and non-cultic spheres and as an exemplary 'instructing' of the Israelites about the importance and seriousness of the divine statutes. The veto on intoxicating drinks for officiating priests may be understood as in the interests of a correct performance of the priestly duties. Probably, too, there is a deeper concern to steer clear of foreign cultic practices; for the cultic 'intoxication', the 'alcoholic ecstasy', was probably not unknown to the religions surrounding the Israelites and could from these infiltrate into the Israelites' worship (cf., e.g., the Babylonian creation-song III 134–8 and Isa 28.7, 8).

The rest of the chapter (vv. 12–20) appends special instructions to the sacrifices of ch. 9. In so doing it repeats from other Old Testament regulations some things which a later writer found missing, or incorrectly carried out. Here is a remarkable attempt to reconcile the deviations of different Old Testament traditions with one another by supplementary material. [12–13] Chapter 9 left it an open question what was done with the remains from the people's meal offering (v. 17). Chapter 10.12, 13 adds, on the basis of 6.16, 17 (cf. also the addition in 2.3), that the remainder, consisting of unleavened bread, was to be eaten by Aaron and his surviving sons—i.e. by the priests. [14–15] In ch. 9 nothing was said about the ultimate destination of the breast-parts taken from the people's peace offering (v. 31). Chapter 10.14, 15 adds, on the basis of 7.30–34, that these parts were likewise to be eaten by Aaron and his sons. Here, the wording of this passage links it rather closely with 7.30–34, particularly by its use, not of the unusual plural of ch. 9 ($\underline{h}\bar{a}z\bar{o}t$ = 'breast-parts'), but of the singular $\underline{h}\bar{a}ze$ which also occurs in ch. 7. It certainly looks as though originally, as in ch. 9, only 'the breast' was mentioned, for 'breast' and 'thigh' in vv. 14 and 15 are named in different sequence, and v. 15 only mentions the 'waving', applicable to the breast but not to the thigh. In that case, as in 9.21, the 'thigh that is offered' was perhaps added later. [16–20] Lastly, an original emendation to the sacrificial procedures of ch. 9 is provided by the concluding section

vv. 16–20. It concerns the people's sin-offering he-goat (9.15). This was to be offered 'like the first'—i.e. like the young ox in the sin offering of Aaron and his sons (9.8–11); and with this the parts not offered on the altar had to be burnt 'outside the camp' (9.11). But that did not correspond to the arrangements of 6.24–30, according to which the rest of the sacrificial animal was burnt in the priestly sin offering (cf. 4.11, 12), but in the case of the 'lay' sin offering was to be handed over to the officiating priest. Moses later (v. 16a) discovered the 'mistake' in the sacrificial actions in ch. 9, although he must be thought of as present at the sacrifices of ch. 9 (cf. 9.6), and reproached Aaron and his sons with it (vv. 16b, 17), pointing out that the special case of 6.30 did not apply (v. 18a with (partly) verbal correspondence)—i.e. the case of a priestly sin offering, in which, according to 4.5, 6, some of the blood from the animal was to be brought into the holy place. Thereupon Aaron excused himself in an allusive and therefore not very clear explanation (v. 19), which, however, satisfied Moses (v. 20). Aaron pointed out that 'they' (this must cover Aaron's sons, including Nadab and Abihu, although Aaron himself had been the chief officiant) had indeed presented 'their' offering rightly; but that 'such things as these' (this must be an allusion to Nadab and Abihu's error) had happened. It would therefore certainly not have been 'well pleasing' to God if he (vv. 17, 18 would also, on the basis of 6.29a, include his surviving sons), involved in the guilt of his two elder sons, had enjoyed his share of the sin offering. The protest put forward in vv. 16–20 is not quite complete. If—following 6.24–30—the failure to distinguish between priests' and people's sin offering was criticized, the lack of 'blood-sprinkling' inside the holy place required by 4.5, 6, and referred to in v. 18a (following 6.30) in the priestly sin offering of 9.8–11, should also have been censured. We are dealing in 10.8–20 with loose and unsystematically attached additions that were gradually appended, probably one after another, in an order which can be no longer determined.

# IV

## 'CLEANNESS' REGULATIONS

### Lev. 11.1–15.33

#### (a) CLEAN AND UNCLEAN ANIMALS: 11.1–47

**11** ¹And the LORD said to Moses and Aaron, ²'Say to the people of Israel, These are the living things which you may eat among all the beasts that are on the earth. ³Whatever parts the hoof and is cloven-footed and chews the cud, among the animals, you may eat. ⁴Nevertheless among those that chew the cud or part the hoof, you shall not eat these: The camel, because it chews the cud but does not part the hoof, is unclean to you. ⁵And the rock badger, because it chews the cud but does not part the hoof, is unclean to you. ⁶And the hare, because it chews the cud but does not part the hoof, is unclean to you. ⁷And the swine, because it parts the hoof and is cloven-footed but does not chew the cud, is unclean to you. ⁸Of their flesh you shall not eat, and their carcasses you shall not touch; they are unclean to you.

9 'These you may eat, of all that are in the waters. Everything in the waters that has fins and scales, whether in the seas or in the rivers, you may eat. ¹⁰But anything in the seas or the rivers that has not fins and scales, of the swarming creatures in the waters and of the living creatures that are in the waters, is an abomination to you. ¹¹They shall remain an abomination to you; of their flesh you shall not eat, and their carcasses you shall have in abomination. ¹²Everything in the waters that has not fins and scales is an abomination to you.

13 'And these you shall have in abomination among the birds, they shall not be eaten, they are an abomination: the eagle, the ossifrage, the osprey, ¹⁴the kite, the falcon according to its kind, ¹⁵every raven according to its kind, ¹⁶the ostrich, the nighthawk, the sea gull, the hawk according to its kind, ¹⁷the owl, the cormorant, the ibis, ¹⁸the water hen, the pelican, the vulture, ¹⁹the stork, [the heron] according to its kind, the hoopoe, and the bat. ²⁰All winged insects that go upon all fours are an abomination to you. ²¹Yet among the winged insects that go on all fours you may eat those which have* legs above their feet, with

* Cf. BH.

89

which to leap on the earth. <sup>22</sup>Of them you may eat: the locust according to its kind, the bald locust according to its kind, the cricket according to its kind, and the grasshopper according to its kind. <sup>23</sup>But all other winged insects which have four feet are an abomination to you.

24 'And by these you shall become unclean; whoever touches their carcass shall be unclean until the evening, <sup>25</sup>and whoever carries any part of their carcass shall wash his clothes and be unclean until the evening. <sup>26</sup>Every animal which parts the hoof but is not cloven-footed or does not chew the cud is unclean to you; every one who touches them shall be unclean. <sup>27</sup>And all that go on their paws, among the animals that go on all fours, are unclean to you; whoever touches their carcass shall be unclean until the evening, <sup>28</sup>and he who carries their carcass shall wash his clothes and be unclean until the evening; they are unclean to you.

29 'And these are unclean to you among the swarming things that swarm upon the earth: the weasel, the mouse, the great lizard according to its kind, <sup>30</sup>the gecko, the land crocodile, the lizard, the sand lizard, and the chameleon. <sup>31</sup>These are unclean to you among all that swarm; whoever touches them when they are dead shall be unclean until the evening. <sup>32</sup>And anything upon which any of them falls when they are dead shall be unclean, whether it is an article of wood or a garment or a skin or a sack, any vessel that is used for any purpose; it must be put into water, and it shall be unclean until the evening; then it shall be clean. <sup>33</sup>And if any of them falls into any earthen vessel, all that is in it shall be unclean, and you shall break it. <sup>34</sup>Any food in it which may be eaten, upon which water* may come, shall be unclean; and all drink which may be drunk from every such vessel shall be unclean. <sup>35</sup>And everything upon which any part of their carcass falls shall be unclean; whether oven or stove, it shall be broken in pieces; they are unclean, and shall be unclean to you. <sup>36</sup>Nevertheless a spring or a cistern holding water shall be clean; but whatever touches their carcass shall be unclean. <sup>37</sup>And if any part of their carcass falls upon any seed for sowing that is to be sown, it is clean; <sup>38</sup>but if water is put on the seed and any part of their carcass falls on it, it is unclean to you.

39 'And if any animal of which you may eat dies, he who touches its carcass shall be unclean until the evening, <sup>40</sup>and he who eats of its carcass shall wash his clothes and be unclean until the evening; he also who carries the carcass shall wash his clothes and be unclean until the evening.

41 'Every swarming thing that swarms upon the earth is an abomination; it shall not be eaten. <sup>42</sup>Whatever goes on its belly, and whatever goes on all fours, or whatever has many feet, all the swarming things that swarm upon the earth, you shall not eat; for they are an abomination.

43 'You shall not make yourselves abominable with any swarming thing that swarms; and you shall not defile yourselves with them, lest

*I.e. from any such vessel.

you become unclean. [44]For I am the LORD your God; consecrate your-selves therefore, and be holy, for I am holy. You shall not defile your-selves with any swarming thing that crawls upon the earth. [45]For I am the LORD who brought you up out of the land of Egypt, to be your God; you shall therefore be holy, for I am holy.'

46 This is the law pertaining to beast and bird and every living creature that moves through the waters and every creature that swarms upon the earth, [47]to make a distinction between the unclean and the clean and between the living creature that may be eaten and the living creature that may not be eaten.

THE CHAPTER HANDLES in great detail the subject of the cultic cleanness or uncleanness of animals. Its only parallel in the Old Testament is the section Deut. 14.3–21, where the same subject is discussed but in essentially shorter form. There can be no doubt of the literary connection between these two pieces, shown by their partial verbal correspondence. Certainly, the nature of the connec-tion is hard to determine, for the two pieces—especially Lev. 11—are not from one mould. Looked at broadly, Deut. 14.3–21, concentrat-ing on the question of eatability or non-eatability, appears more self-contained and original. On the other hand, the unassimilated col-lection of detailed enumerations and short summary compositions in Deut. 14 points to the taking over of separate sections from Lev. 11, to be sure not probably from the final stage of this chapter as we now have it, but from an earlier form. Deuteronomy 14.3–21—and in large part Lev. 11—are cast in the plural address and therefore belong to the elements taken in later to the Deuteronomic law; they probably date from the exile. The chapter Lev. 11 has had a lengthy history of gradual build-up and is, from what has just been said, more ancient in its older portions and more recent in its later ones than Deut. 14.3–21. Nothing more exact can be said owing to the complete lack of datable stages. Judged by its subject-matter it must contain old, perhaps even primitive, regulations which someone—perhaps when the Jerusalem cultus came to an end and with it the practices belonging to the royal days—began to write down and then pro-gressively expanded over some time through further detailed precepts.

The lack of unity in Lev. 11 is shown even by the alterations in the phrasing. The prevailing form is the didactic second person plural address, the style of the priestly instruction (tōrā), which forms the basis of the chapter. Alongside are sentences in impersonal objective form (e.g. vv. 24b, 25), apparently priestly professional knowledge in set form. These sentences, with their formal address and frequent and often lengthy enumerations, do not suggest the writing down of actually given instruction; rather, they look like collections of material for such instruction to be given by the teaching priest; and sentences bearing on priestly professional knowledge have also found their way into this collection. The lack of unity in Lev. 11 is also shown by the unsystematic juxtaposition of different points of view. First it deals with the distinction between clean and unclean animals from the point of view of eating their meat; soon, however, the question of uncleanness through contact intrudes; and finally farther on the additional matter of uncleanness arising from contact with dead animals. These different points of view are not clearly separated, but intermingle. The whole has become, then, in its present state, a loose collection of important information first for the priest himself, and for those he would have to instruct, and also for the 'layman', on the question of cleanness and uncleanness in animals.

The distinction between clean and unclean animals (except for the birds) follows definite external bodily features, and partly also peculiarities of their way of life or behaviour. We must not, however, assume that these external features are the real ground of the distinction; they served rather for a tolerably simple and superficial classification. The real ground is to be sought in the cultic field, for we are dealing throughout with the ideas of 'cultically clean' and 'cultically unclean'. The real 'unclean' was all that did not accord with Israel's lawful cultus, all that—outside the cultic field in the narrower sense—was forbidden for the Israelites, bound as they were to their God by their worship, and might therefore not be eaten. This point of view concerned primarily those animals playing a part in certain foreign cults of the surrounding world as 'holy' animals, and animals for sacrifice, or important in idolatrous practices (spells and magic); or animals appearing to be specially connected with the powers working against God ('Chaos'). The eating of such animals, even if not actually bound up with any cultic or magical practices or the like, would have had for the Israelites relationships with illegitimate cultic practices and 'powers' (cf. I Cor. 10.28). This point of departure for the distinction was probably no longer generally recognized in later times; and so there was preserved this simple and traditional classification into 'clean' and 'unclean' animals, a classification both simple and authoritative.

[1] After Aaron had been instituted to his priestly office he was

addressed direct by Yahweh, and not only through the intermediary, Moses (v. 1; cf. 13.1, 15.1). Both received instructions to be passed on in their teaching to the Israelites. **[2–8]** These concerned first the edibility of certain animals, which were first reviewed in parallel sections, the large animals living on land (vv. 2b–8) and the water-animals (vv. 9–12). (The introductory sentence in v. 26 is taken up again in v. 9a, with similar phrasing.) First the positive and then the negative aspects of the matter are dealt with point by point. The large land-animals allowed to be eaten are classified in summary fashion according to their external features (v. 3a). There is no detailed enumeration here, but there is one in Deut. 14.4b, 5, preceding the summary description (v. 6a = Lev. 11.3a). According to this, and following out the classifying features, it was allowable to eat cattle and animals from the flock as well as wild game. To avoid any doubts, vv. 4–7 then append a list of those animals who show one, but not the other, of the distinguishing features and were therefore not allowed to be eaten. In this connection there crops up in a stereotyped concluding formula a solemn declaration of 'uncleanness' from time to time (vv. 4bβ, 5b, 6b, 7b); to which is appended in the veto on eating, in the context of v. 8, the veto on touching the carcass. This meant that a dead 'unclean' animal, wherever found, must be simply left where it was for the animals and birds of prey. **[9–12]** The section on the water-animals is positive (v. 9b) and negative (vv. 10–12), and shortly and summarily phrased. It refers expressly to all water-animals, whether in the 'seas' (which includes the Mediterranean as well as inland seas) or in the 'brooks', i.e. especially the water-courses fed by perennial springs. In the negative part we meet the concept *šeqeṣ*, translatable as 'abomination'—a dramatic expression for that which must in all cases be shunned. The shortened word-for-word repetition of v. 10 in v. 12 shows that the intervening v. 11 came in as a later addition, adding once again to the veto on eating the veto on touching the carcass, though in the case of water-animals this was of less practical importance than for the large land-animals. The features given show that amongst the water-animals fish in general were allowed to be eaten.

**[13–23]** The section on the winged animals (vv. 13–23) is differently phrased and arranged from the two preceding sections. Presumably it was added later. In general, and in the stereotyped concluding formulae (vv. 20b, 23b), it does not employ the concept of 'uncleanness', but, like the section on the water-animals, the term 'abomination'. It places the forbidden (vv. 13–20) before the permitted (vv. 21, 22). For the birds it gives, instead of a classification by definite features, a detailed enumeration (vv. 13b–19) with a wealth of bird-names appearing to a large extent only here and in the almost verbally parallel passage in Deut. 14.12b–18. Their special meanings are still largely a matter of conjecture. In the forbidden class v. 20 adds to the birds, in summary form, four-legged animals with wings, and so insects. Verses 21, 22 give exceptions to the last group— winged animals that might be eaten. Here the attempt at classification by external features is taken up again, and the characteristic of 'legs with which to leap' (v. 21b) is introduced. The enumeration following in v. 22 shows that this characterization extends to include the genus of the locust, for which the Old Testament had special expressions designating the different kinds and stages. These occur in v. 22, but their meaning is no longer capable of exact definition. In the bird section there was no express indication of those freely allowed to be eaten. Naturally they included all not in the list of the forbidden, for example the doves, which even had a part to play in sacrifices (cf. 1.14; 5.7). In the small winged animals section, too, there was at first no indication of a positive content. The verbal correspondence of v. 23 and v. 20 shows that the intervening vv. 21, 22 were later additions, and have brought in with them the repetitions of the older text of v. 20 and v. 23. This would mean that at first all four-legged and winged small animals were summarily forbidden; only later on was the passage added allowing the eating of locusts.

[24–28] At v. 24 style and theme undergo a brief change. After a linking phrase in v. 24a, still in the plural address, calling general attention to the fact that what follows is still dealing with the matter of cultic uncleanness in animals, so important to the Israelites, possible cases of uncleanness and their results are considered in objectively phrased third person sentences. It is now no longer a question of eating animal flesh, but of uncleanness through contact and the like. And although it remains at first quite undefined what kind of animals are being considered, it is clear that we are dealing at any rate no longer only, or principally, with the last-mentioned winged animals, but with all the previously mentioned kinds of animal, and especially, as the context of the sentences shows, with the large land-animals. Here, vv. 24b, 25 make a distinction, pursued farther on, between the two cases of 'touching' a carcass, quite possibly by accident, and 'carrying' or 'lifting' the carcass or any part of it. Both cases entail 'uncleanness till the evening'—i.e. for the day in question. This was apparently because this 'uncleanness' came to an end of itself with the close of day, without any 'cleansing' procedure. Only in the case of 'carrying' or 'lifting', apparently, was an immediate washing of the clothes required. From this whole passage we seem to gather indirectly that contact with or carrying of the carcass of 'clean' animals (apart from the slaughtered sacrificial animal) had no 'polluting' effect (but cf. vv. 39, 40). Verse 26a furnishes the explanation of uncleanness for animals similar to those enumerated in vv. 4–7, yet not quite the same. This is by way of preparation for a following sentence about touching—not, be it observed, a carcass—but touching as such in itself (v. 26b). A supplement, superfluous if the main rule in v. 3 is sensibly applied, pronounces the animals who 'go upon their paws', i.e. the species of dogs, cats and bears, to be 'unclean' (v. 27a) and adds again the sentences about 'touching' and 'carrying' a carcass (vv. 27b, 28). In these supplements objectively phrased sentences are mixed with the uncleanness explanations which have the second person plural address (vv. 26aβ, 27aβ, 28b).

[29–38] The section vv. 29–38 deals with small animals. First the unclean animals are enumerated (vv. 29b, 30). The address is didactic, but as the question of edibility was not here actually under discussion, the phrasing differs from vv. 4aα, 10, 13a. Joining on to this we have in vv. 31b–38 an exposition, generally phrased in objective sentences suggestive of priestly professional knowledge, of the defiling effects which may possibly be produced by dead animals of this kind. In this case there is not only contact with known beings to be considered (v. 31b), but also contact varying with the nature of the case with objects of household furniture and other fittings in house or garden. Household utensils, if they had been rendered unclean through contact with a small animal—e.g. a dead mouse—must be rinsed in water and even then remained unclean—i.e. unusable—till the evening. Earthenware vessels, especially those for storing water or grains, were to be broken and their contents withdrawn from use—this time obviously for good (v. 33). Food and drink prepared with water from an unclean vessel, before the vessel's uncleanness had been noticed, might no longer be consumed (v. 34). Even baking-ovens and cooking-hearths made of stone, clay tiles or clay, must be taken to pieces and then rebuilt (v. 35). An exemption was made for cisterns and springs (v. 36), likewise for a heap of seed-corn in house or garden, or seeds laid out ready for sowing in the fields. Obviously it is a question here of a certain limit set by the most elementary demands of practical living to the consequences of the cleanness-uncleanness regulations. The necessary water-supply and the indispensable cultivation of the fields in order to ensure the year's crops could not be endangered by any declaration of uncleanness. Cheap earthenware vessels and small household equipment, along with easily set up baking and cooking arrangements, could be declared unclean; but for the not so easily replaceable household gear only a short period of uncleanness and the possibility of 'cleansing' were provided. All the more so, water and seed, where contact with a small dead animal would be specially easy, could not be allowed to become unusable. The exception to this exception in v. 38 is not very clearly based; was water-soaked seed so thoroughly impregnated with uncleanness by a small dead animal that there would in this case be no question of its not being treated as unclean?

[39–42] A further supplement (vv. 39, 40), with mixed phrasing, lays down all the same (cf. vv. 24–28 and above pp. 94f.) that a carcass, even of a 'clean' animal, has the same contaminating effect as that of an 'unclean' animal. Verses 41, 42 append to vv. 29, 30 the missing veto on eating and add classifying details of the external features of unclean small animals, perhaps in order to include expressly the animals 'going on the belly', i.e. the snakes (cf. the similarly worded phrase in Gen. 3.14).

[43–47] In the concluding paragraph (vv. 43–47) the first part (vv. 43–45) refers especially to the smaller animals. It warns against the uncleanness of those animals, and points to the holiness of Yahweh which requires of the Israelites to keep themselves 'holy', in phrases peculiar to certain parts of the Law of Holiness. This part is a supplement, as is apparent from its restriction to the small animals and the lack of corresponding sections dealing with the other classes, as well as from detailed peculiarities in the phrasing. Even the passage vv. 46, 47, concluding and bringing together the whole, was a later addition, as can be seen from the divergencies in phrasing from what goes before. It is worth noting that it considers the eatability or noneatability of different animals to be the main theme of this chapter.

(*b*) UNCLEANNESS RESULTING FROM CHILDBIRTH: 12.1–8

12 ¹The Lord said to Moses, ²"Say to the people of Israel, If a woman conceives, and bears a male child, then she shall be unclean seven days; as at the time of her menstruation, she shall be unclean.

<sup>3</sup>And on the eighth day the flesh of his foreskin shall be circumcised. <sup>4</sup>Then she shall continue for thirty-three days in the blood of her* purifying; she shall not touch any hallowed thing, nor come into the sanctuary, until the days of her purifying are completed. <sup>5</sup>But if she bears a female child, then she shall be unclean two weeks, as in her menstruation; and she shall continue in the blood of her purifying for sixty-six days. <sup>6</sup>And when the days of her purifying are completed, whether for a son or for a daughter, she shall bring to the priest at the door of the tent of meeting a lamb a year old for a burnt offering, and a young pigeon or a turtledove for a sin offering, <sup>7</sup>and he shall offer it before the LORD, and make atonement for her; then she shall be clean from the flow of her blood. This is the law for her who bears a child, either male or female. <sup>8</sup>And if she cannot afford a lamb, then she shall take two turtledoves or two young pigeons, one for a burnt offering and the other for a sin offering; and the priest shall make atonement for her, and she shall be clean.'

The address to Moses only in the introductory formula (vv. 1, 2aα) perhaps indicates that this short chapter was only later added to the whole complex of the cleanness regulations (cf. above p. 93 and 11.1). It deals, in the objective phrasing of priestly professional knowledge, with the cultic uncleanness following upon birth. It makes a distinction between the birth of a boy (vv. 2aβb–4) and the birth of a girl (v. 5), and adds an instruction about the offerings to be brought for cleansing, thus bringing these two cases together again (vv. 6, 7). The concluding formula in v. 7b shows v. 8 to be a quite clearly recognizable later addition. The sexual processes, especially birth, were also reckoned 'unclean' far beyond the circle of Israel, because mysterious powers were seen to be at work in them, having little or no connection with the official cults. How far Israel had any consciousness of the background beliefs, and how far she was only following traditional customs, we cannot any longer know. The age of the written form of Lev. 12 cannot be determined. The simple occurrence of 'the priest' in v. 6 (and 8), and the slight and later redaction by a priestly writer evident in the syntactically incomplete addition of 'the tent of meeting' (v. 6), both point to it as the work of a pre-Priestly writer. We should note the difference in assessment of 'uncleanness' after the birth of a boy and after a girl. The cultic inferiority of the female sex is expressed in giving the female birth a double 'uncleanness' effect, shown also in the double period required in this case before the mother is once more clean (cf. vv. 2b, 4a, with v. 5aβb).

The birth was always followed by a short period of 'uncleanness'

*Reading *ṭoḥᵒrāh* for *ṭoḥᵒrā*.

L.–G

for the mother, equal to the 'uncleanness' following menstruation (v. 2bβ). There follows a longer time—in the case of a boy separated from the first period by his circumcision on the eighth day after birth, as noted in the formally phrased but clumsily inserted addition, v. 3. This longer period formed an interval between cleanness and uncleanness, during which the mother, having regard to 'the blood of her cleansing'—i.e. presumably the processes leading gradually to her recovery and cleansing—had to abstain from all contact with 'any hallowed thing' (v. 4 and—shortened, but with the same meaning— v. 5b). A modest burnt offering and sin offering would, at the end of this period, reinstate full cultic cleanness (vv. 6, 7a). It is part and parcel of the subject-matter, but all the same remarkable, that in this case the woman herself, and not her husband, appears with an offering. The priest, naturally, reserved to himself the usual functions in the sin and burnt offerings (cf. chs. 1 and 4). The supplementary v. 8 reduces the requirement for the burnt offering in a case of special poverty, without thereby impairing the full efficacy of the sacrificial procedure (cf. 5.7–13).

### (c) UNCLEANNESS ARISING FROM 'LEPROSY': 13.1–14.57

**13** [1]The LORD said to Moses and Aaron, [2]'When a man has on the skin of his body a swelling or an eruption or a spot, and it turns into a leprous disease on the skin of his body, then he shall be brought to [Aaron] the priest [or to one of his sons the priests,] [3]and the priest shall examine the diseased spot on the skin of his body; and if the hair in the diseased spot has turned white and the disease appears to be deeper than the skin of his body, it is a leprous disease; when the priest has examined him he shall pronounce him unclean. [4]But if the spot is white in the skin of his body, and appears no deeper than the skin, and the hair in it* has not turned white, the priest shall shut up the diseased person for seven days; [5]and the priest shall examine him on the seventh day, and if in his eyes the disease is checked and the disease has not spread in the skin, then the priest shall shut him up seven days more; [6]and the priest shall examine him again on the seventh day, and if the diseased spot is dim and the disease has not spread in the skin, then the priest shall pronounce him clean; it is only an eruption; and he shall wash his clothes, and be clean. [7]But if the eruption spreads in the skin, after he has shown himself to the priest for his cleansing, he shall appear again before the priest; [8]and the priest shall make an examination, and if the eruption has spread in the skin, then the priest shall pronounce him unclean; it is leprosy.

[9]'When a man is afflicted with leprosy, he shall be brought to the

---

*Reading šeʿārāh for šeʿārā.

priest; [10]and the priest shall make an examination, and if there is a white swelling in the skin, which has turned the hair white, and there is quick raw flesh in the swelling, [11]it is a chronic leprosy in the skin of his body, and the priest shall pronounce him unclean; he shall not shut him up, for he is unclean. [12]And if the leprosy breaks out in the skin, so that the leprosy covers all the skin of the diseased person from head to foot, so far as the priest can see, [13]then the priest shall make an examination, and if the leprosy has covered all his body, he shall pronounce him clean of the disease; it has all turned white, and he is clean. [14]But when raw flesh appears on him, he shall be unclean. [15]And the priest shall examine the raw flesh, and pronounce him unclean; raw flesh is unclean, for it is leprosy. [16]But if the raw flesh turns again and is changed to white, then he shall come to the priest, [17]and the priest shall examine him, and if the disease has turned white, then the priest shall pronounce the diseased person clean; he is clean.

18 'And when there is in the skin of one's body a boil that has healed, [19]and in the place of the boil there comes a white swelling or a reddish-white spot, then it shall be shown to the priest; [20]and the priest shall make an examination, and if it appears deeper than the skin and its hair has turned white, then the priest shall pronounce him unclean; it is the disease of leprosy, it has broken out in the boil. [21]But if the priest examines it, and the hair on it is not white and it is not deeper than the skin, but is dim, then the priest shall shut him up seven days; [22]and if it spreads in the skin, then the priest shall pronounce him unclean; it is diseased. [23]But if the spot remains in one place and does not spread, it is the scar of the boil; and the priest shall pronounce him clean.

24 'Or, when the body has a burn on its skin and the raw flesh of the burn becomes a spot, reddish-white, or white, [25]the priest shall examine it, and if the hair in the spot has turned white and it appears deeper than the skin, then it is leprosy; it has broken out in the burn, and the priest shall pronounce him unclean; it is a leprous disease. [26]But if the priest examines it, and the hair in the spot is not white and it is no deeper than the skin, but is dim, the priest shall shut him up seven days, [27]and the priest shall examine him the seventh day; if it is spreading in the skin, then the priest shall pronounce him unclean; it is a leprous disease. [28]But if the spot remains in one place and does not spread in the skin, but is dim, it is a swelling from the burn, and the priest shall pronounce him clean; for it is the scar of the burn.

29 'When a man or woman has a disease on the head or the beard, [30]the priest shall examine the disease; and if it appears deeper than the skin, and the hair in it is yellow and thin, then the priest shall pronounce him unclean; it is an itch, a leprosy of the head or the beard. [31]And if the priest examines the itching disease, and it appears no deeper than the skin and there is no black hair in it, then the priest shall shut up the person with the itching disease for seven days, [32]and on the seventh day the priest shall examine the disease; and if the itch has not spread, and there is in it no yellow hair, and the itch appears to be no deeper than the skin, [33]then he shall shave himself, but the itch he shall not shave;

and the priest shall shut up the person with the itching disease for seven days more; [34]and on the seventh day the priest shall examine the itch, and if the itch has not spread in the skin and it appears to be no deeper than the skin, then the priest shall pronounce him clean; and he shall wash his clothes, and be clean. [35]But if the itch spreads in the skin after his cleansing, [36]then the priest shall examine him, and if the itch has spread in the skin, the priest need not seek for the yellow hair; he is unclean. [37]But if in his eyes the itch is checked, and black hair has grown in it, the itch is healed, he is clean; and the priest shall pronounce him clean.

38 'When a man or a woman has spots on the skin of the body, white spots, [39]the priest shall make an examination, and if the spots on the skin of the body are of a dull white, it is tetter that has broken out in the skin; he is clean.

40 'If a man's hair has fallen from his head, he is bald but he is clean. [41]And if a man's hair has fallen from his forehead and temples, he has baldness of the forehead but he is clean. [42]But if there is on the bald head or the bald forehead a reddish-white diseased spot, it is leprosy breaking out on his bald head or his bald forehead. [43]Then the priest shall examine him, and if the diseased swelling is reddish-white on his bald head or on his bald forehead, like the appearance of leprosy in the skin of the body, [44]he is a leprous man, he is unclean; the priest must pronounce him unclean; his disease is on his head.

45 'The leper who has the disease shall wear torn clothes and let the hair of his head hang loose, and he shall cover his upper lip and cry, "Unclean, unclean." [46]He shall remain unclean as long as he has the disease; he is unclean; he shall dwell alone in a habitation outside the camp.

47 'When there is a leprous disease in a garment, whether a woollen or a linen garment, [48]in warp or woof of linen or wool, or in a skin or in anything made of skin, [49]if the disease shows greenish or reddish in the garment, whether in warp or woof or in skin or in anything made of skin, it is a leprous disease and shall be shown to the priest. [50]And the priest shall examine the disease, and shut up that which has the disease for seven days; [51]then he shall examine the disease on the seventh day. If the disease has spread in the garment, in warp or woof, or in the skin, whatever be the use of the skin, the disease is a malignant leprosy; it is unclean. [52]And he shall burn the garment, whether diseased in warp or woof, woollen or linen, or anything of skin, for it is a malignant leprosy; it shall be burned in the fire.

53 'And if the priest examines, and the disease has not spread in the garment in warp or woof or in anything of skin, [54]then the priest shall command that they wash the thing in which is the disease, and he shall shut it up seven days more; [55]and the priest shall examine the diseased thing after it has been washed. And if the diseased spot has not changed colour, though the disease has not spread, it is unclean; you shall burn it in the fire, whether the leprous spot is on the back or on the front.

56 'But if the priest examines, and the disease is dim after it is

washed, he shall tear the spot out of the garment or the skin or the warp or woof; ⁵⁷then if it appears again in the garment, in warp or woof, or in anything of skin, it is spreading; you shall burn with fire that in which is the disease. ⁵⁸But the garment, warp or woof, or anything of skin from which the disease departs when you have washed it, shall then be washed a second time, and be clean.'

59 This is the law for a leprous disease in a garment of wool or linen, either in warp or woof, or in anything of skin, to decide whether it is clean or unclean.

14 ¹The LORD said to Moses, ²"This shall be the law of the leper for the day of his cleansing. He shall be brought to the priest; ³and the priest shall go out of the camp, and the priest shall make an examination. Then, if the leprous disease is healed in the leper, ⁴the priest shall command them to take for him who is to be cleansed two living clean birds and cedarwood and scarlet stuff and hyssop; ⁵and the priest shall command them to kill one of the birds in an earthen vessel over running water. ⁶He shall take the living bird with the cedarwood and the scarlet stuff and the hyssop, and dip them and the living bird in the blood of the bird that was killed over the running water; ⁷and he shall sprinkle it seven times upon him who is to be cleansed of leprosy; then he shall pronounce him clean, and shall let the living bird go into the open field. ⁸And he who is to be cleansed shall wash his clothes, and shave off all his hair, and bathe himself in water, and he shall be clean; and after that he shall come into the camp, but shall dwell outside his tent seven days. ⁹And on the seventh day he shall shave all his hair off his head; he shall shave off his beard and his eyebrows, all his hair. Then he shall wash his clothes, and bathe his body in water, and he shall be clean.

10 'And on the eighth day he shall take two male lambs without blemish, and one ewe lamb a year old without blemish, and a cereal offering of three tenths of an ephah of fine flour mixed with oil, and one log of oil. ¹¹And the priest who cleanses him shall set the man who is to be cleansed and these things before the LORD, [at the door of the tent of meeting.] ¹²And the priest shall take one of the male lambs, and offer it for a guilt offering, along with the log of oil, and wave them for a wave offering before the LORD; ¹³and he shall kill the lamb [in the place where they kill the sin offering and the burnt offering, in the holy place; for the guilt offering, like the sin offering, belongs to the priest; it is most holy.] ¹⁴The priest shall take some of the blood of the guilt offering, and the priest shall put it on the tip of the right ear of him who is to be cleansed, and on the thumb of his right hand, and on the great toe of his right foot. ¹⁵Then the priest shall take some of the log of oil, and pour it into the palm of his own left hand, ¹⁶and dip his right finger in the oil that is in his left hand, and sprinkle some oil with his finger seven times before the LORD. ¹⁷And some of the oil that remains in his hand the priest shall put on the tip of the right ear of him who is to be cleansed, and on the thumb of his right hand, and on the great toe of his right foot, upon the blood of the guilt offering; ¹⁸and the rest of the oil that is in the priest's hand he shall put on the head of him who is to be cleansed.

Then the priest shall make atonement for him before the LORD. ¹⁹The priest shall offer the sin offering, to make atonement for him who is to be cleansed from his uncleanness. And afterward he shall kill the burnt offering; ²⁰and the priest shall offer the burnt offering and the cereal offering on the altar. Thus the priest shall make atonement for him, and he shall be clean.

21 'But if he is poor and cannot afford so much, then he shall take one male lamb for a guilt offering to be waved, to make atonement for him, and a tenth of an ephah of fine flour mixed with oil for a cereal offering, and a log of oil; ²²also two turtledoves or two young pigeons, such as he can afford; the one shall be a sin offering and the other a burnt offering. ²³And on the eighth day he shall bring them for his cleansing to the priest, [to the door of the tent of meeting,] before the LORD; ²⁴and the priest shall take the lamb of the guilt offering, and the log of oil, and the priest shall wave them for a wave offering before the LORD. ²⁵And he shall kill the lamb of the guilt offering; and the priest shall take some of the blood of the guilt offering, and put it on the tip of the right ear of him who is to be cleansed, and on the thumb of his right hand, and on the great toe of his right foot. ²⁶And the priest shall pour some of the oil into the palm of his own left hand; ²⁷and· shall sprinkle with his right finger some of the oil that is in his left hand seven times before the LORD; ²⁸and the priest shall put some of the oil that is in his hand on the tip of the right ear of him who is to be cleansed, and on the thumb of his right hand, and the great toe of his right foot, in the place where the blood of the guilt offering was put; ²⁹and the rest of the oil that is in the priest's hand he shall put on the head of him who is to be cleansed, to make atonement for him before the LORD. ³⁰And he shall offer, of the turtledoves or young pigeons such as he can afford, ³¹*one for a sin offering and the other for a burnt offering, along with a cereal offering; and the priest shall make atonement before the LORD for him who is being cleansed. ³²This is the law for him in whom is a leprous disease, who cannot afford the offerings for his cleansing.'

33 The LORD said to Moses and Aaron, ³⁴'When you come into the land of Canaan, which I give you for a possession, and I put a leprous disease in a house in the land of your possession, ³⁵then he who owns the house shall come and tell the priest, "There seems to me to be some sort of disease in my house." ³⁶Then the priest shall command that they empty the house before the priest goes to examine the disease, lest all that is in the house be declared unclean; and afterward the priest shall go in to see the house. ³⁷And he shall examine the disease; and if the disease is in the walls of the house with greenish or reddish spots, and if it appears to be deeper than the surface, ³⁸then the priest shall go out of the house to the door of the house, and shut up the house seven days. ³⁹And the priest shall come again on the seventh day, and look; and if the disease has spread in the walls of the house, ⁴⁰then the priest

*The opening six words of the Hebrew text are due to dittography and are not translated.

shall command that they take out the stones in which is the disease and throw them into an unclean place outside the city; [41]and he shall cause the inside of the house to be scraped round about,* and the plaster that they scrape off they shall pour into an unclean place outside the city; [42]then they shall take other stones and put them in the place of those stones, and he shall take other plaster and plaster the house.

43 'If the disease breaks out again in the house, after he has taken out the stones and scraped the house and plastered it, [44]then the priest shall go and look; and if the disease has spread in the house, it is a malignant leprosy in the house; it is unclean. [45]And he shall break down the house, its stones and timber and all the plaster of the house; and he shall carry them forth out of the city to an unclean place. [46]Moreover he who enters the house while it is shut up shall be unclean until the evening; [47]and he who lies down in the house shall wash his clothes; and he who eats in the house shall wash his clothes.

48 'But if the priest comes and makes an examination, and the disease has not spread in the house after the house was plastered, then the priest shall pronounce the house clean, for the disease is healed. [49]And for the cleansing of the house he shall take two small birds, with cedarwood and scarlet stuff and hyssop, [50]and shall kill one of the birds in an earthen vessel over running water, [51]and shall take the cedarwood and the hyssop and the scarlet stuff, along with the living bird, and dip them in the blood of the bird that was killed and in the running water, and sprinkle the house seven times. [52]Thus he shall cleanse the house with the blood of the bird, and with the running water, and with the living bird, and with the cedarwood and hyssop and scarlet stuff; [53]and he shall let the living bird go out of the city into the open field; so he shall make atonement for the house, and it shall be clean.'

54 This is the law for any leprous disease: for an itch, [55]for leprosy in a garment or in a house, [56]and for a swelling or an eruption or a spot, [57]to show when it is unclean and when it is clean. This is the law for leprosy.

In the widely ranging section chs. 13 and 14 is brought together all that falls under the aspect of cultic cleanness and uncleanness in the field covered by the very broad word 'leprosy'.† A rough subdivision of the whole, indicated by the new introduction in 14.1, 2a, is constituted by the concentration of ch. 13 mainly on the declaration of cleanness and uncleanness by means of definite signs, whereas ch. 14 deals with measures for getting rid of the uncleanness and effecting a recovery from it. It was the priest's business to pronounce on the state of cleanness or uncleanness; hence it is a case here of recording the priestly professional knowledge in writing (cf. the relevant

*So BH. [Noth reads *yaqṣū*, 'they shall scrape'; cf. next clause. Ed.]
†[The term 'leprosy' is preserved here, as in the English translations: but it is clear from these chapters that a much wider range of conditions is indicated. Ed.]

phrasing of the introduction, 13.1), in an impersonal case-law style. The conditional clause gives the indications, and the following clause sets out the measures to be taken in consequence. The instructions for the relevant measures, important for both priest and 'layman' (cf. the absence of Aaron from the introductory formula 14.1), are in general cast in an impersonal ritual style, suitable to the subject-matter. However, this prevailing style is not evenly maintained, and even the distinction between diagnosis and treatment is not carried through in systematic detail. This shows that the whole complex is not a single composition. The basic material would seem to be the details about human 'leprosy'—these are widest in scope and far the most prominent—i.e. all kinds of human skin-diseases. In this basic material the subdivisions according to the symptoms (13.2–46) and cleansing measures (14.2–32) is fairly clearly carried out. Over against this the sections about 'leprosy' in materials (13.47–59) and houses (14.34–53, with a new heading in 14.33) are seen to be secondary. In these latter sections the determination of uncleanness is closely intermingled with the consequences arising. Likewise in these sections the most startling discrepancies of style occur. Chapter 13.55, 57 have the second person singular address; 14.34 has God speaking in the first person with the second person plural. At all events the basic material dealt with has hardly formed a completely unified picture from the beginning. The details show it to be the result of a process of growth, in the course of which what seemed most important on the theme of uncleanness through skin-diseases and the requisite counter-measures for cleansing was written down, and then amplified by further details.

The whole was slightly edited in the direction of P when it was fitted into its present context. Almost throughout it talks simply of 'the priest', who has to make observations and act according to the cultic cleansing rites; only at the first mention of 'the priest' in 13.2 has a reference to Aaron and his priestly sons been inserted. And in 14.11, 23, where the formula 'before Yahweh' occurs, each time the 'entrance to the tent of meeting' is also mentioned. At least the basic form of both chapters can be claimed comprehensively as 'pre-Priestly': a more exact dating of the first draft and of its further amplifications is no longer possible. Chapter 14.13 (cf. 6.25b, 26; 7.2a, 6b, 7) takes an obviously secondary, because badly inserted, glance back at the sacrificial instructions of chs. 1–7.

The contents cover the cultically polluting effects of human skin-diseases. The infected man was no longer whole, and therefore no longer fit for the cult: his outward appearance was deformed. Fundamentally, every disease, as far as it was visible in the body, excluded a man from the cultic community for as long as it was present. In practice, skin-diseases played a specially large part. They occurred with special frequency, and they did not in themselves keep an infected man away from bodily participation in cultic proceedings. Besides, special care was needed in this field to test for what was diseased and therefore ranked as unclean, and what was not. For this, a complicated case-law had in course of time been developed. Any question of a possible therapy for healing the disease was entirely excluded from the priestly professional field of vision: the priest had only to declare the marks of a disease present or absent or no longer present, as determined by the corresponding bodily irregularity, and then apply the requisite cultic and ritual measures. Even the isolating of sick people (13.46) was not so much for hygienic reasons, but served—by analogy from the infectious nature of certain diseases, known by experience—to prevent the spreading of cultic uncleanness. Because attention was confined to observing certain external indications, ignoring any deeper causes, it was possible to make the strange transference of the ideas of 'leprosy' to certain appearances in materials and houses. The secondary nature of this transference is shown by the application of bodily ideas (e.g. 'healing', 14.48) to inanimate objects. The inclusion of materials and houses is not only, as mentioned above, secondary from a literary point of view, as in chs. 13, 14, but also secondary in subject-matter.

[13.2–46] Chapter 13.2–46 develops a very difficult priestly casuistry for judging suspicious skin abnormalities, calculated to enable the priest to pronounce in a concrete case 'clean' or 'unclean'. In certain cases no immediate decision was to be made: the priest had to wait and see how the symptoms would develop. Then a kind of 'quarantine' of seven days (vv. 4, 21, 26, 31), or if need be twice seven days (vv. 5, 33) had to be applied to the suspect, during which he was 'shut up', i.e. excluded from all contact with others on account of suspicions of an 'infectious' uncleanness; but we are unfortunately not told where and how this segregation was effected. In the whole section we meet a number of special expressions, occurring for the most part here only, and no longer capable of exact definition. They can only be rendered with approximate probability. Everything is included under the idea of ṣāra'at (with some other derivatives from the same stem), usually rendered 'leprosy'. Yet it is doubtful whether it is here a matter of the real incurable disease of leprosy, for the possibility is envisaged of a disappearance and healing of the signs of illness. The characteristic symptoms of real leprosy at an advanced stage are not mentioned. It is clearly rather a variety of virulent or non-virulent skin-diseases that is being considered here, having cultically 'unclean' effects; but not enough is said about the attendant symptoms for us to be able to define them more precisely. The features for the priestly determination of cleanness or uncleanness are confined to rather simple stereotyped external phenomena and—in certain cases—their development over a limited period. With the priest's determination of cleanness or uncleanness his task is for the time being complete. Cultic measures are not in the first place contemplated. Only in a case where, after the two weeks' observation, a state of 'cleanness' has finally been declared, is a washing of the clothes also required (vv. 6, 34), since there had been all the same an unjustified suspicion of uncleanness. For the person who has been declared definitely 'unclean', however, vv. 45, 46 prescribe in conclusion that he should make the changes in outward appearance usual in mourning for the dead. To the already-mentioned (10.6) rending of the clothes and letting the hair hang loose this passage adds the covering of the beard (cf. Ezek. 24.17, 22), probably to make himself unrecognizable to the mysterious powers who hover round him even as they do round those who mourn for the dead. Further, he is to call out the word 'Unclean', after he has been declared unclean, as a public warning to others; and he is to 'sit' alone and apart from the company of others—presumably with food and drink brought to him by them—until he shall be again declared clean. (The mention of the 'camp' in v. 46 is perhaps a later addition, having regard to the situation in the wilderness assumed in the P-narrative.)

[47–59] The 'leprosy' in textiles and leather, dealt with in 13.47–59, a section added later, probably meant mildew, amongst other things. An external resemblance to human skin diseases was the reason for declaring a state of cultic uncleanness according to certain corresponding indications and for describing these as 'a leprous disease'. A closer definition of the 'leprosy', which only comes in here and in 14.44 with reference to the 'leprosy' in a house, can no longer be arrived at with any certainty. The determination of cleanness or uncleanness followed a procedure similar to that for human 'leprosy': evidently this is a secondary transference of the idea of human 'leprosy' to material objects (cf. especially the phrasing in v. 55b). In this section the establishment of the facts goes hand in hand with the arrangements for further treatment. A declaration of uncleanness resulted in the destruction by burning of the whole object in question (v. 52). Verses 53–58 deal with some minor cases with doubtful or less serious symptoms; and the treatment of the respective objects is correspondingly differentiated. From the literary point of view this section does not run quite smoothly: v. 54b looks like an addition, intruding awkwardly between v. 54a and v. 55; and vv. 55, 57, 58 introduce a second person singular address which does not belong to the general framework.

[14.1–32] Chapter 14.2–32 deals once more with human 'leprosy' and the cleansing rites required of a person whose 'leprosy'-marks had been healed and who could therefore be declared 'clean' again. Nothing had been done by way of healing, except simply to wait for it; and the priest had now to verify the fact. The conditions assumed are those of 13.45, 46—a life excluded from contact with others. [2–3] With this in view, vv. 2b and 3a contain two concurrent announcements. The regulation in v. 2b was most likely the original one. It laid down that the patient must be brought to the priest— presumably by someone else who had gathered the facts of his supposed cure and was for the present sufficiently convinced of them to be prepared to take responsibility for at any rate a temporary removal of the restrictions; whereas v. 3a, with a view to the strict maintenance of the imposed segregation, makes the priest 'go out' to the patient on receipt of some corresponding information. [4–9] If the priest declared the disease to be at an end, a cleansing rite must first be fulfilled (vv. 4–9) and then a sacrificial procedure carried out (vv. 10–31). The cleansing rite, with its very crude ideas of the effectiveness of magic, aimed at the removal of all cultic uncleanness caused by the disease, once the disease-marks had disappeared. It led to the recovery of 'cleanness', as the end of v. 9 expressly states, and was thus far a conclusive procedure requiring no further amplification. It was preserved—because of a presumably fairly ancient tradition—when, probably later on, the sacrificial procedure came in, also aiming at the re-establishment of cultic 'cleanness', as stated at the end of v. 20. This could have meant—and was perhaps originally intended to mean—that the less ancient sacrificial procedure replaced the cleansing rite. The latter consisted of two elements: first, the sprinkling of a cleansing liquid over the person to be cleansed; then the transference of the uncleanness to a bird, which was then allowed to fly away. The cleansing fluid was prepared in an earthenware vessel with the blood of a bird of an unspecified kind, and all manner of ingredients to which was ascribed a cultically cleansing action (vv. 4b, 6a); (cf. the same ingredients in the cleansing liquid of Num. 19.6). At first sight the part played by the 'living' water (vv. 5b, 6b) is not quite clear—that is, spring-water as distinguished from cistern-water. Probably this spring-water was ready drawn in an earthenware vessel to serve as a basis for the cleansing liquid (so at any rate in the rather differently phrased parallel passage vv. 51, 52). It was then mixed with the bird's blood and other cleansing remedies. The subject of these actions is not always very clearly indicated. In v. 7 the priest, although not expressly named, must be the subject. The same applies to v. 6. In vv. 4 and 5, however, the priest only gave the required instructions for the preparatory procedure to someone who had then to carry them out. The person to be cleansed, whom one might imagine the most likely, cannot, however—at any rate from the phrasing of v. 4aβb—be intended, and probably not in v. 5aβb either. Some other member of his family might be meant, assumed to be present at the cleansing rite. At all events the priest had then to pour the prepared cleansing remedies into the mixture of water and blood standing ready to hand (v. 6) and to undertake the cleansing spraying of the patient (v. 7a). Then he had to release the second—unspecified—bird (v. 7b), after dipping it in the cleansing liquid and bringing it in mysterious fashion into relationship with the cleansing process (v. 6b), so that it would bear away with it into space the 'uncleanness' that had entered into the cleansing liquid. A double washing of clothes, cutting of the hair, and washing down of the body for a space of seven days, during which the person to be cleansed was already partly taken back again into human society, finally completed the whole blood-rite (vv. 8, 9).

[10–20] In the sacrificial proceedings that now followed (vv. 10–20), the most important part was the 'guilt offering', for which far the most detailed instructions were formulated. The 'guilt offering', which had perhaps originally been an integral part of the cleansing procedure (cf. above pp. 58f. and 7.1–7), served to get rid of the 'guilt'. At any rate in this particular case it is at once clear that there is no question of subjective guilt, but only of an objective 'taint' caused by the in no way blameworthy cultic uncleanness. In the present context only the ritual to be carried out with the animal's blood is of interest: nothing is said of any burning of sacrificial portions on the altar (cf. 7.3–5), probably because it is assumed as a matter of course. The final destination of the remains from the sacrificial animal is only mentioned in the later supplement, v. 13aβb (cf. above p. 104). The action with the blood consisted of an application of blood from the sacrifice to the 'extremities' (cf. 8.23f. and above pp. 71f.) of the body of the person to be cleansed, which was clearly held to possess atoning power (v. 14). This was followed by an exactly corresponding application of oil (v. 17), after this oil had been consecrated for this special purpose by a sevenfold sprinkling 'before Yahweh' (v. 16). The oil, as was probably the case in the 'anointing' with oil, was expected to have a life-renewing effect. This was still further heightened by the priest's pouring finally on to the person's head all the oil remaining in his left hand (v. 18). To round off the sacrificial procedure there was in addition a sin offering (v. 19a) and a burnt offering together with a meal offering (vv. 19b, 20a). Both of these are only briefly mentioned: their ritual is assumed to be well known. In other respects the detailed instructions in vv. 10–20 are very uneven. Only the parts that seemed important for the particular purpose are dealt with in detail. First of all in v. 10, in comparative detail, the preparation of the required material for all the following sacrifices is discussed. Of the three sacrificial animals, one, according to v. 12 a fully grown male sheep, served for the 'guilt offering'. It is not stated subsequently how the other fully grown ram and the young ewe were to be distributed between sin offering and burnt offering. For the meal offering, which was additional to the burnt offering, some grain, 'three tenths' (of an ephah?), i.e. nearly half a bushel, were required; the oil procedure, on the other hand, only required the small amount of 1 lōg (liquid measure), i.e. about a pint. Then the officiating priest had to present all this material with the person to be cleansed 'before Yahweh' (v. 11), and in addition carry out for the 'guilt offering' and for the oil offering the gesture of 'waving' these important materials 'before Yahweh' (v. 12). In what follows it is again not quite clear who the operating subject is. The priest not being expressly named in 13aα, the slaughtering of the sacrificial animal was perhaps the business of the person to be cleansed or one of his family (cf. above on v. 4). The strange double occurrence of the words 'the priest' in vv. 15a and 15b repeated in the parallel passage v. 26 might indicate that originally v. 15a did not contain the subject, 'the priest', nor was it understood. The priestly procedure with the oil is described with unusual fullness of detail in vv. 15b–18a because it occurred only in this context, and there could not therefore be a tacit reference to a well-known ritual existing elsewhere.

[21–31] Verses 21–31 describe how a poor man, unable to afford the not inconsiderable outlay necessary for the sacrificial procedure of v. 10, could carry out the cleansing requirements at less expense. In the requisite 'guilt offering' and the oil ritual, it is true, no reduction was permissible, for it was here a matter of the main elements in the procedure, which were not allowed to be reduced. Verses 23–29 repeat the instructions for them *in extenso*, with almost the same wording. For the sin offering and burnt offering, however, the usually required smaller animals could each be replaced by two doves (v. 22), elsewhere (cf. 1.14–17) prescribed for sacrifice. Moreover, the material needed for the meal-offering supplement and the burnt offering could be reduced to a third of the quantity required in v. 10. Here and in the corresponding cases (5.7–13 and 12.8) nothing is said about the circumstances in which these reduced sacrificial requirements might be permitted; nor how the man in question was to show that 'his means did not suffice' and that he thus had a right to carry out a fully valid and effective sacrifice 'at a reduced rate'. Probably it was held sufficient that he was generally known to be 'a poor man', who for some reason or other was not in possession of his full share of arable land and other property in the community in which he lived.

[33–53] For the 'leprosy' in houses (vv. 33–53) the same is true as for 'leprosy' on materials and leather (13.47–59). It is a question again of appearances externally suggestive of human skin-diseases, and therefore having the same cultically polluting effect, to be treated therefore in a corresponding manner. In practice it must have been lichen or mildew and the like. From the literary and from the subject-matter standpoint this section is certainly secondary to those dealing with human diseases. It assumes a settled way of life in civilized conditions, and arose and took shape naturally with civilization at a time which we can no longer specify. It was subsequently incorporated into the context of the P-narrative, which assumes Israel to be still at Sinai. This was effected by altering the introduction in vv. 33, 34, where the 'I' of Yahweh conflicts with the second person plural address. It was regarded as instructions for conditions that were still to come. For the rest, the section contains the whole detailed case-law covering the declaration of fact by the priest and his subsequent adoption of counter-measures obviously copying the procedure for human diseases.

When a 'leprosy' had been diagnosed a house was either partly 'repaired' or completely pulled down. When the 'disease' had been pronounced 'healed' (v. 48) and the house pronounced 'clean' by the priest, a cleansing rite had to be performed (vv. 49–53), corresponding exactly to the cleansing rites for human 'leprosies' (cf. vv. 4–7). There is no question of an appended sacrificial procedure by analogy with vv. 10ff. It may perhaps be concluded from this that the section about the house 'disease' presupposes an earlier stage of the cleansing regulations for human 'diseases', in which the cleansing ritual was sufficient and the appended competing sacrificial procedures (cf. above pp. 107f.) were not yet provided. One detail shows the strongly formalistic treatment of all that concerned 'cleanness' and 'uncleanness'. According to v. 36a the suspected house was to be cleaned out before the arrival of the priest to pronounce uncleanness in a given case, so that the household contents should not also become 'unclean'. This can only be understood to mean that the priest did not have to declare an already existing cleanness or uncleanness: cultic 'cleanness' or 'uncleanness' only began at the priest's pronouncement 'clean' or 'unclean'. Here also (cf. 11.36, 37 and above pp. 95f.) the practical needs of daily life come in to modify the extreme rigour of the cleanness-uncleanness regulations: the valuable household contents were to be rescued from a suspected house before the priest's declaration of uncleanness made it too late.

### (d) UNCLEANNESS ARISING FROM BODILY DISCHARGES: 15.1–33

15 [1]The LORD said to Moses and Aaron, [2]'Say to the people of Israel, When any man has a discharge from his body, he [his discharge] is unclean. [3]And this is the law of his uncleanness for a discharge: whether his body runs with his discharge, or his body is stopped from discharge, it is uncleanness in him. [4]Every bed on which he who has the discharge lies shall be unclean; and everything on which he sits shall be unclean. [5]And any one who touches his bed shall wash his clothes, and bathe himself in water, and be unclean until the evening. [6]And whoever sits on anything on which he who has the discharge has sat shall wash his clothes, and bathe himself in water, and be unclean until the evening. [7]And whoever touches the body of him who has the discharge shall wash his clothes, and bathe himself in water, and be unclean until the evening. [8]And if he who has the discharge spits on one who is clean, then he shall wash his clothes, and bathe himself in water, and be unclean until the evening. [9]And any saddle on which he who has the discharge rides shall be unclean. [10]And whoever touches anything that was under him shall be unclean until the evening; and

he who carries such a thing shall wash his clothes, and bathe himself in water, and be unclean until the evening. [11]Any one whom he that has the discharge touches without having rinsed his hands in water shall wash his clothes, and bathe himself in water, and be unclean until the evening. [12]And the earthen vessel which he who has the discharge touches shall be broken; and every vessel of wood shall be rinsed in water.

13 'And when he who has a discharge is cleansed of his discharge, then he shall count for himself seven days for his cleansing, and wash his clothes; and he shall bathe his body in running water, and shall be clean. [14]And on the eighth day he shall take two turtledoves or two young pigeons, and come before the LORD [to the door of the tent of meeting] and give them to the priest; [15]and the priest shall offer them, one for a sin offering and the other for a burnt offering; and the priest shall make atonement for him before the LORD for his discharge.

16 'And if a man has an emission of semen, he shall bathe his whole body in water, and be unclean until the evening. [17]And every garment and every skin on which the semen comes shall be washed with water, and be unclean until the evening. [18]If a man lies with a woman and has an emission of semen, both of them shall bathe themselves in water, and be unclean until the evening.

19 'When a woman has a discharge of blood which is her regular discharge from her body, she shall be in her impurity for seven days, and whoever touches her shall be unclean until the evening. [20]And everything upon which she lies during her impurity shall be unclean; everything also upon which she sits shall be unclean. [21]And whoever touches her bed shall wash his clothes, and bathe himself in water, and be unclean until the evening. [22]And whoever touches anything upon which she sits shall wash his clothes, and bathe himself in water, and be unclean until the evening; [23]whether it is the bed or anything upon which she sits, when he touches it he shall be unclean until the evening. [24]And if any man lies with her, and her impurity is on him, he shall be unclean seven days; and every bed on which he lies shall be unclean.

25 'If a woman has a discharge of blood for many days, not at the time of her impurity, or if she has a discharge beyond the time of her impurity, all the days of the discharge she shall continue in uncleanness; as in the days of her impurity, she shall be unclean. [26]Every bed on which she lies, all the days of her discharge, shall be to her as the bed of her impurity; and everything on which she sits shall be unclean, as in the uncleanness of her impurity. [27]And whoever touches these things shall be unclean, and shall wash his clothes, and bathe himself in water, and be unclean until the evening. [28]But if she is cleansed of her discharge, she shall count for herself seven days, and after that she shall be clean. [29]And on the eighth day she shall take two turtledoves or two young pigeons, and bring them to the priest, [to the door of the tent of meeting.] [30]And the priest shall offer one for a sin offering and the other for a burnt offering; and the priest shall make atonement for her before the LORD for her unclean discharge.

31 'Thus you shall keep the people of Israel separate from their

uncleanness, lest they die in their uncleanness by defiling my tabernacle that is in their midst.'

32 This is the law for him who has a discharge and for him who has an emission of semen, becoming unclean thereby; 33also for her who is sick with her impurity; that is, for any one, male or female, who has a discharge, and for the man who lies with a woman who is unclean.

Apart from the introductory formula in vv. 1, 2a, corresponding almost verbatim with that in 11.1, 2a; and apart from the obviously secondary parenetic concluding sentences in v. 31, the chapter is couched in the consistent and objective style of the cleanness-uncleanness case-law. It does not deal with a subject of special priestly professional knowledge, for the priest had only to officiate (vv. 14, 15 and vv. 29, 30) in the cleansing sacrifices for removing an unusual 'uncleanness'; it deals rather with cleanness regulations important for everyone to know, as is pertinently stated in the introductory formula. Naturally the priest had to give information about these rules; and in priestly circles they may well have been formulated and finally fixed in written shape. There is an almost complete lack of any points of attachment for dating these rules in their present form; but it is clear once again that there has been a slight redaction towards P, indicated by the mention of the tent of meeting in vv. 14 and 29, which must have come in at a later stage.

The whole is divided by the clearly parallel introductory conditional clauses v. 2bα and v. 19aα into two sections, the first concerning the 'man' and the second the 'woman'. [18] The sentence in v. 18 was probably inserted as a later addition. In the conditional clause it appears to refer to the woman, but in fact refers to man and woman equally. It does not belong to the framework of the whole in that it does not treat as elsewhere of unusual or abnormal sexual processes. For the rest, this chapter deals in some detail with the cultically polluting effect caused by sexual 'discharges', and with the measures to be taken in regard to them. [2–15] With the men, it is primarily a case of a morbid 'discharge' (vv. 2b–15), not more exactly described or defined, and perhaps used in a kind of collective sense. Such a 'discharge' made not only the man 'unclean' but also everything in direct or indirect contact with him. People rendered unclean by such contact must wash their clothes and bodies and remain unclean for that day. Belongings must be either destroyed (v. 12a) or, if seeming too valuable for destruction, at least be thoroughly washed (v. 12b). If it was a question of costly objects, they must be declared

L.–H

unclean for an indefinite period of time (vv. 4a, 4b, 9). When the morbid condition had ceased, and after a waiting period of seven days and a washing of clothes and body (v. 13), the men could regain cultic cleanness by a modest sacrifice of two doves as a sin offering and burnt offering. [16-17] The case of pollution, shortly handled in vv. 16, 17, required only ablutions and only involved uncleanness for one day. [19-24] In the women's case (vv. 19-24) the polluting effects of the regular menstruation are first dealt with, for the woman herself and for her contacts with persons and things. It lasted in all seven days. On the expiry of these seven days the uncleanness was deemed to have ended. This case, being a 'regular' one, needed no special cleansing ceremony or 'atoning' sacrificial procedure. [25-30] Very different was the case dealt with in vv. 25-30—an irregular discharge of blood lasting beyond the usual period of menstruation, or altogether outside the menstrual period (v. 25a). Here, the same uncleanness ordinances were in force as for menstruation (vv. 25b, 26, 27). When the abnormal phenomena had ended, however, the corresponding regulations (vv. 13-15) must be obeyed, with a waiting period of seven days (v. 28) and the bringing of two doves as a sin offering and burnt offering (vv. 29, 30).

# V

## THE GREAT CLEANSING RITUAL

### Lev. 16.1–34

**16** ¹The LORD spoke to Moses, after the death of the two sons of Aaron, when they drew near before the LORD and died; ²and the LORD said to Moses, 'Tell Aaron your brother not to come at all times into the holy place within the veil, before the mercy seat which is upon the ark, lest he die; for I will appear in the cloud upon the mercy seat. ³But thus shall Aaron come into the holy place: with a young bull for a sin offering and a ram for a burnt offering. ⁴He shall put on the holy linen coat, and shall have the linen breeches on his body, be girded with the linen girdle, and wear the linen turban; these are the holy garments. He shall bathe his body in water, and then put them on. ⁵And he shall take from the congregation of the people of Israel two male goats for a sin offering, and one ram for a burnt offering.

6 'And Aaron shall offer the bull as a sin offering for himself, and shall make atonement for himself and for his house. ⁷Then he shall take the two goats, and set them before the LORD at the door of the tent of meeting; ⁸and Aaron shall cast lots upon the two goats, one lot for the LORD and the other lot for Azazel. ⁹And Aaron shall present the goat on which the lot fell for the LORD, and offer it as a sin offering; ¹⁰but the goat on which the lot fell for Azazel shall be presented alive before the LORD [to make atonement over it,] that it may be sent away into the wilderness to Azazel.

11 'Aaron shall present the bull as a sin offering for himself, and shall make atonement for himself and for his house; he shall kill the bull as a sin offering for himself. ¹²And he shall take a censer full of coals of fire from the altar before the LORD, and two handfuls of sweet incense beaten small; and he shall bring it within the veil ¹³and put the incense on the fire before the LORD, that the cloud of the incense may cover the mercy seat which is upon the testimony, lest he die; ¹⁴and he shall take some of the blood of the bull, and sprinkle it with his finger on the front of the mercy seat, and before the mercy seat he shall sprinkle the blood with his finger seven times.

15 '[Then he shall kill the goat of the sin offering which is for the people, and bring its blood within the veil, and do with its blood as he did with the blood of the bull, sprinkling it upon the mercy seat and before the mercy seat;] ¹⁶thus he shall make atonement for the holy place, because of the uncleannesses of the people of Israel, and because of their transgressions, all their sins; and so he shall do for the tent of meeting, which abides with them in the midst of their uncleannesses. ¹⁷There shall be no man in the tent of meeting when he enters to make atonement in the holy place until he comes out and has made atonement for himself and for his house and for all the assembly of Israel. ¹⁸Then he shall go out to the altar which is before the LORD and make atonement for it, and shall take some of the blood of the bull [and of the blood of the goat,] and put it on the horns of the altar round about. ¹⁹And he shall sprinkle some of the blood upon it with his finger seven times, and cleanse it and hallow it from the uncleannesses of the people of Israel. ²⁰And so he shall make* an end of atoning for the holy place and the tent of meeting and the altar. Then he shall present the live goat; ²¹and Aaron shall lay both his hands upon the head of the live goat, and confess over him all the iniquities of the people of Israel, and all their transgressions, all their sins; and he shall put them upon the head of the goat, and send him away into the wilderness by the hand of a man who is in readiness. ²²The goat shall bear all their iniquities upon him to a solitary land; and he shall let the goat go in the wilderness.

23 'Then Aaron shall come into the tent of meeting, and shall put off the linen garments which he put on when he went into the holy place, and shall leave them there; ²⁴and he shall bathe his body in water in a holy place, and put on his garments, and come forth, and offer his burnt offering and the burnt offering of the people, and make atonement for himself and for the people. ²⁵And the fat of the sin offering he shall burn upon the altar. ²⁶And he who lets the goat go to Azazel shall wash his clothes and bathe his body in water, and afterward he may come into the camp. ²⁷And the bull for the sin offering and the goat for the sin offering, whose blood was brought in to make atonement in the holy place, shall be carried forth outside the camp; their skin and their flesh and their dung shall be burned with fire. ²⁸And he who burns them shall wash his clothes and bathe his body in water, and afterward he may come into the camp.

29 'And it shall be a statute to you for ever that in the seventh month, on the tenth day of the month, you shall afflict yourselves, and shall do no work, either the native or the stranger who sojourns among you; ³⁰for on this day shall atonement be made for you, to cleanse you; from all your sins you shall be clean before the LORD. ³¹It is a sabbath of solemn rest to you, and you shall afflict yourselves; it is a statute for ever. ³²And the priest who is anointed and consecrated as priest in his father's place shall make atonement, wearing the holy linen garments; ³³he shall make atonement for the sanctuary, and he shall make atone-

*[RSV links 20a with what follows. Ed.]

ment for the tent of meeting and for the altar, and he shall make atonement for the priests and for all the people of the assembly. ³⁴And this shall be an everlasting statute for you, that atonement may be made for the people of Israel once in the year because of all their sins.' And Moses did as the LORD commanded him.

I T IS USUAL to describe this chapter as the 'ritual of the great day of atonement'. That is correct in so far as, according to v. 29b, the cultic procedures described in this chapter were to be repeated each year on the tenth day of the seventh month. According to Lev. 23.27, 28; 25.9 this day was the 'day of propitiation' (*yōm hakkippūrīm*), the so-called 'great day of atonement'; and there is no doubt that in the post-exilic cult this day followed the ritual of Lev. 16. Now the passage vv. 29–31 hardly belongs to the original form of the chapter; the reference to a 'great day of atonement' fixed for a definite date came in accordingly later. It is clear that Lev. 16 contains elements in all probability older than the existence of a 'great day of atonement'. It is evident at the first glance that the chapter is in its present form the result of a probably fairly long previous history that has left its traces in a strange lack of continuity and unity about the whole. The position is indeed so complicated that all attempts hitherto at factual and literary analysis have not led to at all convincing results. But the fact itself, that the chapter came into being through an elaborate process of growth, is generally recognized and accepted.

[1, 2aα] It is not easy to answer the question how the arrangement of the whole indicated in its setting fits into a larger context. The stereotyped formula describing the carrying out of the procedure with which it concludes (v. 34b) can only refer back to the introductory sentences vv. 1, 2aα. These say that Moses passed on the ordinance communicated to him to Aaron, as commanded. These introductory sentences vv. 1, 2aα and thus implies that Moses passed on the ordinance he had been given to Aaron, as commanded. These introductory sentences themselves, however, are not a unity. Verse 1 is a loose have been inserted into the P-narrative already enlarged by later accretions, at an appropriate place; for the ritual containing regulations for the holy place and priesthood seems, from the incident reported in 10.1ff., to be in its right position. The linking-on in v. 1 probably also goes to show that Lev. 16 was incorporated into the P-context before the now-interposed complex of Lev. 11–15 occupied its present place. But the linking introductory sentence v. 1 is now

itself secondary as compared with the competing independent introductory sentence v. 2aα. This ties down the sequel quite generally and
historically to Moses' reception of the law and to Sinai; thus showing
this piece to have been already introduced in a narrative sequence
before v. 1 effected the special linking on to 10.1ff. It must therefore
be reckoned at least possible that 16.2ff. already stood in the P-
narrative antecedent to 10.1ff. and 16.1, and had somehow become
joined on—not inappositely—to the priestly dedication and the first
sacrifices of chs. 8 and 9. But that is in no way certain; and in any
case ch. 16¶, in spite of many connections with the P-narrative, did
not belong to the original substance of P, but was only worked in at
some later stage (with the introductory sentence v. 2aα). This chapter
has had its own early history and must be interpreted from within—
especially as its content is somewhat unusual and peculiar to itself.

In attempting to do this one comes up against unusual difficulties.
There are even numerous and striking unevennesses in form. Here
are a few examples. At one moment it is 'the congregation' (*'ēdā* v. 5),
then 'the assembly' (*qāhāl* v. 17), elsewhere 'the people' (*'am* vv. 15,
24), and finally 'the people of the assembly' (*'am haq-qāhāl* v. 33),
although the meaning throughout is the same. Again, the frequently
occurring verb 'atone' (*kipper*) appears freely in almost all the possible Hebrew constructions—absolute (v. 32a), with accusative (vv.
20a, 33a), with *'al* (vv. 10aβ, 16a, 30, 33b, 34a), with *be'ad* (vv. 6b,
11aβ, 17b, 24bβ). There are some repetitions in particular phrases,
but in most cases no factual reason is perceptible for the change of
construction. In the structure, too, there is a lack of smoothness.
Aaron's ram for the burnt offering in v. 3bβ disappears at one
moment completely into the background and crops up quite briefly
and supplementarily in v. 24bα. In the same place there appears
alongside a burnt offering of the 'people', previously mentioned only
briefly way back in v. 5b. As to the contents, different themes run
parallel and intermingle. The whole begins in vv. 2aβb, 3a with the
provisions for Aaron's entry into the holy place, and this subject is
treated in the sequel in the setting of other contexts, as occasion
serves (vv. 11b–14, 23, 24a). Then all kinds of atoning sacrifices
come again into the foreground (vv. 3b, 5, 11ff.¶), with which
Aaron 'makes atonement' either for himself and his house (v. 6b and
elsewhere) or for the 'holy place' and its furnishings (vv. 16–20a¶),
or for the whole people (v. 17bβ, etc.). A special element is constituted by the transaction with the two he-goats, one of which is

presented as a sin offering and the other sent into the wilderness
(vv. 5, 7–10, 15, 20b–22, 26). It will not do simply to arrange these
irregularities so as to show certain basic material and certain layers
of secondary growth. It must also be remembered that even eluci-
dation of the pre-literary or literary growth-process still cannot
decide the relative ages of the cultic customs and ideas contained in
the separate elements. This can be seen in one particular element—
the procedure with the two he-goats—which appears to presuppose,
at any rate in part, the present state of the chapter, but in its material
makes a distinct impression of antiquity. The whole is held together
by the general viewpoint of cultic 'atonement', and within this
framework the atoning of the priesthood and the holy place come
into the foreground as something special. Perhaps this subject is
really the kernel of the chapter, to which in the course of a fairly
long time, and very unsystematically, many other elements have
attached themselves. Even if we reckon with elements of very ancient
material in Lev. 16, we shall not be able to assign a very early date
to the beginning of its literary fixation. In this chapter, quite otherwise than in Lev. 1–7 and 11–15, the figure of Aaron as the chief
priest is firmly rooted in the definitive form of the chapter. This does
not mean direct dependence upon P, but perhaps only dependence
on the similar, but fairly late, Aaron tradition, hardly to be dated
before Ezekiel. Even the representations of the holy place, as far as
they are at all recognizable in the not very clear pronouncements of
Lev. 16, have reference to the P-narrative; but they are on the other
hand unusually expressed, so that even in this point direct dependence on P is not very likely. The connecting thread is probably not
so much literary as in the history of the tradition. In any case the
whole cleansing ritual must, from the first stages of written consoli-
dation onwards, have been formulated round the primitive image of
the Sinai tradition. The age of its contents, or the contents of its
separate elements, can scarcely be determined with any certainty.

[2aβb–4] Even the opening in vv. 2aβb–4 is remarkably uneven.
Aaron is forbidden to enter the holy place 'at any time'. One would
expect this to be followed by the indication of a particular time or
occasion when entrance was allowed or commanded. Instead of this
v. 3 orders Aaron only to come into the holy place 'with' two animals
for sacrifice, though it is not stated whether he should take these
animals in with him. The whole is a rather inaptly phrased instruction
to Aaron only to enter the holy place on the occasions of a special

sacrifice, which according to v. 34a (cf. vv. 29b–31) took place 'once in the year'. This leaves it doubtful what exactly is meant by the holy place: is the passage about '(the space) within the curtain' in apposition to 'holy place', or does it have a further specialized and restricted meaning? In any case the direction about entry refers to the inner room, divided off by a curtain, the place where the ark stood. Its distinguishing marks show clear relationship with the description of the 'tabernacle' in the P-narrative of Ex. 26 (cf. especially Ex. 26.33, 34). What is striking here is that the expression 'the holy of holies', which appears often in P, and would seem obvious in Lev. 16, is not used, and the word 'holy place' occurs in a sense not usual in P. Much the same is true of the instruction for Aaron's priestly robes which he must wear for entering the 'holy place' (v. 4a; the rather lame v. 4b, putting forward a washing before wearing the holy garments, is perhaps a later addition). This official dress has some connections with the high priest's dress as described in Ex. 28, without precisely resembling it. The parts occupying the foreground of interest in Ex. 28 are here completely lacking; instead, there are the linen breeches, which in Ex. 28.42ff. only crop up in a supplement. The effect of the whole is that a much simpler and plainer dress is prescribed than in Ex. 28, unless one takes Lev. 16.4 to mean that Aaron was not to wear the full regalia in the once-a-year sacrifice in the 'holy place', but only a more modest dress. [5] The preparatory instructions for the sacrificial procedure provided in v. 3b are followed immediately in v. 5 by the requirement that 'the congregation of the people of Israel' should prepare animals for sacrifice. These were clearly for procedures intended to be linked up with the sacrifices in v. 3b. Such an accumulation of different cultic procedures for one specific occasion is not in itself a specially unusual feature in cultic history. Verse 5 would therefore not be so striking if the instructions in the following verses did not so strangely flit to and fro between the people's offering in v. 5 and the priest's offering in v. 3b. Verse 6 deals with the young bull for the sin offering mentioned in v. 3b; vv. 7–10 speak of the two he-goats of v. 5; vv. 11ff. come back to the young bull for the sin offering of v. 3b, v. 11a repeating v. 6 word for word.* This last circumstance shows that in Lev. 16 we have to reckon not only with a pre-history in the tradition of the cult, but also with an earlier literary history. In all probability the verbatim

---

*[This is clear in Noth's translation; RSV differs slightly, 'offer'/'present'. Ed.]

repetition of v. 6 in v. 11a indicates that vv. 7–10 are, from the literary point of view, secondary; and v. 5, being so immediately dependent on vv. 7–10, secondary likewise. This would make the sacrificial procedure provided in v. 3b, with which the entry of Aaron into the 'holy place' was connected, the original basis of the chapter. The sacrificial procedures prepared in v. 5, in which the two he-goats were to play a principal part, are to be regarded as a later accretion. In the received form of this chapter the different elements are so arranged that, substantially, everything as far as v. 5 serves to introduce the preparations, and everything from v. 6 onwards describes the carrying out, of the cultic procedures belonging to this particular day.

[6] Verse 6 first requires the 'bringing in' of the sin offering young bull of v. 3b (in this sense the *wᵉhiqrīb*, here as in v. 11a, is clearly used). This sacrificial procedure is not more exactly described till vv. 11ff. [7–10] The insertion of vv. 7–10 at this point—perhaps on the grounds of the actual customary cultic practice—must be taken to mean that the first procedure with the two goats put forward by the 'congregation' must be carried out before the presentation of the young bull for the sin offering. After these had been presented 'before Yahweh' (v. 7) (the accompanying superfluous mention of the 'tent of meeting' might be secondary), Aaron was to allot each to its special purpose by casting lots, the means by which the divine will was ascertained (v. 8). The drawing of lots was so contrived that two lots (stones or the like), marked one with the name or symbol of Yahweh and the other of Azazel, were shaken and then 'came out' of a vessel (so literally v. 9), first one, then naturally the other. The goat destined for Yahweh was then at once sacrificed as a sin offering, as v. 9b shortly observes, whilst the other was kept ready (v. 10) for the procedure to be carried out later, as described in vv. 20b–22. The remark about 'making atonement' for this goat is in quite the wrong place and probably only came in here by mistake. (With this procedure cf. below p. 124.) [11–14] The present form of the ritual places the sacrifice of one of the sin-offering goats (v. 9b) as the first to be undertaken. Then follows the sacrifice of the young bull as a sin offering (v. 3bα). After the insertion of vv. 7–10, v. 11a, taking up v. 6, serves to introduce the repeated instruction to 'bring in' the sin-offering bull. Before vv. 7–10 were inserted, the *wᵉhiqrīb* of vv. 6a, 11aα must have had the sense of 'presenting', as shown by the continuation in v. 6b = 11aβ, referring as it does to the whole sacrificial

procedure. Verse 6 (= v. 11a) was thus originally an inclusive introductory sentence, followed later (in vv. 11bff.) by the details for
carrying out some specially important acts. According to v. 6b
(= v. 11aβ) this procedure had atoning power (*kipper* with *be'ad*) for
Aaron and 'his house'. By the unusual expression 'house of Aaron'
must be meant the whole priesthood by reason of the fact that the
priestly office was hereditary in the one family. However, in what
follows there is a connection between this atonement of the priesthood, effected through the chief priest and probably from the beginning taking place once a year, and the subject of an atoning cleansing
of the holy place itself and of its furniture. This connection was not
in itself hard to make; for a cultic 'profaning' of the holy place,
necessitating such an atoning act, was most likely to proceed from
the priests who officiated in it. Thus a connection between an atoning
of the priesthood and a cleansing of the holy place lay ready to hand.
But according to the present wording of v. 6 (= v. 11a) the point of
departure for the development of the whole was a sacrifice to atone
for the priesthood; and the instructions for this sacrifice form the
most detailed portion in this ch. 16. There is therefore reason to
think that this sacrifice, from the textual and perhaps even from the
literary point of view, is to be regarded as the kernel. Between the
brief remarks on the slaughtering of the sin-offering bullock by Aaron
(v. 11a), and the instructions for dealing with the blood from the
sacrificial animal in v. 14, the passage about censing the holy place
(vv. 12, 13) looks at first like an intrusion, separating what should
belong together. It could be regarded as a later addition without
thereby making a gap in the original textual continuity. It would
then have been added later on, probably on the basis of later practice, in order to prepare for the unusual blood-ritual in the 'holy of
holies' (v. 14). In any case it would only be meaningful in reference
to v. 14, and by assuming vv. 11b and 14. But if one assumes that this
censing belonged from the start to the material of this ritual—which
is in itself not improbable—then this act, if immediately preparatory
for the blood-sprinkling, could have no other place than between the
slaughter and the blood-sprinkling. It must therefore appear in the
ritual instructions, which naturally enumerated the separate ritual
acts in their proper sequence, at the very place where it is now mentioned. There is then no material reason for doubting the original
unity of the passage vv. 11b–14. The act of burning incense does not
yet assume the special altar of incense in Ex. 30.1–10 (cf. Noth,

*Exodus*, pp. 234f.), but reckons with only one altar, in agreement with the original P-narrative, as in Ex. 27.1–8¶. It rests on the idea of the apotropaic protective power against dangers, inherent in the burning of sweet-smelling substances. In v. 13b this is focused in the thought that the burning of incense would make the the mercy seat above the ark, specially 'dangerous' through the divine presence, invisible. After this precaution the blood-sprinkling could take place, for which Aaron now had to fetch some of the blood from the slaughtered bull in some kind of vessel. This act consisted of a single sprinkling towards the front (east side) of the mercy seat, and a sevenfold sprinkling 'towards the mercy seat' (i.e. in the air). On this very special occasion of the priestly atoning this act was carried out in the 'holy of holies' itself (contrast the other sin offerings in 4.6, 17). Only on this single occasion was the chief priest permitted and enjoined to enter the 'holy of holies' (cf. vv. 2aβb–4). By this procedure the sin-offering blood and the sin offering itself were brought into specially direct contact with the place of the divine presence or appearance, and thus consecrated in a unique fashion. After this the sin offering itself must be presented, according to the usual ritual, intended for the atoning of Aaron and 'his house'. This last receives no further special mention: it was probably held to be already contained in the comprehensive main clause v. 11a. But a remark bearing on it might have been eliminated by the following secondary additions. [17b] It might once have been connected with the sentence v. 17b, which now stands in lonely isolation, where—seemingly in conclusion—there is a further mention of atoning (*kipper* with *be'ad*) for Aaron and his 'house' (worded as in v. 6a = 11aβ), but with the addition of 'all the assembly of Israel'. This expression, occurring here only in Lev. 16, stresses the effect of the solemn priestly sin offering as extending over the whole of Israel. [15] Of the intervening sentences v. 15 is at any rate secondary; it requires an exactly corresponding blood-sprinkling rite to be carried out with the blood from the sin-offering goat (v. 9), just as with the sin-offering bull in the 'holy of holies'. By its specific reference to v. 14 this verse shows itself secondary as compared with vv. 11–14. The procedure with the sin-offering bull for the priests has become extended at a later stage to cover also the sin-offering goat of the people. But this was not at first contemplated in v. 9. It is certain that this originally meant the complete offering of the goat put forward by the 'congregation' (v. 5; in v. 15 'people'). Yet v. 15, surprisingly, contains the first mention of this animal's slaughter.

Verse 9b must then be taken in retrospect as a mere preparation for the offering. This leaves it an open question what should have been 'done' with the sin-offering goat before the slaughter. [16–20a] Verses 16ff. are probably secondary, too: they lay down further atoning actions with the blood of the sin-offering bull (and the subsequently added sin-offering goat—cf. v. 18b), to be carried out by the chief priest in the 'holy place'. (Here, *kipper* with *'al*, except as mentioned above, v. 17b, and in the inclusive final sentence v. 20a, *kipper* + acc.) This obviously has in mind, without expressly saying so, further blood-sprinklings calculated to free the holy place from all 'pollutions' caused by the Israelites' transgressions. These, as the present wording shows, would be not so much offences specifically against ordinances of the holy place as quite generally the Israelites' sins, which affected their relationship to their God, and so indirectly their place of worship. The juxtaposition of 'holy place' and 'tent of meeting' in v. 16 (cf. v. 20a) shows that 'holy place' here means the inner space (cf. above pp. 119f., v. 2aβb), the 'holy of holies' in P. Verse 17a (cf. v. 17b above) again expressly and naturally requires that only the chief priest himself should carry out the atoning actions in 'the holy place' (= 'holy of holies'). During the time of this specially intimate and 'dangerous' procedure, no one was to stay in the tent of meeting. Verses 18, 19 prescribe a further special 'cleansing and hallowing' for the altar standing before the tent of meeting.

[20b–22] In vv. 20b–22 there follows the procedure with the goat. Verse 8 says that it was allotted to Azazel; v. 10, that it was to be held ready for a special purpose. Aaron, representing the community, laid his hands on its head and at the same time confessed over it the sins of Israel (clearly in a quite general sense). These were then laid upon it (vv. 20b, 21abα), and it was led out into the 'wilderness' by a specially appointed 'man' and there let loose, to bear away with it the sins of Israel to an unknown and remote place. This crude procedure for removing the sins of Israel (and cleansing the holy place) was indeed a later addition to the ritual of priestly atonement in the framework of Lev. 16 (cf. above pp. 120f., on vv. 5 and 7–10). It doubtless represents a very ancient rite that once played an independent part outside the present context, and was to be sure originally bound up with a definite *'Sitz im Leben'*. In the present context the 'wilderness' into which the scapegoat is led out and then left to run wild means the wilderness (of Sinai) surrounding Israel's camp at Sinai and during their further sojourn in the wilderness. The rite with the two he-goats may originally have had its home in a holy place in settled living conditions, where there was a 'wilderness' close at hand, which could very easily be the case within range of Israel, either east or west of Jordan; and the fact that in v. 21b$\beta$ a 'man' has to lead the goat into the wilderness may perhaps be an argument for this latter possibility. If the reference then is not to a central, but to a more or less local, holy place, this massive atonement-rite was not in the first place for all Israel, but for some narrower circle of worshippers, and only later taken over for the whole of Israel at a central holy place—no doubt Jerusalem, with its neighbouring 'wilderness of Judaea'. The figure of Azazel remains an enigma. It is remarkable that it is not mentioned in the main section vv. 20b–22, but only in the preparatory section vv. 7–10. Here, the one is chosen by lot 'for Azazel' (vv. 8, 10a$\alpha$ and v. 26a$\alpha$). People have usually seen in him a 'desert demon' who is satisfied by the sending of a he-goat and thus rendered harmless. The juxtaposition of Yahweh and Azazel in v. 8 would seem to justify this assumption. This, it is true, makes the whole rite somewhat ambiguous: the gift to Azazel should then have had the apotropaic purpose of warding off this redoubtable desert demon and the dangers that he threatened; whilst the burdening of the he-goat with Israel's trespasses meant the cleansing and atoning removal of these trespasses. Thus it might be asked whether the whole rite had not already had a history before it came into the cleansing ritual of Lev. 16. In that case the handing over of the goat 'to Azazel' would be the primary feature, and the burdening of the goat with Israel's sins a later, although still a very primitive feature. At any rate the occurrence of Azazel, if it belonged to the original substance of the rite, would seem to point to a meaning at first belonging to a limited locality. For the name Azazel, occurring here only, could hardly be a general description for any 'desert demon', but rather that of a demonic being thought of as inhabiting and casting his spell upon a particular wilderness. With this local limitation the 'scapegoat' ritual will have been different in kind from the Passover ritual; though comparable in its apotropaic purpose, it was markedly different in its detailed procedure.

[23–28] The section vv. 23–28 brings by way of supplement—probably secondary in essence from the literary point of view—far more detailed instructions for completing the complicated ritual. The passage vv. 23, 24a ignores the scapegoat interlude; it therefore probably originates from the stage before the insertion of the sections dealing with the two goats. At the end of the cleansing procedure, which had finally led Aaron to the altar in front of the tent of meeting (v. 20a), he should have taken off and left his official robes (cf. v. 4a) in this tent, and after washing himself should have put on his everyday clothes. By the later addition of v. 24b at any rate the last remark has been twisted to mean that Aaron should exchange his special dress, needed for the great cleansing ritual referred to in v. 4, for his usual official dress as described in P (Ex. 28). This was for the purpose of completing the still outstanding burnt offering (from vv. 3bβ and 5b) according to the customary ritual. There must originally have been a direction about the burnt offering in accordance with v. 3bβ, but it has dropped out in the later expansions. In v. 24b the subsequent combination of priestly and holy-place atonements with vv. 5, 7ff. is already presupposed. (Here again, as in v. 15, we have 'people' instead of 'congregation' in v. 5.) In v. 25 a missing remark about the sin offering of vv. 3bα, 6, 11–14 is subsequently brought in. As this now means only one sin offering, the sin-offering goat of vv. 9, 15 is ignored. Contrast vv. 27, 28, where something more is said about the parts left over from both sin-offering animals. Verse 26 is a later addition to the scapegoat ritual.

[29–34] The final section (vv. 29–34) first fixes (vv. 29–31) the date of the tenth day of the seventh month for the annual performances of the great cleansing ritual. The phrasing is very near to the passage in the Law of Holiness about the *yōm hak-kippūrīm* (23.27–32a). The position at the end shows the supplementary character of the date-fixing. The same is shown by the fact that the concrete element in the priestly and holy-place atonement has quite disappeared and only the general atoning of Israel—addressed in the second person plural—is considered (and likewise in v. 34a). In this last respect the passage vv. 32, 33 is seen as obviously older, though certainly not original; for it again shows a special interest only in the already secondary element of the holy-place atonement in vv. 16ʃ–20a (*kipper* with acc., as v. 20a). Not till the supplementary v. 33b (*kipper* with *ʿal*) do the 'priests' and 'all the people of the assembly' (this expression occurs only here) come in as objects of the atoning. The description in v. 32a of the chief priest in office is worth noting. It presupposes the end of the Jewish kingdom. Worth noting also is the quite peculiar expression *miqdaš haq-qōdeš* for the 'holy of holies' in v. 33a.

# VI

## THE HOLINESS CODE

### Lev. 17.1–26.46

IN 17.1 THERE begins a series of sections all introduced, in a
manner familiar from the chapters so far dealt with, by a remark
about the words of Yahweh to Moses at Sinai, instructing him to
pass on specific 'laws' and 'ordinances' to Aaron and his sons or to the
Israelites. As far, then, as the indication of framework is concerned,
the remaining chapters proceed in the same fashion. But in 26.3–45
we come to a great announcement of blessings and cursings for
obedience or disobedience to the divine commands. This blessing or
cursing parenesis, most nearly related to Deut. 28.1–68, can only be
understood as the concluding portion of a collection of divine 'laws',
to be sought in the preceding chapters. Now, these chapters do not
in any way form a unity, either in form or in content, but rather a
composite of different material. The same is, however, true of the
Deuteronomic law: by its framework, or by the absence of any
internal divisions marked off by section-headings, it likewise shows
itself to be a book of laws that have received a literary polish. It is
apparent, then, that in the chapters preceding Lev. 26 we can assume
a similar law-book, once an independent literary complex. We can
suppose it to begin with ch. 17, primarily for the simple reason that
we can see elsewhere no other longer collection to which ch. 17 and
the following chapters could once have belonged; but also because,
in spite of all the variety in their contents, the chs. Lev. 17–25 are
bound together by a certain common intention. Now the insertion of
this literary complex is in no way marked outwardly. Hence its
separate sections are provided with the conventional stereotyped
introductory formulae found in Leviticus and even in Numbers. The

opinion that Lev. 17–25, rounded off by Lev. 26, forms an originally independent law-book is fairly generally held; and it is customary, following August Klostermann's proposal, to call this law-book the 'Holiness Code'. This name was suggested by the almost set form of the concluding formulae occurring in parts of this book, speaking of the 'holiness' of Yahweh, which also requires 'holiness' from the Israelites (e.g. 19.2; 20.26). By way of dating this literary complex, the Holiness Code, we can only say for the present that we can merely attempt to fix a time at which the whole of this hypothetical law-book took shape, disregarding the fact that in substance and perhaps even in phrasing certainly much older—perhaps very old—elements have passed over into the separate sections; and disregarding the other fact that the already completed law-book also acquired later supplementary accretions. According to the not very numerous and not very helpful points of attachment for dating, the Holiness Code might be placed in the period between the later days and end of the pre-exilic cultus and its new development in the post-exilic Jerusalem sanctuary—a process taking place perhaps in several stages.

### (a) THE OFFERING OF SACRIFICES AND THE EATING OF MEAT: 17.1–16

**17** [1]And the LORD said to Moses, [2]'Say to Aaron and his sons, and to all the people of Israel, This is the thing which the LORD has commanded. [3]If any man of the house of Israel kills an ox or a lamb or a goat in the camp, or kills it outside the camp, [4]and does not bring it to the door of the tent of meeting, to offer it as a gift to the LORD before the tabernacle of the LORD, bloodguilt shall be imputed to that man; he has shed blood; and that man shall be cut off from among his people. [5]This is to the end that the people of Israel may bring their sacrifices which they slay in the open field, that they may bring them to the LORD, to the priest at the door of the tent of meeting, and slay them as sacrifices of peace offerings to the LORD; [6]and the priest shall sprinkle the blood on the altar of the LORD at the door of the tent of meeting, and burn the fat for a pleasing odour to the LORD. [7]So they shall no more slay their sacrifices for satyrs, after whom they play the harlot. This shall be a statute for ever to them throughout their generations.

[8] 'And you shall say to them, Any man of the house of Israel, or of the strangers that sojourn among them, who offers a burnt offering or sacrifice, [9]and does not bring it to the door of the tent of meeting, to sacrifice it to the LORD; that man shall be cut off from his people.

[10] 'If any man of the house of Israel or of the strangers that sojourn among them eats any blood, I will set my face against that person who eats blood, and will cut him off from among his people. [11]For the life of the flesh is in the blood; and I have given it for you upon the altar

to make atonement for your souls; for it is the blood that makes atonement, by reason of the life. 12Therefore I have said to the people of Israel, No person among you shall eat blood, neither shall any stranger who sojourns among you eat blood. 13Any man also of the people of Israel, or of the strangers that sojourn among them, who takes in hunting any beast or bird that may be eaten shall pour out its blood and cover it with dust. 14For the life of every creature is the blood of it;* therefore I have said to the people of Israel, You shall not eat the blood of any creature, for the life of every creature is its blood; whoever eats it shall be cut off.

15 'And every person that eats what dies of itself or what is torn by beasts, whether he is a native or a sojourner, shall wash his clothes, and bathe himself in water, and be unclean until the evening; then he shall be clean. 16But if he does not wash them or bathe his flesh, he shall bear his iniquity.'

This chapter gives general directions for the slaughtering of animals and the eating of meat, and assumes an idealized situation with Israel encamped at Sinai, and the tent of meeting in the middle of the camp. [3–4] The express reference to 'the camp' in v. 3 certainly does not seem to belong very comfortably to the context, and looks rather like a later clarification; but the tent of meeting (v. 4) clearly belongs to the original substance. This would mean that one single place of worship for Israel might be presupposed and mirrored in the one tent of meeting for Israel encamped at Sinai. This would lead us to find the kernel of the whole in a period when the Deuteronomic demand for one place of worship for Israel was recognized as valid (Deut. 12.13ff.), for it is difficult to believe that the present directions can possibly go back to a primitive time when Israel, or a certain part of the later Israel, before their settlement in the promised land, were once assembled round a single holy place. In the promised land, however, there were at first numerous holy places, at any rate for 'private' worship. Now vv. 3, 4 voice a general demand that every slaughter of a 'clean' animal—i.e. one allowed to be eaten, domestic or from the herd—should be undertaken as a cultic act, that is as a 'peace offering'. Apparently the slaughter itself did not have to be performed at any particular place, but the slaughtered animal with its blood drained off into a vessel had to be brought to the holy place for carrying out the peace-offering ritual (cf. Lev. 3). This demand is in opposition to the 'free permission' to slaughter for food in the Deuteronomic law (Deut. 12.15f.), which merely required the 'pouring out' of the blood of the slaughtered animal. The demand of Lev.

---

*Gk, Syr.; compare Vulg.; Hebrew: 'for the life of all flesh, its blood is in its life'.

17.3f. certainly corresponded to ancient custom (cf. I Sam. 14.32–35), practicable so long as there were everywhere in the country local shrines at which the peace-offering ritual could be carried out. The Deuteronomic law demanded a unified place of worship, and sought means to ensure it through obedience to this requirement. Hence, taking into account the widespread nature of the Israelites' occupation of the country, it gave permission, at once far-reaching and disruptive of all previous traditions, to slaughter animals for 'profane' use (thus later P, according to Gen. 9.1–6). Yet Lev. 17.3f., in spite of the presupposition of one unified place of worship, returns to the ordinance, strictly underlined by the threat that any offender would be 'cut off' (v. 4b$\beta$), requiring every slaughter to be a sacrificial slaughter, according to the pre-Deuteronomic law. This can only mean—if a thorough carrying out of the law was ever intended—that circumstances had to be considered such as might have arisen after 587 BC in the still remaining cultic circles round about Jerusalem; and even in those conditions it might be difficult to comply with the 'ideal' demands of the Holiness Code. After the actual rebuilding of the cultic structure in Jerusalem following the exile, the practice of this requirement would hardly have been possible; and so even P (see above) went back to the Deuteronomic ordinance. In this respect the Holiness Code is therefore seen to be a preserver of ancient cultic traditions, and to be concerned to renew their validity in the time after 587 BC, over against the Deuteronomic innovations. It was perhaps believed possible, in altered conditions, to go back behind these both in the present and for the future; but actual circumstances were soon to show that there could be no going back.

The basic form of the section vv. 3–7 (v. 8 forms a new introduction) is to be found in vv. 3, 4, obviously enlarged in the course of time by further detail. Verse 3 speaks of a 'private' slaughter of an eatable animal suitable for sacrifice, only permissible in the framework of the sacrificial ritual. For 'peace offerings' on the part of a community or the whole people, and more so still for 'burnt offerings', that was moreover understood, and needed no special mention in the present context. In v. 4 the reference to 'the tabernacle of Yahweh' is probably a secondary expansion; so certainly is the 'bloodguilt' arising from a disregard of the ritual requirements. This last is very remarkable, for 'bloodguilt' and guilty 'shedding of blood' are elsewhere in the Old Testament used only of human beings (cf. Gen. 9.6), not of animals; whereas here the killing of an animal not in accordance with sacrificial procedure is compared to the killing of a human being. [5–6] The very loosely attached passage vv. 5, 6 adds a detail to the requirement of vv. 3, 4. Verse 5 assumes that up till now the Israelites have carried out their 'slaughterings' (so—in the sense of *šḥṭ* v. 3—must *zbḥ/zebaḥ* in v. 5a be understood, in contrast to v. 5b) in the open, instead of making them into 'peace offerings' (*zibḥē šelāmīm*); then it briefly recalls the essential elements of the peace-offering ritual (cf. 3.2b–5). [7] Whilst v. 5 goes against the continuance of 'profane' slaughterings, v. 7—again in loose attachment to the preceding—forbids idolatrous peace offerings to the 'he-goats' (literally the 'hairy ones'). This veto is connected with the fact that in late pre-exilic times there had been (according to II Kings 23.8, emended text) near one of the city gates of Jerusalem a cultic centre for the 'he-goats'—probably demons represented in the form of goats—which King Josiah suppressed. After the catastrophe of 587 BC the forbidden cult very likely came to life again, so that such 'goat-demons' were thought of in later times as holding sway over the ruins of destroyed cities (cf. Isa. 13.21; 34.14). At all events, the addition of v. 7 to the more general regulations of vv. 3ff. suggests that there was good reason to sharpen this particular veto. The conditions envisaged seem to have been those in Jerusalem, about the time of the catastrophe of 587 BC.

[8–9] From v. 8 onwards a new heading introduces some further appended regulations. The passage vv. 8, 9 passes beyond the requirement of vv. 3, 4 in now expressly adding the burnt offering to the peace offering in the demand for sacrifice exclusively in front of the tent of meeting. Thus no one would be able to think that because the burnt offering was not mentioned in vv. 3ff. permission was therefore given for a burnt offering (as distinct from a peace offering) to be presented at any place the worshipper might choose (which vv. 3ff. certainly do not intend to imply). Besides this, vv. 8, 9 expressly place alongside the settled population the group of 'strangers', i.e. the group of those, whether Israelites or non-Israelites, who lived without any stake in the land among the settled population, while enjoying their protection and being taken into their cultic community, thus becoming subject to their cultic regulations. Their special mention was always justifiable, for there had always been 'strangers' within the orbit of Israel; but in the unsettled conditions following upon the overthrow of the state of Judah there was doubtless special cause to mention them. [10–14] In vv. 10–14 the veto on any eating of blood is expressed and the reasons for it stated in great detail. This veto is shown by its content to be very ancient; but here it appears as an appendix to vv. 3, 4. The basic form of vv. 10ff. might indeed have originally belonged together with vv. 3ff.; but in the present form it has obviously been much remodelled. In the very first main clause (v. 10a)—taken up from v. 3—the 'strangers' appear again alongside of the natives; and then the awkward appearance of the first person for Yahweh is certainly a result of secondary reshaping. (Verse 10b may originally have run like v. 4bβ.) The argument in v. 11aα is based on the ancient idea that 'life' (*nepeš*), i.e. the life-force, the 'vitality' (of animals and of man) has its specific seat in the blood, and that this 'life' belongs to God and may therefore in no circumstances be appropriated by human beings. The detailed application of this basis in v. 11aβb (first person again for Yahweh) narrows down this general notion into the idea that the blood from a sacrifice is 'given' by God to the Israelites as a means of atonement; and with the coming into prominence of atoning sacrifices in later times, this special role of the blood became particularly important. The conclusion in v. 12 (Yahweh in first person) contains nothing further of importance. Finally vv. 13, 14 (v. 13aα has 'Israelites' instead of 'house of Israel') deal with the case of animals killed in hunting. They could naturally not be 'slaughtered' and sacrificed, but were in part (cf. 11.3ff.) allowed for food, but with the same strict regulations about the blood. It must be drained off on the spot and covered with earth, so that no other creature should by mistake drink any of it. The basis of v. 14aα is materially the same as that of v. 11aα, though it is somewhat divergent in phrasing; and v. 14aβb (with Yahweh in the first person) repeats the ordinance, the reasons for it, and the threatened penalties attached to it. **[15–16]** Finally vv. 15, 16 add to the general theme of meat-eating the case in which someone, a native or a 'stranger' (differently phrased from vv. 8a, 10a, 12, 13a) eats meat from a dead animal, an edible part of a domestic animal, or one from the herd which has been torn by a beast of prey. Such eating is not positively forbidden, but in union with 11.40 it is made the reason for a provisional cultic uncleanness, requiring cultic ablutions (v. 15), the omission of which would have certain undefined consequences (v. 16).

(*b*) PRECEPTS DEALING WITH SEXUAL RELATIONS: 18.1–30
18 ¹And the LORD said to Moses, ²'Say to the people of Israel, I am

the LORD your God. ³You shall not do as they do in the land of Egypt, where you dwelt, and you shall not do as they do in the land of Canaan, to which I am bringing you. You shall not walk in their statutes. ⁴You shall do my ordinances and keep my statutes and walk in them. I am the LORD your God. ⁵You shall therefore keep my statutes and my ordinances, by doing which a man shall live: I am the LORD.

6 'None of you shall approach any one near of kin to him to uncover nakedness. I am the LORD. ⁷You shall not uncover the nakedness of your father, which is the nakedness of your mother; she is your mother, you shall not uncover her nakedness. ⁸You shall not uncover the nakedness of your father's wife; it is your father's nakedness. ⁹You shall not uncover the nakedness of your sister, the daughter of your father or the daughter of your mother, whether born at home or born abroad. ¹⁰You shall not uncover the nakedness of your son's daughter or of your daughter's daughter, for their nakedness is your own nakedness. ¹¹You shall not uncover the nakedness of your father's wife's daughter, begotten by your father, since she is your sister. ¹²You shall not uncover the nakedness of your father's sister; she is your father's near kinswoman. ¹³You shall not uncover the nakedness of your mother's sister, for she is your mother's near kinswoman. ¹⁴You shall not uncover the nakedness of your father's brother, that is, you shall not approach his wife; she is your aunt. ¹⁵You shall not uncover the nakedness of your daughter-in-law; she is your son's wife, you shall not uncover her nakedness. ¹⁶You shall not uncover the nakedness of your brother's wife; she is your brother's nakedness. ¹⁷You shall not uncover the nakedness of a woman and of her daughter, and you shall not take her son's daughter or her daughter's daughter to uncover her nakedness; they are your* near kinswomen; it is wickedness. ¹⁸And you shall not take a woman as a rival wife to her sister, uncovering her nakedness while her sister is yet alive.

19 'You shall not approach a woman to uncover her nakedness while she is in her menstrual uncleanness. ²⁰And you shall not lie carnally with your neighbour's wife, and defile yourself with her. ²¹You shall not give any of your children to devote them by fire to Molech, and so profane the name of your God: I am the LORD. ²²You shall not lie with a male as with a woman; it is an abomination. ²³And you shall not lie with any beast and defile yourself with it, neither shall any woman give herself to a beast to lie with it: it is perversion.

24 'Do not defile yourselves by any of these things, for by all these the nations I am casting out before you defiled themselves; ²⁵and the land became defiled, so that I punished its iniquity, and the land vomited out its inhabitants. ²⁶But you shall keep my statutes and my ordinances and do none of these abominations, either the native or the stranger who sojourns among you ²⁷(for all of these abominations the men of the land did, who were before you, so that the land became defiled); ²⁸lest the land vomit you out, when you defile it, as it vomited out the nation that was before you. ²⁹For whoever shall do any of these

*Gk; Hebrew lacks 'your'.

abominations, the persons that do them shall be cut off from among their people. ³⁰So keep my charge never to practise any of these abominable customs which were practised before you, and never to defile yourselves by them: I am the LORD your God.'

The complex of prohibitions connected with sexual relations has the style of apodeictic law, with second person singular address. Verses 2b–5, 24–30 form an unusually detailed frame for it, with the address in the second person plural, setting before Israel in parenetic terms the warning example of other nations. In general the Old Testament considered 'the Canaanites', i.e. the previous inhabitants of the land promised and given by God to Israel, particularly licentious and promiscuous from the sexual point of view. Their expulsion from the land in favour of Israel was in the Old Testament view of history a punishment for their guilt (cf. Gen. 15.16), and this guilt had consisted especially in this sexual licentiousness. The God of Israel, with his holy name 'Yahweh', would not tolerate such behaviour (cf. vv. 2b, 4b, 5b, 6b, 21bβ, 30b). His 'statutes' and 'judgments' (vv. 4a, 5a, 26aα; cf. 30aα) were severe and relentless in this field especially (v. 29); their infringement would result in Israel's expulsion from the land given to her (v. 28). The secondary framework of the chapter does not appear to be entirely a unity. The mention of Egypt along with Canaan (v. 3a) is unusual in this context, but perhaps is simply based on the consideration that the Israelites, here in their supposed position at Sinai, could not yet have knowledge of the Canaanites as a warning example, but only of the Egyptians, whose way of life is here equated with that of the Canaanites. Verse 5 enjoins obedience to Yahweh's 'statutes' and 'judgments' with a reference to their life-giving effect—i.e. the prevention of sudden death in the framework of 'normal' earthly life. In the concluding section vv. 24–30 the passage vv. 26, 27 looks at first sight like a further detailed repetition of vv. 24, 25. But v. 28 does not join on smoothly to anything going before, and vv. 28, 29 must therefore be regarded as probably a later addition. Lastly, v. 30 gives the impression of a concluding remark finally bringing together all that has been previously said.

The heart of the chapter was no doubt the complex of the apodeictic prohibitions in vv. 7–18, in both form and content a relatively self-contained whole which may originally have been 'decalogical' or 'dodecalogical'. It forbids sexual relations within certain degrees of 'relationship' (there is no reference in the basic form to marriage).

[6] The later prefixed main statement in v. 6, formulated on the lines of 17.3, 8, 10, culminating in 'אֲנִי 'אֲנִי, is in contrast to the following address in the second person plural; it interprets those detailed regulations in the sense of a general prohibition of all sexual relations between blood-relatives. Most of the following details are comprehended in this, but not all. [7–18] Rather, vv. 7–18 exhibit different points of view running in parallel. It can easily be understood that in many of the cases named it was not a question of blood-relationship in the strict sense. And even if the marriage relationship were to be understood in the sense of a blood-relationship, there would still remain the case in v. 11, dealing with the relationship to a daughter of a man and woman if born of another union—the woman obviously not being the mother of the person addressed. (This case had already been dealt with in v. 9.) The daughter is declared to be 'a sister', in a peculiar phrase—perhaps a later addition—because 'begotten by your father'. It looks as though originally it had not been a definitely demarcated circle of blood-relationship that was being considered, but rather those normally living together in the circle of a large family, in tents or houses. The basis of the whole would then seem to have been a tribal code strictly forbidding all promiscuity within this circle. To this code Israel held fast, even in settled conditions, in opposition to the loose-living adherents of 'Canaanitish' city culture and its connections with fertility cults. In the large family group there is involved possibly brothers still living together with their father (v. 14) and with their own already married brothers (v. 16); and on the other hand with their own married sons (v. 15). It is a question of respecting all the marriage bonds existing within the large family unit. In this case the 'nakedness' of a woman was considered to belong to her husband and is unusually so described in vv. (7a), 8b, 14, 16b. The virginity of the unmarried woman living under the protection of the large family circle was to be respected likewise. On the other hand, within the large family unit there naturally arose considerations of blood-relationship, especially when marriage was brought within the conception of a 'blood-relationship'. Such cases have therefore been taken up into the list of prohibitions, in which not so much living in proximity, but rather blood-relationship, forms the assumption of the veto, on the ground that sexual intercourse between near blood-relatives is something unnatural and forbidden by God. Reference to blood-relationship is brought in as the express basis, not only in the secondarily prefixed sentence v. 6,

but also in the special prohibitions of vv. 12, 13; even though the (unmarried) sister of the father (v. 13) might still be living in the family circle, but normally not the mother's sister (v. 13). The following details are also to be noted. In v. 7 the juxtaposition of father and mother is inappropriate: presumably the mention of the 'nakedness' of the father is an addition. Verses 8, 9, 11 tacitly assume the possibility of several wives for one husband. The prohibition of sexual intercourse with a half-sister (v. 9) does not necessarily include a veto on marriage with a half-sister (cf. Gen. 20.12). The phrase in the singular *mōledet bayit 'ō mōledet ḥūṣ* (v. 9) most probably refers to legitimate or illegitimate birth. The basic sentence v. 10b seems to use *'erwā* in the sense of the *šᵉ'ēr* in vv. 12b, 13b; the case in v. 10 corresponds, too, with that of vv. 12, 13 in so far as the granddaughter of a daughter, if born in wedlock, could hardly still belong to the large family circle living all together. (For v. 11 cf. above.) Verse 16 in no way forbids 'levirate marriage' (cf. Deut. 25.5–10); it does not apply at all to marriage, but to sexual intercourse, and moreover assumes that the brother is still alive. Verses 17, 18 deal specially with marriage (cf. *lqḥ* in vv. 17, 18); simultaneous marriage with a woman and her daughter or granddaughter or sister are forbidden, which is understandable, if marriage was also reckoned a 'blood-relationship' (cf. *šᵉ'ēr* in v. 17b). The reference to the lifetime of the woman in v. 18 expressly forbids such marriages only if they are simultaneous. For the rest, vv. 17, 18, dealing with the marriage-bond, are perhaps a later accretion on vv. 7–16.

[19–23] Verses 19–23 give a general veto on all non-permissible and especially unnatural sex relationships. This portion is not very unified (cf. the different reasons given in vv. 20b, 21b, 22b, 23aβbβ), and consists probably of successively added supplements to vv. 7–16 (18). In this context only v. 21 is striking, with its prohibition of handing over to 'Moloch [Molech]' any of 'your seed', whereby the name of the God of Israel would be profaned. The same subject occurs with more detail in 20.2–5 (cf. below pp. 147ff.). Perhaps it was only the key-word 'seed' which brought this verse into the present context.

## (c) A COLLECTION OF PRECEPTS OF GENERAL IMPORTANCE: 19.1–37

19 ¹And the LORD said to Moses, ²"Say to all the congregation of the people of Israel, You shall be holy; for I the LORD your God am holy. ³Every one of you shall revere his mother and his father, and you shall

keep my sabbaths: I am the LORD your God. ⁴Do not turn to idols or make for yourselves molten gods: I am the LORD your God.

5 'When you offer a sacrifice of peace offerings to the LORD, you shall offer it so that you may be accepted. ⁶It shall be eaten the same day you offer it, or on the morrow; and anything left over until the third day shall be burned with fire. ⁷If it is eaten at all on the third day, it is an abomination; it will not be accepted, ⁸and every one who eats it shall bear his iniquity, because he has profaned a holy thing of the LORD; and that person shall be cut off from his people.

9 'When you reap the harvest of your land, you shall not reap your field to its very border, neither shall you gather the gleanings after your harvest. ¹⁰And you shall not strip your vineyard bare, neither shall you gather the fallen grapes of your vineyard; you shall leave them for the poor and for the sojourner: I am the LORD your God.

11 'You shall not steal, nor deal falsely, nor lie to one another. ¹²And you shall not swear by my name falsely, and so profane the name of your God: I am the LORD.

13 'You shall not oppress your neighbour or rob him. The wages of a hired servant shall not remain with you all night until the morning. ¹⁴You shall not curse the deaf or put a stumbling block before the blind, but you shall fear your God: I am the LORD.

15 'You shall do no injustice in judgment; you shall not be partial to the poor or defer to the great, but in righteousness shall you judge your neighbour. ¹⁶You shall not go up and down as a slanderer among your people, and you shall not stand forth against the life* of your neighbour: I am the LORD. ¹⁷You shall not hate your brother in your heart, but you shall reason with your neighbour, lest you bear sin because of him. ¹⁸You shall not take vengeance or bear any grudge against the sons of your own people, but you shall love your neighbour as yourself: I am the LORD.

19 'You shall keep my statutes. You shall not let your cattle breed with a different kind; you shall not sow your field with two kinds of seed; nor shall there come upon you a garment of cloth made of two kinds of stuff.

20 'If a man lies carnally with a woman who is a slave, betrothed to another man and not yet ransomed or given her freedom, an inquiry shall be held. They shall not be put to death, because she was not free; ²¹but he shall bring a guilt offering for himself to the LORD, to the door of the tent of meeting, a ram for a guilt offering. ²²And the priest shall make atonement for him with the ram of the guilt offering before the LORD for his sin which he has committed; and the sin which he has committed shall be forgiven him.

23 'When you come into the land and plant all kinds of trees for food, then you shall count their fruit as forbidden;† three years it shall

---

*Hebrew: 'blood'.

†Hebrew: 'their uncircumcision'. [Noth renders: 'you shall leave their foreskin, namely their fruit, uncut.' Ed.]

be forbidden to you, it must not be eaten. ²⁴And in the fourth year all their fruit shall be holy, an offering of praise to the LORD. ²⁵But in the fifth year you may eat of their fruit, that they may yield more richly for you: I am the LORD your God.

26 'You shall not eat any flesh with the blood in it. You shall not practise augury or witchcraft. ²⁷You shall not round off the hair on your temples or mar the edges of your beard. ²⁸You shall not make any cuttings in your flesh on account of the dead or tattoo any marks upon you: I am the LORD. ²⁹Do not profane your daughter by making her a harlot, lest the land fall into harlotry and the land become full of wickedness. ³⁰You shall keep my sabbaths and reverence my sanctuary: I am the LORD. ³¹Do not turn to mediums or wizards; do not seek them out, to be defiled by them: I am the LORD your God.

32 'You shall rise up before the hoary head, and honour the face of an old man, and you shall fear your God: I am the LORD.

33 'When a stranger sojourns with you in your land, you shall not do him wrong. ³⁴The stranger who sojourns with you shall be to you as the native among you, and you shall love him as yourself; for you were strangers in the land of Egypt: I am the LORD your God.

35 'You shall do no wrong in judgment, in measures of length or weight or quantity. ³⁶You shall have just balances, just weights, a just ephah, and a just hin: I am the LORD your God, who brought you out of the land of Egypt. ³⁷And you shall observe all my statutes and all my ordinances, and do them: I am the LORD.'

This chapter provides for everyone in Israel, for 'all the congregation of the people of Israel' (so the introductory formula in v. 2a), a definite codex of regulations mostly concerned with daily life and its different circumstances and activities. In its transmitted form, this codex is indeed remarkably diverse and disordered. Even the apparently capricious and random alternations between second singular and third plural, often even within one verse and within the same topic, show that the whole probably took shape as part of a fairly long and complicated process. Most of the numerous detailed precepts are only bound together in unity of a kind by the apodeictic style—'thou shalt (or shalt not)', 'ye shall (or shall not)'. The same is true of the contents. It is seen to be relatively self-contained in so far as it deals in general with the right behaviour of individuals (i.e. according to God's will), in the circumstances of daily life within the framework of the community to which he belongs. In detail, however, the different departments of life are arranged very much at random— cultivation of the land, co-operation with justice, the business of buying and selling, personal intercourse with the 'neighbour', behaviour towards demonic powers, and so forth. In view of this it is understandable that it has been asked again and again whether a basic form, to some extent unified in shape and substance, cannot be discerned, to which further precepts have grown on unsystematically in the course of time. It is indeed possible that there lies concealed an apodeictic 'decalogue' or 'dodecalogue' which has gradually been expanded. But no one has so far succeeded in reconstructing this basic decalogue or dodecalogue. There is not even any agreement whether the primary elements of the chapter are to be sought in the sentences with singular, or with plural, address.* In many places the plural sentences are manifestly secondary to the singular ones (cf., e.g., v. 9aα with vv. 9aβb, 10; v. 15aα with vv. 15aβγb, 16–18; v. 19aα with v. 19aβγb); in other places, however, the relationship is reversed (cf. v. 12a with v. 12b, and the complicated relationship in vv. 33, 34). On the whole one gets the impression that the material formulated in the singular has grounds for being reckoned the older; which would fit in with the fact that in the Old Testament apodeictic law in general the singular address was originally the usual one. But it remains an open question whether in this chapter the alternations of primary and secondary correspond at all to the alternations in the form of address; or whether perhaps the whole was not from the beginning a combined series of prohibitions, expressed partly in the singular and partly in the plural. For it is at any rate clear that the chapter contains several series of prohibitions, referring each time to a particular subject, and presenting a fairly clear original unity. It can be assumed that these once possessed an independent existence as short collections of pronouncements on behaviour in each particular relationship. They would be continually recalled to memory by the Israelites, whenever occasion arose. Now this kind of list of prohibitions appears for the most part in the singular (vv. 9aβb, 10; vv. 15aβγ–18; v. 19aβγb), but does also occur in the plural (vv. 11, 12a; vv. 35, 36a). In these circumstances it might well be to the point to give up trying to work out an original basic form and instead simply inquire into the contents and meaning of the single precepts and groups of precepts in their traditional order.

[2] Verse 2aβb stresses, as a preface to the whole, the saying about the 'holiness' of the Israelites, based on the 'holiness' of their God. The expression leaves it undecided whether the 'holiness' of the Israelites is a statement or a demand: 'you are holy' or 'you are to be

*[These are not distinguished in RSV; Authorized and Revised Versions use 'thou', 'ye', etc. Ed.]

holy'. At the head of a long list of precepts there should certainly have stood as the most important the requirement to be in reality, and maintain, what one was in principle. [3–4] The first complex of precepts (vv. 3, 4) is fairly general in content. The sabbath commandment contained in it—supposing this to represent an original unit—shows it to be fairly late. For the plural 'sabbaths' and especially 'my sabbaths' occur—apart from the Holiness Code— particularly in the book of Ezekiel; elsewhere they are found only in late Old Testament writings. It is tacitly assumed that everyone knew what the 'keeping of the sabbath' should consist of; the background is certainly the growing importance, through the time of the exile, of 'sabbath-keeping' (contrast Ex. 20.8); on this subject cf. Noth, *Exodus*, pp. 164f. It is noteworthy that the first place, and therefore special stress, is given to the idea of 'reverence' for parents. Note also the unusual precedence of the mother over the father. And one can at least ask whether perhaps some loosening of the kinship and family arrangements in connection with the end of the old pre-exilic Israel brought into special prominence respect for parents, and particularly for the mother. (Compare further Ex. 20.12 and Noth, *Exodus*, p. 165.) The prohibition of 'turning' to 'idols' belonged to the basic demands on Israel from time immemorial. The word for 'idols', *'elilīm*, really 'non-beings', is in assonance with the word for God, *'elōhīm*, and thus makes the contrast between God, who is all, and the idols, who are 'nothings', all the more effective. The expression 'molten gods' occurs elsewhere only in Ex. 34.17: the whole sentence v. 4aβ is word for word the same as Ex. 34.17, except that it is cast in the plural form of address. Molten statues were probably forbidden for any use whatever in the worship of Yahweh, all foreign cults being already excluded by v. 4aα (cf. Noth, *Exodus*, p. 263, and Ex. 34.17). [5–8] Verses 5–8 deal with the principal part of the 'layman' in the sacrificial system, namely the sacrificial meals connected with the sacrifices. The peace offerings were intended and calculated to be 'well pleasing' (to God), v. 5; this is expressed by an introductory sentence, with plural address, in the parenetic style. This style persists on into the initial phrase of v. 6; for the rest, vv. 6–8 are in the impersonal ritualistic style, and largely correspond in wording and in content with 7.16aβb, 17, 18, only with some detailed enlargement in v. 8. [9–10] The passage vv. 9–10 is introduced by a secondary and shortened dependent clause, in the plural form (v. 9aα). It contains a short list of harvest regulations, expressed in the singular. It forbids complete gleaning of the borders of a field; the picking up of any odd grain which has been left lying after harvest; the stripping bare of the vineyard to recover any grapes that have been overlooked at the first gathering, and the picking up of any fallen grapes; and—in a positively phrased concluding sentence—directs that the remains from harvest shall be for the poor and the stranger, i.e. for those who have no stake in the soil. This social reason has replaced the primitive motive, certainly pre-Israelitic, of leaving these remains for the fertility-spirits of the soil as their share in the crop. [11–12] Verses 11, 12a contain a short list of prohibitions (in the plural). It has some connection with the decalogue sentences of Ex. 20.15, and forbids various kinds of underhand relationship with the people with whom one lives (the word ʿāmīt, 'companion', has already occurred, apart from the Holiness Code, in 6.2; cf. above p. 48). For the prohibition of theft, probably meaning—at least originally—open robbery against human beings, cf. Noth, Exodus, pp. 165f. The supplementary v. 12b (in the singular) brings together the previously mentioned crimes under the idea of 'dishonouring the name of God' (by disobedience to his commands). [13–14] Verses 13, 14a contain another short list of prohibitions, this time in the singular, concluded by a general parenetic sentence in v. 14b. It forbids transactions in which an economically or physically stronger person could use his advantage over weaker and helpless people. Verse 13b assumes that a worker hired by the day is entitled to his wage in the evening, on completion of his work. In v. 14aα (cf. v. 14aβ) there is a basic assumption that a curse uttered, even if the victim of it could not hear it, was nevertheless effective; it is therefore forbidden against a helpless person who was not in a position to take any counter-measures. [15–18] The plural leading sentence (v. 15aα), introduced by a section in the singular (vv. 15–18), deals with right behaviour in the legal community 'in the gate', to which every fully enfranchised Israelite belonged. It is therefore not a question of a special 'self-examination' for judges, but of a code of behaviour applicable to all Israelites in their relations with other members of the community in which they lived. The designation of the other man is noticeably inconsistent: vv. 15b, 17bα have ʿāmīt (companion); vv. 16b, 18aβ rēaʿ (neighbour); v. 17a ʾāḥ (brother); v. 18aα ben-ʿam (fellow countryman). There is no recognizable material difference between these words. On the other hand, there is in Hebrew no law of style proscribing variety in expression, not even in 'legal' texts. It must therefore be assumed that

vv. 15–18 bring together, under the aspect of behaviour in the legal community, sentences of different origin. All partiality is forbidden, even—remarkably—in favour of a 'poor' man (v. 15aβ), for not only fear or anxiety in face of a 'great' man (v. 15aγ), but also sympathy with a 'poor' man, would impair right judgment (v. 15b). The spreading of slanders amongst the other members of the legal community is forbidden, before they enter or in their presence (v. 16a), likewise evil intentions towards another (vv. 16b, 17a), and the giving of decisions out of revenge or lingering anger because of some previous disputes or quarrels (v. 18aα). Verse 17bβ is difficult to understand, with its veto on burdening a person with a 'transgression' (ḥēṭ'). It is not very clear what 'transgression' here means. Is it a slight trespass to be removed by a cultic atonement, without the necessity of bringing it before the legal community? Or is it a previous trespass, which has meanwhile been dealt with, and should not be a permanent 'burden'? Or does it mean a personal trespass against the person addressed, which should not be allowed to count in any way during the handling of a different case before the legal community? All this is brought together in the best-known sentence in Leviticus, the sentence 'thou shalt love thy neighbour as thyself' (cf. Mark 12.31 and parallels), which here relates especially to behaviour in the legal community (cf., however, v. 34a). It takes the presumed 'love of oneself' as the measure of behaviour towards others. [19] Verse 19, after a plural introduction, has a threefold list of prohibitions respecting the coupling of unlikes (cf. Deut. 22.9–11, where the same list recurs, though not in the same strict form). The key-word is kil'āyim, originally perhaps 'double', but here in the sense 'of two different kinds'. At the basis of this intrinsically very ancient, possibly pre-Israelitic, prohibition lies the idea that the union of heterogeneous stock is against the divine ordinance. Concretely, the veto is directed against the pairing of different species of animal (though there were certainly mules in ancient Israel—cf. II Sam. 13.29 and elsewhere—that can scarcely have been imported; in Deut. 22.10 this veto appears with an altered, and probably later, meaning); against the sowing of more than one crop on the same piece of land; and against the production of woven material for clothes from different kinds of thread (wool and linen—so expressly Deut. 22.11). [20–22] In vv. 20–22 there follows, in a casuistic form not elsewhere represented in this chapter, a special case of marriage-law, namely sexual intercourse with a female slave already selected for marriage by someone, but not yet redeemed or liberated by her master for the time being, so that the intended marriage has not yet been legally accomplished. This is not a case of breach of marriage, and does not therefore meet with a death-sentence. There is only 'compensation for damage' to be paid (for the word *biqqōret*, occurring here only, cf. the Accadian stem *baqārum* and its derivatives), either to her present master or to her future partner in marriage; and there is a cultic atonement to be performed in the shape of a 'ram of the guilt offering', which, as there is no mention of sacrifice, was perhaps not delivered in live form but in money equivalent (cf. 5.15ff.). **[23–25]** An apparently very ancient, perhaps pre-Israelitic, commandment in vv. 23–25 concerns the harvesting of fruit from newly planted fruit trees. The analogy of human circumcision (so the expression in v. 23) is applied to them. After an initial period of remaining 'uncircumcised' (v. 23), the fruit must first be offered to Yahweh on the occasion of an 'offering of praise' (Judg. 9.27 mentions a 'festival' in the vineyards at the time of the grape-harvest). This offering to Yahweh would correspond somewhat to human circumcision. Only after this would the crop from these trees be free for normal use. **[26–31]** The section vv. 26–31, generally in the plural, forbids all kinds of idolatrous and superstitious practices, loosely strung together in a series of separate ordinances. First, eating of blood (i.e. appropriating the 'life' of an animal; cf. above p. 132); likewise augury and witchcraft, without any closer definition (v. 26); then all manner of customs concerned with the dead (vv. 27, 28a), such as the cutting of the ends of the hair all round one's head and the making of incisions and tattooings on one's body. These were probably in origin an attempt to make oneself unrecognizable in face of the dangers emanating from the 'soul' of a dead person. Verses 27b, 29, cast in singular, must be considered from a literary standpoint secondary. The sentence v. 27b, assuming the wearing of a beard as normal, adds to the precept about the hair (v. 27a) a corresponding one about the beard. Verse 29 deals, as its phrasing shows, with 'cultic prostitution', which had been and still was customary among the 'Canaanites', and to which a man might devote his daughter. For Israel, because regarded as a special characteristic of the 'Canaanitish' cults, it was considered abominable 'wickedness'. Verse 30 is in the plural, not as a prohibition but as an injunction; it is so generally expressed in its references to the 'sabbaths' (cf. v. 3aβ) and the holy place that it looks like a stranger among the objective detailed regulations to which v. 31 belongs, with its prohibition of all relationships with the spirits of the dead and other such spirits (cf. on this subject I Sam. 28.3ff.). From these people expected to obtain uncanny knowledge (*yiddeʿōnī*, literally 'knowing ones', regularly in the Old Testament named together with *'ōb* = spirits of the dead). [32] Verse 32 stands in isolation, phrased in the singular, enjoining honour and respect for the aged, outside as well as inside the small or large family circle (cf. v. 3aα). Verse 32aα might originally have had a specific meaning—that one should make room for an old man if he wants to sit or lie down somewhere, whilst v. 32aβ, in more general terms, requires a respectful bearing. [33–34] Verses 33, 34 are again isolated, or have strangely mixed singular and plural address. They forbid the 'oppression' of a guest, that is, making use of the economic advantage of a full land-owning citizen over a dispossessed Israelite or non-Israelite who looks to him for protection and the assurance of a livelihood. In v. 34 the plural elements can easily be seen as unusually detailed reasons added later; we are justified in assuming that the real main sentence v. 33b, as well as the beginning of the conditional clause v. 33a which belongs to it, was originally in the singular. The real reason then would lie in the requirement of v. 34 to love the stranger 'as thyself' (cf. v. 18aβ). [35–36] Lastly, the passage vv. 35, 36 requires honesty in buying and selling and the use of 'just'—correct, not falsified—weights and measures for measuring goods to be sold and weighing out money to be paid (for ephah and hin cf. pp. 45, 171, and on the same subject Deut. 25.13–16 and Ezek. 45.10). The reference to 'right judgment' in v. 35a, verbally equivalent to v. 15aα, might well be a secondary addition, out of place in the context of vv. 35, 36a.

### (d) SEXUAL AND OTHER TRANSGRESSIONS PUNISHABLE BY DEATH: 20.1–27

20 ¹The LORD said to Moses, ²ᶜSay to the people of Israel, Any man of the people of Israel, or of the strangers that sojourn in Israel, who gives any of his children to Molech shall be put to death; the people of the land shall stone him with stones. ³I myself will set my face against that man, and will cut him off from among his people, because he has given one of his children to Molech, defiling my sanctuary and profaning my holy name. ⁴And if the people of the land do at all hide their eyes from that man, when he gives one of his children to Molech, and do not put him to death, ⁵then I will set my face against that man and against his family, and will cut them off from among their people, him and all who follow him in playing the harlot after Molech.

6 'If a person turns to mediums and wizards, playing the harlot after them, I will set my face against that person, and will cut him off

from among his people. ⁷Consecrate yourselves therefore, and be holy; for I am the LORD your God. ⁸Keep my statutes, and do them; I am the LORD who sanctify you. ⁹For every one who curses his father or his mother shall be put to death; he has cursed his father or his mother, his blood is upon him.

10 'If a man commits adultery with the wife of* his neighbour, both the adulterer and the adulteress shall be put to death. ¹¹The man who lies with his father's wife has uncovered his father's nakedness; both of them shall be put to death, their blood is upon them. ¹²If a man lies with his daughter-in-law, both of them shall be put to death; they have committed incest, their blood is upon them. ¹³If a man lies with a male as with a woman, both of them have committed an abomination; they shall be put to death, their blood is upon them. ¹⁴If a man takes a wife and her mother also, it is wickedness; they shall be burned with fire, both he and they, that there may be no wickedness among you. ¹⁵If a man lies with a beast, he shall be put to death; and you shall kill the beast. ¹⁶If a woman approaches any beast and lies with it, you shall kill the woman and the beast; they shall be put to death, their blood is upon them.

17 'If a man takes his sister, a daughter of his father or a daughter of his mother, and sees her nakedness, and she sees his nakedness, it is a shameful thing, and they shall be cut off in the sight of the children of their people; he has uncovered his sister's nakedness, he shall bear his iniquity. ¹⁸If a man lies with a woman having her sickness, and uncovers her nakedness, he has made naked her fountain, and she has uncovered the fountain of her blood; both of them shall be cut off from among their people. ¹⁹You shall not uncover the nakedness of your mother's sister or of your father's sister, for that is to make naked one's near kin; they shall bear their iniquity. ²⁰If a man lies with his uncle's wife, he has uncovered his uncle's nakedness; they shall bear their sin, they shall die childless. ²¹If a man takes his brother's wife, it is impurity; he has uncovered his brother's nakedness, they shall be childless.

22 'You shall therefore keep all my statutes and all my ordinances, and do them; that the land where I am bringing you to dwell may not vomit you out. ²³And you shall not walk in the customs of the nation which I am casting out before you; for they did all these things, and therefore I abhorred them. ²⁴But I have said to you, "You shall inherit their land, and I will give it to you to possess, a land flowing with milk and honey." I am the LORD your God, who have separated you from the peoples. ²⁵You shall therefore make a distinction between the clean beast and the unclean, and between the unclean bird and the clean; you shall not make yourselves abominable by beast or by bird or by anything with which the ground teems, which I have set apart for you to hold unclean. ²⁶You shall be holy to me; for I the LORD am holy, and have separated you from the peoples, that you should be mine.

27 'A man or a woman who is a medium or a wizard shall be put to death; they shall be stoned with stones, their blood shall be upon them.'

*Hebrew repeats 'if a man commits adultery with the wife of'.

L.–K

This chapter is largely identical in content with ch. 18, but the form is different. Chapter 18 expresses prohibitions in an apodeictic form ('thou shalt not'), without regard to the consequences of any infringements: ch. 20 regards them from the point of view of punishment by death to be meted out to the offender. The closeness of these two chapters, within the larger whole of the Holiness Code, though separated by the very different ch. 19, presents a problem. A literary dependence of one on the other would be difficult to suppose, for each chapter is too clearly marked out as to some extent independent and self-contained, each with its own arrangement and development from an original nucleus. It must, then, be assumed that the same subject-matter has been treated in different fashion by lists of precepts, each of which originally had its own particular *Sitz im Leben*. As far as the Holiness Code is concerned, this only shows that it was a book of laws obviously without much plan, and was brought into being by loosely stringing together existing complexes of precepts.

The basis of ch. 20 was obviously a series of *mōt yūmat* statutes (see below) (vv. 9ff.). The framework of the chapter shows this. At the beginning (vv. 1, 2aα) there is merely the stereotyped introductory formula in which the stress on the 'Israelites' is striking and unexplained, for it seems to presuppose some preceding ordinances not intended for the 'Israelites'. But not till vv. 7, 8 do we get a parenetic injunction comparable with 18.2b–5; 19.2αβb and seeming to indicate that this was once the true beginning. Verses 22–26 contain the concluding addresses, corresponding to 18.24–30 (cf. also 19.37), to which v. 27 would seem to be an obvious later addition. Thus the section vv. 9–21 is seen to be the kernel, in which the *mōt yūmat* phrase is the constant element, and that with special reference to sexual offences. We are dealing then with a 'list of offences worthy of death' (*mōt yūmat* = 'he (the offender) is to be summarily put to death', or 'is to be punished by death'). Such a list is principally to be found in the Book of the Covenant in Ex. 21.12–17¶ (cf. Noth, *Exodus*, pp. 179f.), in an obviously more primitive form, with a participial subject to the *mōt yūmat* sentence, defining the matter of the offence. This strict form appears, somewhat loosened and lightened, in Lev. 20, especially by *'iš* (*'iš*) *'ašer* . . . ('anyone who' . . .), introducing a dependent clause, instead of a participle. This seems to be equivalent to the *mōt yūmat* construction for ritual prescriptions (cf. 17.3, 8, 10, 13). This is certainly a sign of later development. Elsewhere, too, in Lev. 20.9ff. there are traces of later expansion of old forms, especially in the inconsistent connection of the *mōt yūmat* sentence with other stereotyped sentences such as the 'casting out' formula, the 'blood' formula (see below) and the like. No absolute dating even of the basic material of 20.9ff. can be derived from its contents, in view of the 'timelessness' of the material in most of the precepts. The *mōt yūmat* construction as such occupies a special position between 'apodeictic' and 'casuistic'. The *mōt yūmat* pronouncement is itself apodeictic. Its unconditional nature, however, does not apply to the actual or potential delinquents in the particular case considered, but to the community for the time being, who were in all circumstances responsible for carrying out the death-sentence. The separate cases, however, are distinguished—either by a participle or by a dependent clause—in a manner related to that of the leading clauses of case-law. They hardly belonged to conditions of justice 'in the gate', but rather to the cultic community, in pre-Deuteronomic times the local cultic community. When the latter met to consider offences that had been committed, these 'lists of offences worthy of death' may well have been recited before the assembly.

[2–5] In vv. 2aβb–5 there has been placed next to the list of special offences worthy of death introduced by vv. 7, 8 a special case, standing first. It has already occurred in 18.21a in the form of an apodeictic prohibition, where, however, it appears very loosely fitted in with the list of sexual transgressions (cf. above pp. 135f.). It is handled first in the basic *mōt yūmat* sentence v. 2aβ, to which a remarkably long sequence of broader details is appended (vv. 2b–5). The subject is an idolatrous practice defined as 'giving' one's 'seed' to 'Molech'. Mention of this occurs elsewhere only in II Kings 23.10; Jer. 7.31; 32.35. A comparison of all these passages shows a fairly fixed terminology. Instead of 'give' it is more often 'hand over' (*heˁᵉbîr*, really 'allow to be handed over'; so II Kings 23 and Jer. 32, and in Lev. 18 both side by side); in II Kings 23 there is the addition 'in fire' or 'with fire' (*bā'ēš*); and in Jer. 7 simply 'to burn with fire'. As the object of this cultic burning, instead of 'seed' (so Lev. 18.20), II Kings 23 has 'son and daughter' and the passage in Jeremiah 'sons and daughters'. This would seem to point to a child-sacrifice. All the passages except Jer. 7 characterize it as a cultic proceeding—*lmlk* (vocalized in the Massoretic text as *lam-molek* and translated 'for Molech'). Now, in Punic the word *mlk* exists as a designation for a particular kind of sacrifice; and this technical term might come from the Phoenician home of the Punic people ['*Poeni*'] and so from the 'Canaanitish' surroundings of the

Old Testament. This seems to suggest that we should see *mlk* as a sacrificial term in the Old Testament passages also, and translate *lmlk* 'as a *mlk*-sacrifice'. Admittedly, Lev. 20.5 would be against this, for it has not *lmlk*, but *ham-molek*, and by the context *ham-molek* must be understood as the name of a god, after whom they 'went a-whoring' in this horrible cult. Now vv. 2b–5 certainly contain secondary detailed additions to v. 2aβ; but it is worth considering whether these details, secondary indeed, but fairly contemporary as the subject-matter shows, do not rest on a thorough misunderstanding of the expression *lmlk*, by which it would most probably have been taken as the name of the divine receiver of these child-sacrifices. It remains questionable whether the Massoretic *lam-molek* [RSV: 'to Molech'] may not represent a later distortion of an original *lam-melek* = 'for the king' ('king' as a divine title was quite current in the Ancient East); or whether *molek* (Septuagint in II Kings 23 and Jer. 32 Μολοχ, whence Vulgate 'Moloch') is not to be regarded as a kindred form of *melek*, used for this special case. In all probability, for those practising this cult *molek/melek* = king was not a special designation for Yahweh, but the title for a foreign god, by which he was worshipped. In II Kings 23 and Jer. 7 and 32 this cult is specially localized at a cultic centre bearing the enigmatic name of *tōpet*, situated in the 'valley of Hinnom', which ran west, south-west, and south past Old Jerusalem; this at a time towards the end of the monarchy in Judah. Even if Josiah had suppressed this cult, as II Kings 23.10 says, the passages from Jeremiah show that it had come to life again in the period after Josiah. We are dealing, then, apparently with an idolatrous local cult of the Jerusalem district, which there was good reason to forbid emphatically about 600 BC (cf. the 'goat-demon' cult in 17.7, above p. 131). The further details in vv. 2b–5 are obviously not a unity. Verse 2b prescribed death by stoning, in which the whole community (the apparent meaning of the somewhat vague expression 'the people of the land') had on principle to take part, in order to cut off the offender from their circle. In tension with this is the announcement of v. 3, phrased with the 'I' of Yahweh, according to which Yahweh himself will turn against the offender (for the expression 'set the face against' cf. 17.10) and 'cut him off', though it is not said how that will happen. Verses 4, 5 clearly resolve this tension: if 'the people of the land' would not themselves note and punish the offence, then Yahweh himself would undertake the 'cutting off' of the evildoer and his whole kindred. (For the 'contagion' involving the whole tribe or

family through the guilt of a crime worthy of death, cf., e.g., Josh.
7.24.) Verse 5, probably as a later addition, explains the 'family' as
the group of those who have followed him (the offender) in 'playing
the harlot' (i.e. have taken part in the idolatrous cult). As the expression 'to go a-whoring after 'has elsewhere in the Old Testament as its
customary object foreign gods or cults, the observation has later been
added that they 'have gone a-whoring after Molech'. [6] Verse 6
appends as a secondary addition to this whole section on 'Molech-
worship' a threat of punishment for 'turning to mediums and wizards',
because this also involved illegitimate cultic practices (on this subject
cf. 19.31 and above, pp. 143f.). The last half of the sentence is not in
the *mōt yūmat* construction, but has the 'I' of Yahweh as subject and
the 'cutting off' phrasing, as in vv. 3a, 5.

[7–8] The introductory passage vv. 7, 8 is followed in vv. 9–21 by a
'list of offences worthy of death' concerned with sexual transgressions.
Not only is the old strict *mōt yūmat* formula apparently softened (cf.
above pp. 146f.), but there is also a lack of any consistent scheme of
clear arrangement. In the course of time all kinds of enlargement have
gathered round an original nucleus. The material as we now have it
hardly warrants the assumption that it was originally based on a ten-
or twelvefold unified list. [9] Verse 9 presents a problem: first, because
of the quite unusual, and apparently inappropriate, causal linking by
means of *kī* ('for') with the introductory sentences vv. 7, 8; and then,
because of the content, which does not fit on to what follows. It almost
looks as though v. 9 is quoting a well-known example of the *mōt yūmat*
sentence (cf. Ex. 21.17 in the original strict phrasing, and for the
subject-matter Deut. 27.16, in the framework of the *'ārūr* (cursed)
sequence there). It would thus seem to be using it as the basis of the
'holiness' saying and 'holiness' demand of vv. 7, 8, meaning in effect:
'Holiness' is to be taken very seriously in Israel: there are strictly
valid sentences like the *mōt yūmat* sentence on the cursing of parents;
and the following sentences must be taken as equally important with
this one, which is inserted by way of illustration. The generally valid
*mōt yūmat* sentence in v. 9bα is followed in v. 9 by the 'conviction-
formula' which the spokesman of the cultic assembly was accustomed
to pronounce, showing that in a concrete case the use of the *mōt
yūmat* sentence was justified. The conclusion in v. 9bβ constitutes the
'blood-formula': *dāmāw bō* (in plural form in vv. 11bβ, 12bβ, 13bβ,
16bβ, 27bβ). This formula (not quite equivalent to 'his blood be upon
his own head'—e.g. Josh. 2.19) originally served to fix the evidence

of guilt in cases of manslaughter: 'his blood (i.e. the traces of the blood shed by him) is still upon him—as visible evidence of the deed he has done'. Later, the formula was transferred to evidence for other than capital crimes; and finally (Lev. 20) it has acquired the fairly general meaning 'he is convicted of an offence worthy of death'. [10] Verse 10 opens the list of the sexual offences worthy of death. It deals with unfaithfulness in marriage (cf. 18.20). The singular *mōt yūmat* sentence refers to the adulterous man; only in the supplementary v. 10bβ is the woman in question brought in on the grounds of a probably later view, that she is to be viewed not only as the object, but also as a fellow subject, in the proceedings for adultery. [11] In v. 11 (for subject-matter cf. 18.8) the *mōt yūmat* sentence, under the same view, is cast in the plural (really dual) form, although the dependent clause is still in the singular. The 'conviction-formula' has already been inserted with it.

[12–13] This is true of v. 12 (cf. 18.15) and v. 13 (cf. 18.22). Here (as also in vv. 14, 17) the concrete 'conviction-formula' has been replaced by a general saying about the 'shamefulness', 'abomination' and the like of the particular action. [14] Verse 14 (cf. 18.17a) appears to refer to marriage (*lqḥ*); the substitution of the demand for burning in place of the *mōt yūmat* pronouncement lifts it out of the general framework, as does the appearance of second person plural address at the end. This would indicate that the verse did not belong to the basic form of the 'list of offences worthy of death'. [15] In v. 15 (cf. 18.23a) only the last sentence (again second person plural) is a probably secondary addition; it regards the animal, too, as incurring 'objective guilt'. [16] The same view also underlies the present form of v. 16 (cf. 18.23b). There has certainly been some secondary alteration to suit v. 15, by which the relevant division in v. 15 between the ideas 'to punish with death' and 'to kill' between man and animal respectively is abandoned, and both ideas are applied without distinction between woman and animal. At the back of this there may have been a sentence corresponding to v. 15a, relating this time to the woman. [17] Verse 17 is to be taken with v. 14 (see above), inasmuch as the subject seems here again to be marriage (*lqḥ*) (contrast 18.9), and there is no *mōt yūmat* pronouncement, which is here replaced by the 'casting away' formula. For the rest, this verse, with its strange mixture of singular and plural, its broad spread of detail, and its inclusion of more or less fixed formulae, does not belong to the general framework. [18] The same is true of v. 18 (for the subject-matter cf. 18.19), where again the beginning, referring to the man, and the continuation, referring to both the participants, are remarkable. [19] Verse 19 (cf. 18.13, 12) corresponds in its 'thou shalt' formulation to the section 18.7ff., and is here foreign to the context; only the sentence giving the reason passes over into the third person, first in the singular, for the man, then in the plural, in reference to both. [20–21] Verses 20, 21 are a further appendix, dealing no longer with 'offences worthy of death', but with transgressions punishable (by God) with childlessness. Verse 20, from its wording, refers to sexual intercourse and v. 21 to marriage (*lqh*). Does this reject 'Levirate marriage' (Deut. 25.5–10) (contrast Lev. 18.16), and declare it to be unworkable, seeing that the whole intention was the raising of children? On the whole, in the section vv. 10–21 there have come in towards the end more and more secondary accretions to what was not in point of content a very well-rounded basic form.

[22–26] For the concluding parenesis vv. 22–26 cf. 18.24–30. This passage can hardly come from one mould. Verse 25 in particular shows this: after v. 24b has announced that God has 'separated' his people from amongst the other peoples, and that they must therefore not behave like the other peoples, especially not like the former inhabitants of the land, who here again are reckoned particularly lascivious in the sexual field, v. 25 introduces a free variation on the theme of 'separation'. It makes reference to a subject not dealt with at all in this chapter—the 'separation' demanded of Israel between clean and unclean animals; concluding with the observation that it is Yahweh who has 'separated' the unclean animals.

[27] The supplementary v. 27 reverts once more to the subject of v. 6, but in contrast to v. 6 introduces it with a *mōt yūmat* sentence, phrased in the plural and thus certainly differing from the original style. Besides, there is unique reference to transactions with 'mediums' and 'wizards', as the passage is now worded;* it appears to be assumed that people could have such demonic beings 'in them', that is, 'be possessed' by them. We leave open the question whether it is here a matter of a subjective and responsible transgression or only an 'objective guilt'. In any case such people were to be cast out from the community of Israel and stoned.

---

*[For 'who is . . .' Noth has 'when a medium or a wizard is in them'. Ed.]

### (e) THE HOLINESS OF PRIESTS: 21.1–24

21 [1]And the LORD said to Moses, 'Speak to the priests, the sons of Aaron, and say to them that none of them shall defile himself for the dead among his people, [2]except for his nearest of kin, his mother, his father, his son, his daughter, his brother, [3]or his virgin sister who is near to him because she has had no husband,* he may defile himself. [4]He shall not defile himself for a woman married† to a husband among his people and so profane himself. [5]They shall not make tonsures upon their heads, nor shave off the edges of their beards, nor make any cuttings in their flesh. [6]They shall be holy to their God, and not profane the name of their God; for they offer the offerings by fire to the LORD, the bread of their God; therefore they shall be holy. [7]They shall not marry a harlot or a woman who has been defiled; neither shall they marry a woman divorced from her husband; for the priest is holy to his God. [8]You shall consecrate him, for he offers the bread of your God; he shall be holy to you; for I the LORD, who sanctify you, am holy. [9]And the daughter of any priest, if she profanes herself by playing the harlot, profanes her father; she shall be burned with fire.

10 'The priest who is chief among his brethren, upon whose head the anointing oil is poured, and who has been consecrated to wear the garments, shall not let the hair of his head hang loose, nor rend his clothes; [11]he shall not go in to any dead body, nor defile himself, even for his father or for his mother; [12]neither shall he go out of the sanctuary, nor profane the sanctuary of his God; for the consecration of the anointing oil of his God is upon him: I am the LORD. [13]And he shall take a wife in her virginity. [14]A widow, or one divorced, or a woman who has been defiled, or‡ a harlot, these he shall not marry; but he shall take to wife a virgin of his own people, [15]that he may not profane his children among his people; for I am the LORD who sanctify him.'

16 And the LORD said to Moses, [17]'Say to Aaron, None of your descendants throughout their generations who has a blemish may approach to offer the bread of his God. [18]For no one who has a blemish shall draw near, a man blind or lame, or one who has a mutilated face or a limb too long, [19]or a man who has an injured foot or an injured hand, [20]or a hunchback, or a dwarf, or a man with a defect in his sight or an itching disease or scabs or crushed testicles; [21]no man of the descendants of Aaron the priest who has a blemish shall come near to offer the LORD's offerings by fire; since he has a blemish, he shall not come near to offer the bread of his God. [22]He may eat the bread of his God, both of the most holy and of the holy things, [23]but he shall not come near the veil or approach the altar, because he has a blemish, that he may not profane my sanctuaries; for I am the LORD who sanctify them.' [24]So Moses spoke to Aaron and to his sons and to all the people of Israel.

*lāh, 'for her', is probably an addition. [RSV puts the phrases from 'who is near' to 'defile himself' in brackets. Ed.]
†Insert lib‘ūlat (cf. BH) before ba‘al, 'husband'.
‡Adding w⁰ before zōnā (cf. BH).

This chapter, affirming the 'holiness' of the priests through a whole sequence of negative pronouncements in the impersonal style of cultic regulations, is divided into two parts by the headings in v. 1abα and vv. 16, 17a, an external division which corresponds to the contents. The first part, vv. 1bβ–15, gives some prohibitions limiting or forbidding for the officiating priest certain ritual defilements in the family circle. It is a question of a defiling contact with the dead, which does indeed render the 'layman' 'unclean' for a time, but is not forbidden to him. Furthermore this passage deals with the limitations in marriage possibilities for the priests, which do not apply to 'laymen'. The priests were thus subject to higher standards of 'holiness', and this grading of 'holiness' is respected within the priesthood itself, for the special section vv. 10–15, referring to the chief priest, sets for him still stricter holiness requirements in the province named than for other priests. The second part, vv. 17b–23, requires bodily wholeness for the practice of the priestly office and gives a catalogue of bodily defects excluding from this office. All this concerns internal rules for the priesthood, subjects of special professional knowledge. The phrasing of the headings corresponds with this. Presupposing the situation at Sinai, it puts forward these regulations through the agency of Moses to the 'sons of Aaron' (v. 1abα) or 'Aaron' (vv. 16, 17a) as the high priest, who is responsible for seeing that no unfit person officiates as a priest. The later supplementary heading v. 24 says that Moses handed on these regulations to 'all the people of Israel', as well as to Aaron and his sons. This is because in the end the whole of Israel is apostrophized—as a secondary element in this chapter—with the meaning that she must respect the special 'holiness' of the priests (v. 8) and is to that extent a participant in this subject.

The chapter offers certain points of contact for an approximate dating. The subject of the special (ritual) 'holiness' of the priests themselves is certainly very old, and to some extent 'timeless'; one can well imagine that such rules not only gained oral currency within the priesthood from generation to generation quite early on, but were also definitely formulated or fixed in writing. Especially is this true of the assumption made in the second part (vv. 16–23) of the hereditary nature of the priestly office in a family. On the grounds of family kinship there was an expectation of office, which might, however, not be realized if bodily imperfections were present. All this had been given to Israel before she became a state (cf. Judg. 18.30b; I Sam. 1.3b and elsewhere). But the putting together of the rules as they appear in Lev. 21 can, even in their basic form, hardly be pushed back further than early exilic times. This is supported by the in part almost verbal correspondence with the regulations for the cultic personnel in Ezekiel's sketch of the future (cf. v. 2b with Ezek. 44.25b and v. 14 with Ezek. 44.22abα). Yet the similarity in arrangement and phrasing is not so great as to suppose a literary dependence on the part of one side or the other. One must conjecture that here and in Ezekiel we are dealing with two independent collations and expositions of rules which were in force. Further, in support of this, there is the appearance of the chief priest in vv. 10–15, and the manner in which he is depicted. The content shows at once that the picture is that of a unified priesthood, with a hierarchical head, and points to post-Deuteronomic times. On the other hand, the high priest's office is so circumstantially defined in v. 10a that one must conclude a settled designation of the chief priest's office to have been not yet fully established, as it was later in Haggai (1.1, etc.) and Zechariah (3.1, etc.) in the title *hak-kōhēn hag-gādōl*, probably for the first time. The expression in Lev. 21.10a is an early form of this title; for here, too, we have the characterizing adjective *gādōl* = 'great', admittedly not, as it later became, an element in a technical term, but in the framework of a description which required further distinguishing features. The exact meaning of *gādōl* in this context is uncertain: the wording, which puts *gādōl* in relationship with 'his brothers', turns our thoughts to length of years; but the very general word *gādōl* can also point to position and rank. In any case the designation 'the greatest among his brethren' was not clear enough to remove the necessity—or at least desirability—of the qualifications that follow in the relative clause. This relative clause can thus scarcely be claimed as a later addition: it designates the chief priest as 'anointed' and, contrary to later usage, still confines anointing exclusively to the chief priest (cf. 'the anointed priest' in 4.3ff. and above p. 38), and refers the 'filling of hands' ['consecrated'] (cf. Noth, *Exodus*, pp. 230f.) to the institution specifically of the chief priest. Moreover, it makes the act of institution consist especially of the vesting with the 'clothes', i.e. with a definite official garb, not here more precisely described. This relative clause gives a *terminus a quo*; for the anointing of the chief priest was not transferred from the king to the chief priest of the Jerusalem sanctuary until after the end of the Davidic kingdom. Thereby the chief priest stepped into the cultic functions of the former king. The basic form of Lev. 21 was thus probably put together in the course of the exile. The reference to Aaron (and his sons) and thus to Sinai is only to be found in the framework (and in an obvious supplement in v. 21); the basic form only mentions 'the priest' or 'the chief priest' and 'the holy place' (v. 12), and not the 'tent of meeting'. Even the basic form is not from one mould, but put together from previously formulated groups of separate rules, as shown particularly by the alternation between singular and plural sentences (cf. vv. 1bβ, 2, 3, 4, with v. 5 and elsewhere).

[1–4] Verses 1bβ–4 forbid the (ordinary) priest to incur 'defilement' from a 'soul', i.e. one who is dead and whose 'soul', according to the widely held belief, still remained in the vicinity of the corpse. In practical terms it is a matter of the preparation of the corpse for burial; or perhaps only entry into a room or a house where someone had died and where the corpse still lay, awaiting burial. The principal clause v. 1bβ names no subject, but the context shows that it must be 'the priest'. The lack of subject shows this passage (vv. 1bβff.) to be an excerpt from an older and more extensive collection of priestly rules, at the beginning of which the subject had been named. Exceptions from the main rule are allowed in vv. 2–4: they concern the nearest relatives, as far as they belonged to the narrower family circle and lived near one another. This is obviously the meaning of *qārēb* = 'near', 'close at hand'; cf. v. 3, where it is not a question of the 'nearness' of the degree of relatedness, which would be the same for married as for the unmarried sister. Verse 4 in the text as we have it is unintelligible: according to the conjecture adopted in the above translation, v. 4 would refer, in contrast to v. 3, to the married sister; but even this conjectural reading is not very satisfying, and its content—according to v. 3—is superfluous. Thus we are led to suppose a badly phrased supplement, intended to bring out once again the distinction between unmarried and married sister, already made in v. 3. [5] Verse 5, in plural form, forbids the priests to take part in some special and probably widespread mourning customs, varying in the detail of their performance. Chapter 19.27, 28 (cf. above p. 143) forbids these not only for the priests but also for all Israelites. [6] In v. 6 what has gone before is motivated, in the style of the Law of Holiness, by the 'holiness' requirement. This is especially valid for the priests, who have to offer the sacrifice here designated as 'the bread of God'—a remarkable term, doubtless based on an impressive and ancient idea. [7] Verse 7a—again in the plural—imposed on the priests, once again by virtue of their 'holiness', limitations in marriage (*lqh* in the clear sense of 'take [to wife]' = marry), restrictions which did not apply to lay Israelites. They might only marry a virgin; only a woman widowed by the death of her husband is, by the wording of v. 7a, excepted from this rule (cf. on the one hand v. 14 and on the other Ezek. 44.22). The singular phrasing of the reason-clause in v.7b might lead one to suppose that the plural sentences vv. 5, (6) and 7a have come in as a later supplement between vv. 1bβ–3, (4) and 7b. [8] The parenesis in v. 8, with its address to Israel, clearly does not belong to the framework. It again characterizes the sacrifice as 'the bread of God', as in v. 6, and is certainly a later secondary addition. It requires of Israel respect for the special 'holiness' of the priests. [9] The casuistic sentence v. 9 stands in isolation, both in form and content; its loose subject-relationship with v. 7 must once have led to its being inserted at this point. It poses the case of the prostitution of a priest's daughter (we can no longer discover whether this is in practice a survival of the 'Canaanitish' custom of 'cultic prostitution'), states the 'defiling' effect on the priestly father, and formulates the regulation punishment.

[10–15] For the chief priest (v. 10a; see above pp. 153f.) vv. 10b–15 draw up corresponding but still stricter holiness rules. Verse 10b forbids him—beyond the requirements of v. 5—even the apparently most harmless mourning customs (cf. 10.6, which corresponds in wording). Verse 11 denies him even the exceptions conceded in vv. 2, 3, (4). He might not leave the holy place at all (v. 12), which assumes that he lived within the holy precincts. This meant for him—beyond all other priests—a specially exacting standard of holiness which demanded not only no possible contact with '(dead) persons', but also absolutely no contact with unclean objects. In the marriage precepts for the chief priest, even marriage with a widow is forbidden (this as a supplement to the requirements of v. 7). Ezekiel 44.22 takes up a position midway between Lev. 21.7 and 21.13, 14: there, marriage with a widow is forbidden to all priests, with the exception of a priest's widow.

[17–21] The kernel of the section vv. 16–23 is the list of bodily imperfections which exclude from the exercise of the priestly office (vv. 18b–20). This list contains a sequence of rare or even unique words whose exact meaning is no longer certain, and which can therefore be only tentatively rendered. Within the framework of vv. 17b, 18a, 21 the one normative sentence is repeated with remarkable frequency—something that can hardly be original. What we should expect to be primary is the most simply and shortly phrased; and this we find in v. 18a (without the connecting *kī* at the beginning). The more detailed sentences in v. 17b (addressed to Aaron, to connect on to the introductory formula vv. 16, 17a), and in v. 21, again have the striking description of the sacrifice as 'the bread of God'. They contain nothing that goes materially beyond v. 18a. [22–23] The passage vv. 22, 23 is probably an accretion, which again begins with the expression 'bread of God'. It concedes to those whose family connections would predestine them to priesthood, but whose physical defects rule them out from officiating as priests, the right to participate in the priestly share of the sacrificial gifts; but not without sharpening (v. 23) the negative requirements. Verse 23 contains the expression 'enter within the veil'. This does not look as though it refers to the 'curtain' in the 'tent of meeting', which divided off—according to P's account—the 'holy of holies' (cf. Ex. 26.31–33), especially as 'approaching the altar' is mentioned only after this. Taking v. 23 at its face value, one must rather imagine a curtain at the entrance to an inner part of the holy precincts. The plural 'my sanctuaries' in v. 23 is also striking: it can only mean 'holy localities' or 'holy furnishings' within the precincts of the one holy place here under consideration.

(*f*) THE HOLINESS OF CULTIC GIFTS AND OFFERINGS: 22.1–33

22 ¹And the LORD said to Moses, ²"Tell Aaron and his sons to keep away from the holy things\* of the people of Israel, which they dedicate to me, [so that they may not profane my holy name;] I am the LORD. ³Say to them, "If any one of all your descendants throughout your generations approaches the holy things, which the people of Israel dedicate to the LORD, while he has an uncleanness, that person shall be cut off from my presence: I am the LORD. ⁴None of the line of Aaron who is a leper or suffers a discharge may eat of the holy things until he is clean. Whoever touches anything that is unclean through contact with the dead or a man who has had an emission of semen, ⁵and whoever touches a creeping thing by which he may be made unclean or a man from whom he may take uncleanness, whatever his uncleanness may be—⁶the person who touches any such shall be unclean until the evening and shall not eat of the holy things unless he has bathed his body in water. ⁷When the sun is down he shall be clean; and afterward he may eat of the holy things, because such are his food. ⁸That which dies of itself or is torn by beasts he shall not eat, defiling himself by it: I am the LORD." ⁹They shall therefore keep my charge, lest they bear sin for it

\*[Noth renders 'gifts' throughout this chapter; see commentary. Ed.]

and die thereby when they profane it: I am the LORD who sanctify them.

10 'An outsider shall not eat of a holy thing. A sojourner of the priest or a hired servant shall not eat of a holy thing; ¹¹but if a priest buys a slave as his property for money, the slave may eat of it; and those that are born in his house may eat of his food. ¹²If a priest's daughter is married to an outsider she shall not eat of the offering of the holy things. ¹³But if a priest's daughter is a widow or divorced, and has no child, and returns to her father's house, as in her youth, she may eat of her father's food; yet no outsider shall eat of it. ¹⁴And if a man eats of a holy thing unwittingly, he shall add the fifth of its value to it, and give the holy thing to the priest. ¹⁵The priests shall not profane the holy things of the people of Israel, which they offer to the LORD, ¹⁶and so cause them to bear iniquity and guilt, by eating their holy things: for I am the LORD who sanctify them.'

17 And the LORD said to Moses, ¹⁸'Say to Aaron and his sons and all the people of Israel, When any one of the house of Israel or of the sojourners in Israel presents his offering, whether in payment of a vow or as a freewill offering which is offered to the LORD as a burnt offering, ¹⁹to be accepted you shall offer a male without blemish, of the bulls or the sheep or the goats. ²⁰You shall not offer anything that has a blemish, for it will not be acceptable for you. ²¹And when any one offers a sacrifice of peace offerings to the LORD, to fulfil a vow or as a freewill offering, from the herd or from the flock, to be accepted it must be perfect; there shall be no blemish in it. ²²Animals blind or disabled or mutilated or having a discharge or an itch or scabs, you shall not offer to the LORD or make of them an offering by fire upon the altar to the LORD. ²³A bull or a lamb which has a part too long* or too short you may present for a freewill offering; but for a votive offering it cannot be accepted. ²⁴Any animal which has its testicles bruised or crushed or torn or cut, you shall not offer to the LORD or sacrifice within your land; ²⁵neither shall you offer as the bread of your God any such animals gotten from a foreigner. Since there is a blemish in them, because of their mutilation, they will not be accepted for you.'

26 And the LORD said to Moses, ²⁷'When a bull or sheep or goat is born, it shall remain seven days with its mother; and from the eighth day on it shall be acceptable as an offering by fire to the LORD. ²⁸And whether the mother is a cow or a ewe, you shall not kill both her and her young in one day. ²⁹And when you sacrifice a sacrifice of thanksgiving to the LORD, you shall sacrifice it so that you may be accepted. ³⁰It shall be eaten on the same day, you shall leave none of it until morning: I am the LORD.

31 'So you shall keep my commandments and do them: I am the LORD. ³²And you shall not profane my holy name, but I will be hallowed among the people of Israel; I am the LORD who sanctify you, ³³who brought you out of the land of Egypt to be your God: I am the LORD.'

---

*[Noth renders, 'with a slit ear', i.e. 'mutilated'. Ed.]

The division of this chapter is clear; it falls into sections each with a clearly discoverable content; but within the separate sections there is to an unusually strong degree a lack of cohesion in structure and formulation. It is predominantly couched in the impersonal ritual style; but this is frequently broken into by other styles. Thus there have arisen sentences of peculiar formlessness, both in construction and connection. One gets the impression that from particular points of view all kinds of rules of different origin have been put together and interpreted, then carried further and enlarged. In general it deals with cultic ordinances, not closely linked in time by their subject-matter, but inserted into the framework of the Holiness Code by reason of the numerous stereotyped concluding formulae and showing in detail numerous relationships to other parts of the the Holiness Code, especially to chs. 17 and 21. The inner divisions are marked by the headings in vv. 1, 2aα, 17, 18a, 26; the first heading indicates that the pricsts arc being addressed through the agency of Moses, and the second, the priests together with the Israelites; whilst the third heading names no special audience.

The first section treats of 'holy things' (Heb. *q°dāšīm*). This general idea refers in practice in this context (as in 21.22) to the priests' share in the sacrificial gifts brought to the holy place (hence the translation of *q°dāšīm* by 'holy gifts'), that is especially the remains of the meal offerings not burnt on the altar (cf. especially 7.9, 10 and above pp. 54f., 60) and the priestly share in the peace offerings (cf. 7.31–34 and above pp. 64f.). Chapter 21.1–16 deals with thc two questions: in what circumstances the priests may 'eat' or 'not eat' 'holy gifts'; and who belongs to the circle of those allowed to eat them. [1–3] We are thus dealing here with internal priestly rules, as the heading in vv. 1, 2aα indicates. The answer to the first question is that the 'holy gifts' may only be 'eaten' by priests in a condition of cultic cleanness. This simple rule is carried into very circumstantial detail. Even the heading in vv. 2aβb, 3aα does not continue through in a unified manner: in v. 2bα a secondary and intervening clause has been inserted. The priests are here enjoined to 'hold themselves' or 'hold themselves back' (probably the basic meaning of the stem *nzr*) from the 'holy gifts', i.e. to pay due respect to their special 'holiness'. The detailed exposition begins in v. 3 with a general passage. In its present context it relates to the theme of this section; but its wording, taken by itself, gives no hint of this relationship. This is particularly so if, as seems probable, the relative clause standing in the middle is taken as a later addition, which the present context would indicate. For these legal definitions, with their 'cutting off' formula, do not mention priests, but 'any man' (amongst the Israelites), nor 'eating', but only 'drawing near'. Originally, the *qᵉdāšīm* probably did not indicate specifically 'holy gifts', but generally 'holy things', and went on to threaten with 'cutting off' any contact at all of somebody 'clean' with something 'unclean'. It is to be noticed that this is not 'cutting off', as usual, from 'amongst the people' but from the circle to which Yahweh's 'countenance' is turned, because the 'countenance' of Yahweh cannot tolerate any infringement of 'holiness'. [4–7] From v. 4, v. 3 later acquired its special meaning; for v. 4 speaks unequivocally of 'eating' of the 'holy gifts' on the part of the 'descendants of Aaron', though one may question whether in place of Aaron there was not originally the word 'priests', which in the ancient received text [cf. BH] does in parts still appear alongside of the name Aaron. Verses 4–7, in very varied phrasing, enumerate various possible cultic uncleannesses which would prevent the 'eating' of 'holy gifts'. They might consist of intrinsic uncleanness (v. 4aαbβ) or acquired uncleanness—through contact with unclean persons or animals (vv. 4bα, 5). The scattered references to the cleanness to be aimed at (vv. 4aβ, 6bβ, 7a), certainly represent details added later to the main theme. It is noteworthy that in v. 6 the general word 'person' crops up, not indicating in the first place a priest. This suggests that the passage vv. 6, 7abα applied first of all to Israelites generally who wished to take part in a peace-offering feast; and it is striking that by the wording of v. 6aβ the uncleanness appears to come to an automatic end 'in the evening', whereas v. 6bβ requires a washing. (Was this contemporary, or a later addition?) These cleansing possibilities refer only, as the subject-matter shows, to uncleanness acquired through contact and not to uncleanness inherent in the person. In the present context the observation in v. 7bβ makes vv. 6, 7 also refer to the priest; for he alone was dependent for his sustenance on the 'holy gifts'. [8] Verse 8 is loosely connected, being only vaguely concerned with the subject, for it too deals with an eating veto, in an intrusive sentence to the effect that 'he' (the priest, by the present context, though not expressly mentioned) may not eat of a dead animal or one killed by a beast of prey. In 11.40a; 17.15f. such eating was not categorically forbidden to a 'layman': it only rendered him unclean, and requiring cleansing. [9] The direct plural sentence in v. 9 sharpens the foregoing regulations with a threat that their neglect would mean 'sin' (*ḥēṭ'*) as a perpetual burden and therefore 'death'. This leaves it open whether the death punishment was to be inflicted in a direct stroke from God or by cultic judicial sentence. It is not clear to what the masculine singular suffixes in v. 9aβ refer; whilst the suffix in *bō* could go with *ḥēṭ'* (to be condemned to death for sin), the other two suffixes (and the suffix in *bō*) have no other masculine singular to go with, as the text now stands, except the *laḥmō* in v. 7bβ, which fits in particularly well in subject-matter with *yᵉhallᵉlūhū*. This fact would seem to indicate that v. 8 has come in as a secondary addition between vv. 7 and 9. All the same, the construction of v. 8 remains careless and incomplete.

[10–16] In vv. 10–16 the principal clause v. 10a is enlarged on in some detail. Repeated in v. 13b, it forbids the eating of the 'holy' (the singular of the expression for 'holy gifts' discussed above) by a 'stranger', that is, anyone not belonging to the circle authorized to take part in the priestly share of the cultic gifts. This circle is, however, defined in family terms: reckoned as belonging to it are all members of the priestly tribes—not only the officiating priests themselves, but all members of their families, including the women and children. Verses 10b–14 discuss against this background one or two special cases that might appear doubtful. According to v. 11 the slaves belonged to the *familia*, as was also customary outside the priestly families, the newly purchased slaves as well as those 'born in the house'—that is, the children of existing male and female slaves. In contrast to this v. 10b tells us that the 'sojourners' (artisans and the like) and the daily workers hired by the hour had no right to any share in the 'holy'. The same, according to v. 12, was true for the priest's daughter married to a man who was not a priest, for by her marriage she had separated herself from the priestly family. On the other hand, v. 13 tells us that one who had been married to a non-priest but had then become widowed or separated could return to her father's priestly *familia*, if she was childless, and return thereby to the right of participation. This leaves it tacitly understood that if she had children she remained in the *familia* of the former husband. This ruling rests presumably on a general legal practice, valid also outside the priesthood but not attested elsewhere, that a childless widow or separated woman might or must return again to her father's *familia*. Verse 14 poses the case of an unauthorized person eating 'by mistake', i.e. unwittingly and unintentionally (for this expression cf. 4.2 and above p. 37) of the 'holy' (here again singular). This implies that

L.–L

the priest was allowed to take his share of the 'holy' away with him out of the holy premises. The offender had to replace what he had taken by mistake and unauthorized (in kind or perhaps in money value) and add a further fifth of the value (cf. 5.16; 6.5) as compensation for his offence, which was indeed objective rather than subjective. The parenetic concluding passage vv. 15, 16, like v. 9, is again in the plural; v. 16 says that the priest's non-observance of these regulations about 'eating' the 'holy gifts' would involve all Israel in blame.

[17–25] The section vv. 17–25 requires only animals 'without blemish' to be brought for private sacrifice. It is intended for the information of the 'layman', who needs to know what defects in an animal would take away its 'unblemished' character. The kernel of the section is thus vv. 22–24a, which contain a catalogue of bodily abnormalities rendering an animal unsuitable for sacrifice. This catalogue, not very unified or self-contained in expression and therefore probably to be regarded as a gradual growth, contains a list of very rare special expressions, of somewhat uncertain meaning (cf. the catalogue in 21.18b–20, where some of these special expressions also occur). The non-observance of the requirements for animals 'without blemish' would not indeed be reckoned a punishable offence in the offerer (there is here no question of that); but, as is constantly repeated, it would remove from the sacrifice the character of 'well-pleasingness' to God ('well pleasing'—Heb. *rāṣōn* derived from the verb *rṣh*) which was its intention, and thereby make it practically useless (cf. 7.18). 'Vows' and 'freewill offerings' (Heb. *nēder* and *nᵉdābā*) both came into consideration: that is, offerings in fulfilment of a vow made in a moment of distress or simply brought quite spontaneously by an individual. Of this type the greater number are peace offerings. As private offerings they were of less weight than the official and obligatory offerings (cf. 7.16). They were also subject to an order of importance (v. 23b), inasmuch as the vow taken had made the 'vow offering' a duty, whereas the freewill offering was brought without any kind of compulsion. But even in the last case the 'unblemished' requirement for the animal must on principle be observed if the offering was to be 'well pleasing'. All the more so, naturally, was this requisite for official and dutiful offerings. The priests had to be well informed on this subject, for they had a share in the proceedings by having to sprinkle the blood and burn the fat parts on the altar (cf. the peace-offering ritual of ch. 3) and in general oversee the due performance of the sacrifices. They are therefore appropriately named before the 'Israelites' in vv. 17, 18a. In detail, this section has no strict form: it consists of a medley of singular and plural sentences and sentences in third and second person. Even the first linked sentence in vv. 18b, 19 is without unity. The main clause v. 18bα, in the style of the cultic rules in 17.3, 8, 10, 13, introduces, like the rules in ch. 17, an order for private sacrifices applying to everyone; but it has no corresponding dependent clause, being merely followed by extremely disconnected fragmentary sentences, strung together and reiterating key-words such as those requiring the sacrificial animal to be 'without blemish' and 'well pleasing'. Verse 18bβ, with its isolated third person plural exposition, deals with vow and freewill offerings brought as burnt offerings. Verses 21ff. then deal expressly with burnt offerings, which must be 'without blemish'. Verse 23 puts forward a more stringent idea of 'without blemish' for a vow offering than for a freewill offering. In the passage vv. 24b, 25a, again very clumsily expressed, it appears to be stated that an offering as the 'food of God' must in general be 'without blemish', whether the animal was taken from the offerer's own herds or was bought from a stranger.

[26–30] Verse 26 is followed by vv. 27–30, which, introduced by a short fresh heading, are supplementary verses of mixed content. Verse 27 tells us that an animal was not suitable for sacrifice until at least eight days old: before that it was considered to belong to its mother. It may be that this regulation and the direction in v. 28 forbid a custom, usual in foreign cults, of sacrificing an animal and its young at one and the same time. This may perhaps be a question of a veto on the fertility rites well known in the cultic world surrounding Israel. The rule in vv. 29ff., that a thank offering was only 'well pleasing' when the meat from the peace offering was eaten on the same day, agrees in content with 7.15 (cf. also 19.5f.). It is perhaps only recalled at this point because 7.16 had somewhat relaxed this strict requirement in the vow offerings and freewill offerings considered in the section vv. 17–25.

[31–33] As usual, a parenesis with plural address rounds off the whole in vv. 31–33.

### (g) THE CALENDAR OF FEASTS: 23.1–44

23 ¹The LORD said to Moses, ²'Say to the people of Israel, The appointed feasts of the LORD which you shall proclaim as holy convocations, my appointed feasts, are these. ³Six days shall work be done;

but on the seventh day is a sabbath of solemn rest, a holy convocation; you shall do no work; it is a sabbath to the LORD in all your dwellings.

4 'These are the appointed feasts of the LORD, the holy convocations, which you shall proclaim at the time appointed for them. [5]In the first month, on the fourteenth day of the month in the evening,* is the LORD's passover. [6]And on the fifteenth day of the same month is the feast of unleavened bread to the LORD; seven days you shall eat unleavened bread. [7]On the first day you shall have a holy convocation; you shall do no laborious work. [8]But you shall present an offering by fire to the LORD seven days; on the seventh day is a holy convocation; you shall do no laborious work.'

9 And the LORD said to Moses, [10]'Say to the people of Israel, When you come into the land which I give you and reap its harvest, you shall bring the sheaf of the first fruits of your harvest to the priest; [11]and he shall wave the sheaf before the LORD, that you may find acceptance; on the morrow after the sabbath the priest shall wave it. [12]And on the day when you wave the sheaf, you shall offer a male lamb a year old without blemish as a burnt offering to the LORD. [13]And the cereal offering with it shall be two tenths of an ephah of fine flour mixed with oil, to be offered by fire to the LORD, a pleasing odour; and the drink offering with it shall be of wine, a fourth of a hin. [14]And you shall eat neither bread nor grain parched or fresh until this same day, until you have brought the offering of your God: it is a statute for ever throughout your generations in all your dwellings.

15 'And you shall count from the morrow after the sabbath, from the day that you brought the sheaf of the wave offering; seven full weeks shall they be, [16]counting fifty days to the morrow after the seventh sabbath; then you shall present a cereal offering of new grain to the LORD. [17]You shall bring from your dwellings two loaves of bread to be waved, made of two tenths of an ephah; they shall be of fine flour, they shall be baked with leaven, as first fruits to the LORD. [18]And you shall present with the bread seven lambs a year old without blemish, and one young bull, and two rams; they shall be a burnt offering to the LORD, with their cereal offering and their drink offerings, an offering by fire, a pleasing odour to the LORD. [19]And you shall offer one male goat for a sin offering, and two male lambs a year old as a sacrifice of peace offerings. [20]And the priest shall wave them with the bread of the first fruits as a wave offering before the LORD, with the two lambs; they shall be holy to the LORD for the priest. [21]And you shall make proclamation on the same day; you shall hold a holy convocation; you shall do no laborious work: it is a statute for ever in all your dwellings throughout your generations.

22 'And when you reap the harvest of your land, you shall not reap your field to its very border, nor shall you gather the gleanings after your harvest; you shall leave them for the poor and for the stranger: I am the LORD your God.'

*Hebrew: 'between the two evenings'.

23 And the Lord said to Moses, 24'Say to the people of Israel, In the seventh month, on the first day of the month, you shall observe a day of solemn rest, a memorial proclaimed with blast of trumpets, a holy convocation. 25You shall do no laborious work; and you shall present an offering by fire to the Lord.'

26 And the Lord said to Moses, 27'On the tenth day of this seventh month is the day of atonement; it shall be for you a time of holy convocation, and you shall afflict yourselves and present an offering by fire to the Lord. 28And you shall do no work on this same day; for it is a day of atonement, to make atonement for you before the Lord your God. 29For whoever is not afflicted on this same day shall be cut off from his people. 30And whoever does any work on this same day, that person I will destroy from among his people. 31You shall do no work: it is a statute for ever throughout your generations in all your dwellings. 32It shall be to you a sabbath of solemn rest, and you shall afflict yourselves; on the ninth day of the month beginning at evening, from evening to evening shall you keep your sabbath.'

33 And the Lord said to Moses, 34'Say to the people of Israel, On the fifteenth day of this seventh month and for seven days is the feast of booths* to the Lord. 35On the first day shall be a holy convocation; you shall do no laborious work. 36Seven days you shall present offerings by fire to the Lord; on the eighth day you shall hold a holy convocation and present an offering by fire to the Lord; it is a solemn assembly; you shall do no laborious work.

37 'These are the appointed feasts of the Lord, which you shall proclaim as times of holy convocation, for presenting to the Lord offerings by fire, burnt offerings and cereal offerings, sacrifices and drink offerings, each on its proper day; 38besides the sabbaths of the Lord, and besides your gifts, and besides all your votive offerings, and besides all your freewill offerings, which you give to the Lord.

39 'On the fifteenth day of the seventh month, when you have gathered in the produce of the land, you shall keep the feast of the Lord seven days; on the first day shall be a solemn rest, and on the eighth day shall be a solemn rest. 40And you shall take on the first day the fruit of goodly trees, branches of palm trees, and boughs of leafy trees, and willows of the brook; and you shall rejoice before the Lord your God seven days. 41You shall keep it as a feast to the Lord seven days in the year; it is a statute for ever throughout your generations; you shall keep it in the seventh month. 42You shall dwell in booths for seven days; all that are native in Israel shall dwell in booths, 43that your generations may know that I made the people of Israel dwell in booths when I brought them out of the land of Egypt: I am the Lord your God.'

44 Thus Moses declared to the people of Israel the appointed feasts of the Lord.

The calendar of feasts in the Holiness Code has its counterpart in Deut. 16. The relationship of these two calendars to one another is

*Or 'tabernacles'.

complicated, as will be seen in the following examination of some of the details. But even by itself this chapter is not a self-contained unity: the competing headings and cross-headings show this at a glance. The first heading in v. 2aβb, already composite in its inconsistent mixture of third and first persons for Yahweh, is followed by another in v. 4. This can be easily explained by the later addition of the Sabbath-ordinance of v. 3. It did not, moreover, really belong to the calendar of feasts, which deals apart from this with the once-a-year 'feasts'; and v. 38a does not make reference to it. It is striking that vv. 37, 38 form a concluding passage, but are followed by vv. 39–43, once more dealing with the 'feast of booths' already treated in vv. 33–36. This points clearly to an inner inconsistency in the whole. On the one hand there are fairly short regulations for the celebration of particularly and precisely dated times in the course of the year (so especially vv. 5–8; also vv. 23ff.); on the other hand there are very detailed ritual precepts for carrying out festival customs on some not exactly dated occasions (so especially vv. 9–21; also vv. 40ff.). These incongruities are not easily explained by the literary-critical assumption of different 'sources'. It is at once clear that the short regulations for the dated feasts formed the skeleton of the whole, without giving it any cohesion. At all events it is worth considering whether these regulations are to be regarded as the basic form which was not then united to another 'source', but was at the most amplified by secondary accretions. But even this reconstruction is not very satisfying, for the 'basic form' is extremely meagre: thus the essential matter of the chapter only came into being with the accretions. Besides, there are too many detailed cross-connections between the two elements just described not to suggest the thesis that the whole is essentially a literary unity. Its peculiar features must have other than a literary origin.

Indeed, we have every inducement to interpret the literary internal disunity of the calendar of feasts in Lev. 23 along historical lines, starting from the history or pre-history of the great cultic feasts, which did not follow only one course. The precisely dated feasts of Lev. 23 are concentrated in the first and seventh months. With some simplification one can provisionally detect a double rhythm of feasts in the course of the cultic year. But the long section of ritual precepts in vv. 9–21 develops this into a threefold rhythm. Now this mixture of twofold and threefold rhythm in the feasts is not altogether foreign to the rest of the Old Testament. The ancient provisions in Ex. 23.14–

17; 34.18, 22, 23 recognize a threefold group of feasts, closely bound up with the natural yearly cycle of agriculture and harvest. In all probability these dated from the pre-Israelitic cultic tradition of the land; but they were also destined to be celebrated by Israel according to these old precepts after she had become settled in Canaan. The line of descent from that point leads directly to the Deuteronomic calendar of feasts in Deut. 16.1–17; only here, going beyond Ex. 23 and 34, the first of these feasts, the Feast of Unleavened Bread, seems closely bound up with the Passover-slaughter of the previous evening. This has arisen through a development that has meanwhile taken place, which the present chapter (vv. 5–8) takes for granted and does not need to discuss. The programme of the future in the Book of Ezekiel (45.21–25) contains, however, a twofold list of the great feasts, one of which (Passover/Feast of Unleavened Bread) was to be celebrated in the first, and the other ('The Feast' purely and simply), in the seventh month—which exactly corresponds to the double character of the dating in Lev. 23. Now a literary connection between the Holiness Code and the Book of Ezekiel on this point is most improbable, as is shown by the disparity of the details mentioned in this context. The similarities must therefore go back to a cultic tradition prior to both of them. The Book of Ezekiel, mentioning these two feasts in reference to the cultic duties of its *nāśî'*, the replacement for the former Davidic king, would seem to indicate a Jerusalem cultic tradition. This, with its dates following the Babylonian spring calendar and numbering of the months, cannot in its present form be earlier than late pre-exilic times; its material, however, may quite possibly be older. The calendar of feasts in the Holiness Code is thus to be understood as framed with the purpose of combining this Jerusalem tradition with the ancient threefold agrarian feasts still preserved in Deuteronomy. It starts from the Jerusalem tradition, which it reproduces fairly shortly in a formulation presumably derived from Jerusalem priestly circles, without having occasion to elaborate the details; it then amplifies this tradition with a glance back to the old threefold festivals, especially in the detailed ritual precepts of vv. 9–21, which were probably formulated anew. The foregoing all points to a dating of this calendar in the time of the 'exile'. It then remained normative for post-exilic times (cf. especially Num. 28–29). The dependence on previous traditions explains most of the formal differences, such as 'objective' and impersonal precepts alongside of instructions with second person plural address. Apart from vv. 2aβb, 3, literary questions only arise in v. 22 and in the passage vv. 39–43.

[1–3] The sentence on the sabbath (v. 3), following on the main heading vv. 1, 2aα, and with its own introduction (v. 2aβb), is certainly a later addition, intended to give weight to the growth in importance of the sabbath that had come about during and after the exile, but not quite fitting in with the following feast-calendar dealing with the annually celebrated feasts. This supplement works with phrasing taken essentially from what follows.

[5–8] The section on the Passover/Feast of Unleavened Bread (vv. 5–8) is prefaced by the original heading for the feast-calendar that follows. In it, the word $mō'ēd$ is used, first plural in its usual sense of 'feast', then singular in its basic meaning 'subject of agreement', 'agreed time', 'appointed time'. There occurs besides the technical term $miqrā'$ $qōdeš$, frequently repeated in the sequel. It means literally 'holy calling', but what is intended by that is not immediately clear. It obviously has its own position in the feast-calendar of Lev. 23, occurring here for the first time and only recurring elsewhere in connection with this feast-calendar. Apart from Ex. 12.16, this is only in Num. 28; 29. We may compare also Isa. 1.13, where in a context enumerating 'cultic festivals' the 'calling of assemblies' is mentioned (with $miqrā'$, but without $qōdeš$, as object of the verb $qr'$, as in the relative clause of Lev. 23.4b). If then $miqrā'$ $qodeš$, as it appears, was introduced by the calendar in the Holiness Code, there would be a link with an older—perhaps specifically Jerusalem (Isaiah)— use of the word $miqrā'$. It is remarkable in the Holiness Code and the portions depending on it that the expression is regularly bound up with the requirement of rest from work on the day in question. Traditionally, $miqrā'$ $qodeš$, by reason of a possible meaning of the verb $qr'$ = 'called together', is rendered 'holy feast-assembly [convocation]', 'feast-assembly at the holy place', and understood in the sense of a gathering together of the worshippers at the holy place. True, the expression does not in itself say that, at all events not unequivocally (Num. 10.2b, quite differently phrased, cannot be adduced without further discussion). It is thus worth considering whether it should not be taken in its simplest sense—a public 'proclamation' provided on each occasion of the day of rest, so that everyone should take note of this requirement. This requirement in itself would represent a transference of the ancient sabbath arrangements to the chief festival days of the year (in the feasts extending over several days, at any rate on the most important days). It occurs for the first time in the Holiness Code, and was perhaps one of its innovations; and to carry it into practice, a somewhat restricted circle must be assumed for the cultic community (cf. above p. 129). So important was it in the Holiness Code that the 'holy proclamations' summoning to rest from work are, according to the heading in v. 4, a direct characterization of the 'feasts of Yahweh'. In vv. 5–8 the Passover/Feast of Unleavened Bread, for which Deut. 16.1 (cf. Ex. 23.13; 34.18) still gives only a special month as the appointed time, is fixed for a definite date, probably on the grounds of an inherited Jerusalem tradition (cf. above p. 166). The fifteenth day of the month—reckoned according to the lunar month—was the middle of the month and day of full moon. The beginning of the feast on that day was followed according to ancient tradition (Ex. 23.15; 34.18) by a seven-day eating of unleavened bread. The evening before, which, however, was reckoned cultically part of the feast (cf. v. 32 and below p. 173), there took place the slaying of the Passover. On the basis of an older tradition, presupposed in Deut. 16.1ff., this took place 'at the time of evening twilight'—the technical term *bēn hā-ʿarbāyīm*, used elsewhere, too, to fix the time of the Passover slaying (Ex. 12.6; Num. 9.3, etc.), probably means at dusk. Of the original meaning of the Passover slaying as an apotropaic rite (cf. Noth, *Exodus*, pp. 89ff.) and the Feast of Unleavened Bread as a cultic celebration of the beginning of harvest (cf. Noth, *Exodus*, pp. 190f.), the Holiness Code has nothing to say. It is enough for it that the provided cultic rites should be carried out at the appointed times, and nothing is said even about the place of the Passover slaughter and the Feast of Unleavened Bread, which the Deuteronomic law had moved from the individual family, where it was previously celebrated, to the one central sanctuary. This last is certainly assumed to be the cultic place for the presentation of the 'offering by fire' to Yahweh (v. 8a) to be offered daily throughout the feast. For the Holiness Code, the 'proclamation' is obviously of special importance, and the rest from work on the first and last days of the seven-day Feast of Unleavened Bread (vv. 7, 8b). The dating in vv. 5, 6a is in an impersonal and objective style; the few detailed precepts (vv. 6b–8) are given as instructions in the second person plural.

[9–21] There now follows a section dealing with the bringing of harvest offerings. It has a new introductory formula (vv. 9, 10aα), and corresponds with the seasons of the year; it was probably newly phrased in the Law of Holiness, with second person plural address throughout. The ancient 'harvest home' (Ex. 23.16a) or 'feast of weeks' (Deut. 16.10) is introduced (or reintroduced) into the list of feasts by these harvest gifts. Here detailed ritual prescriptions are given couched in the form of an address, very different from the old severe ritual style. This feast is not fixed for a particular date, but has kept its close link in time and content with the harvest year, vv. 15, 16a simply connecting it firmly in time with the preliminary offering of the first sheaf. [9–14] This offering of the first sheaf of the new harvest is required in principle and in general in Ex. 23.19a; 34.26a, and has a counterpart in the offering 'of the first fruits of the field' according to the detailed regulations of Deut. 26.1–11. Incidentally— though this is not expressly stated—it must have been a barley-sheaf, for barley is usually the first of the grains to be reaped (cf. *Illustrated World of the Bible Library*, vol. 1, p. 198). Leviticus 23 gives precise regulations for this offering. In v. 10aβ this regulation is represented as having been made even before the entry into the land promised by Yahweh (here in the first person, then third person in what follows). They were to bring in 'to the priest', that is into the holy place, the first sheaf—i.e. a bundle of the first ears to be reaped. Probably each landowner had to do this. The expression 'to the priest' raises the supposition that it is based on an ancient sentence, dealing with the many still-existing sanctuaries throughout the land. But here the whole procedure is unified, both in time and place, as the sequel shows. For v. 12 must surely be understood as follows: the priest would receive the sheaves brought in to him gradually and offer them on an appointed day to Yahweh, by the symbolical 'waving before Yahweh' (cf. Noth, *Exodus*, p. 233). He would then on this same day offer for all a common burnt offering. Now this day was 'the morrow after' the Sabbath, from which day future reckoning was to be made—again for all in common—as vv. 15, 16a announce. Why this precise day is chosen for the cultic procedure remains uncertain: was it perhaps as the beginning of the six-day working week, and thus specially suitable for the custom of bringing in the newly reaped corn? In the absence of exact dating the possibility remains that the time of this 'sheaf-waving' could vary from year to year, according as the ripening of the harvest varied. The essence of the matter was that this cultic act must take place at a time near to the Feast of Unleavened Bread, as being the ancient feast of the beginning of harvest. It is not, however, brought into any temporal relation with the latter. That was not possible, not only because the date of the beginning of harvest remained and was bound to remain dependent on natural circumstances, but also because, as v. 6 tells us, the Feast of Unleavened Bread had meanwhile been fixed for a particular date, while the 'sheaf offering' remained tied to a particular week-day. The method of carrying out the 'sheaf offering' in the one holy place would suggest limitations of space. The sheaf burnt offering required by v. 12b is stated in v. 13 to need a supplementary meal offering of the usual kind, of two tenths of an ephah (for the ephah as a dry measure see above p. 45); that would be, in comparison with the customary meal-offering supplement (cf. Ex. 29.39f.; Num. 28.4f., etc.), a double quantity. In addition to this there was a supplementary drink offering of wine, not provided for in the ritual of Lev. 1–7, which was probably to be poured out before the altar, and was about a quarter of a hin in quantity (hin as a liquid measure = about 6 litres). Verse 14 says that before this cultic duty had been carried out nothing might be eaten from the new harvest, either in the form of baked bread or in the form of roast ears of corn, or as (probably) raw grains of corn rubbed in the hand.

[15–21] Exactly seven weeks after this cultic act (vv. 15, 16a; v. 16a, with its 'fifty days', reckons in both the first and last days) a bigger cultic festival had to take place (vv. 16b–21). This was related to the great cultic feasts in the first and seventh months by the 'proclamation' and rest from work (v. 21a), but was less prominent owing to its restriction to a single day. We are dealing—although this designation is not mentioned in Lev. 23—with the ancient 'harvest home' or 'feast of weeks' (see above) at the end of the corn harvest. This again is not dated, but is firmly linked in point of time with the 'sheaf offering', and thus occupied a probably variable position between the dated feasts. The fixing at 'seven weeks' after the beginning of harvest belonged to the older tradition for this feast; it appears in Deut. 16.9 and forms the basis of the title 'feast of weeks' occurring in Ex. 34.22a and recurring in Deut. 16.10. The first element in this feast, in keeping with its character, was a cultic offering of harvest produce, here in v. 16b designated 'new grain', in v. 17b 'first fruits', and in v. 20a 'bread of the first fruits'. This offering, according to v. 17, was to consist of ready-baked bread—not, as in the Feast of Unleavened Bread at the start of harvest, of unleavened cakes, but of loaves of bread made of leavened dough—

as normally eaten; for it was now a question of the whole harvest yield for daily use in the coming year. Verse 17, phrased in places in a rather set style, requires 'two' of these to be offered; this probably means that all landowners ('from their dwellings') should give two loaves. Verses 18, 19 add a general and larger offering, presumably for all, with burnt offering and appropriate meal and drink offering (v. 18), sin offering (v. 19a), and peace offering (19b). All the animals required for these sacrifices were, in the wording of v. 20a, to be solemnly offered by the priest by 'waving before Yahweh'; how this symbolic action was to be carried out 'over the bread of the first fruits' is not easily conceived, but that is no sufficient ground for assuming that the text has received secondary additions. It is harder to explain how two further sheep have come in (v. 20β), obviously not identical with the peace-offering sheep of v. 19a, of whose further use nothing is said. If v. 20aβ is to be taken specially with v. 20b, which is not exactly obvious, but not impossible, these two sheep could be regarded as a cultic gift set aside for the priest. By the requirement of 'proclamation' and rest from work (v. 21) this whole procedure of presenting and sacrificing is aligned in the Holiness Code to the great feasts of the first and seventh months, and so inserted into the list of yearly feasts, where it occupies admittedly a subordinate place, owing to its limitation to a single day. [22] The section on the 'harvest home' has in v. 22 a secondary addition corresponding verbally with 19.9, 10b, even including the pointless alternation of plural and singular address. It has certainly been taken over from there, under the impression that these sentences, too, are dealing with harvest regulations, but without noticing that this supplement does not fit in with the framework of a calendar of feasts. (The instructions in 19.10a referring to the grape harvest were not, by reason of their subject-matter, taken over as well.)

[23–25] Verse 23 begins the detailed instructions for the feast-days in the seventh month, each provided with its separate introductory formula (vv. 23, 24a, 26, 33), just as the section vv. 9–21 had received its own introduction in vv. 9, 10aα. Verses 24, 25 deal, without specifically saying so, with the New Year's Day. According to Ex. 23.16bα; 34.22b, the old autumnal grape-harvest festival had been celebrated at the turn of the year. Even after the Babylonian spring year had been introduced for the official reckoning of year and month—probably shortly before the exile—the cultic beginning of the year kept its place in the autumn, and was henceforward celebrated in the 'seventh month'; and the only concession to the new calendar was the fixed dating on the first day of the month. For this day, as we learn in v. 24, there was again the 'proclamation' and rest from work and moreover a 'fire offering to Yahweh' not more precisely described. The day was distinguished by a solemn 'blast of trumpets' (*tᵉrū'ā*), i.e. a loud blast on (ram's) horns (*šōpār*; cf. 25.9) used as wind instruments. This may well have originally had an apotropaic significance; later however, it may be supposed, it came to mean merely the festive introduction to a new period of time. Verse 24, in its singular form and set-phrase style—'memorial, remembrance through noise (of blowing)'—does not unfortunately make it at all clear what the 'memorial' was. Not even the logical subject of the idea 'memorial' can be fixed with any certainty: was Yahweh to be 'reminded' of his people by the blast of trumpets, or was Israel to 'remember' her God and his benefits?

[26–32] According to vv. 27–32 there followed on the tenth day of the seventh month the 'day of atonement' (*yōm hak-kippūrīm*), which is designated by this technical term only here and in 25.9 in the Old Testament. In 25.9, dated likewise on the tenth day of the seventh month, it is regarded in point of time as the beginning of the year. As its name indicates, it was the day of a great 'atoning', and according to 16.29 (which does not use the term 'day of atonement' but names the date as the tenth day of the seventh month) the great ancient cleansing ritual of Lev. 16 was intended and drawn up for this day. The connection with the year's cycle would seem to be original, for a great atonement was peculiarly fitting at this particular season. Why this atonement was separated from the great autumn feast at the turn of the year, made independent, and transferred precisely to a point five days before the beginning of this feast—this can no longer be ascertained. The separation and independent institution of New Year's Day (vv. 24, 25) would appear to be a further step, beyond 25.9, in the division of the original New Year and autumn feasts. Besides the dating and naming and the summary requirement for presenting a 'fire offering for Yahweh' (v. 27b, as v. 8a), and the rest from work, there is special mention of 'afflicting yourselves' (v. 27aβ). The technical term for this means literally 'to lower, bow down one's soul (= oneself)'. This must certainly indicate something concrete. It is mostly rendered 'to mortify oneself', with particular reference to fasting, though Hebrew has a special unambiguous word for 'fasting' (*ṣōm*). This matter no longer admits of certain decision: probably definite abstinences are intended, in the sense of a 'penance' in preparation for the 'atonement'. There is no reference at all to—not even a hint of—the contents of the ritual in Lev. 16; rather, it is the other way round, for the supplementary passage 16.29–31 clearly alludes to 23.26–32. The special sharpening of the 'self-affliction' by the use of the 'cutting off' formula in v. 29 might well be a supplementary detail. This applies all the more to the threat of punishment for the non-observance of the rest from work requirement in v. 30; with its first person for Yahweh, it clearly does not belong to the framework. The concluding formula in v. 31b shows v. 32 to be an appendage, though its contents are worth noting, for it fixes the time limits of the 'Day (of Atonement)' as 'from evening to evening' (cf. Ex. 12.18), doubtless taking note of an ancient division of the day. This brings out very clearly the discrepancy between a new 'modern' calendar, with numbered months and days obviously beginning in the morning, and an older use, still preserved in worship, reckoning the days from evening to evening.

[33–36] For the 'feast of booths' vv. 34b–36, in parallel with the Passover/Feast of Unleavened Bread (vv. 5–8), only note the most important matters shortly, the detail of the cultic festival obviously being assumed to be well known. The only special feature is the eighth day (v. 36b), which comes in as a supplement to the seven feast-days (so explicitly vv. 34b, 36a). Comparison with v. 8 shows without doubt that we are dealing with an eighth feast-day, coming in to join the seven, and not simply a last day of the seven-day series, calculated by some different and special method of reckoning (cf. also Num. 29.35–38, where, following Lev. 23, the eighth day is explicitly reckoned). This uneven juxtaposition of the seven-day period (vv. 34b, 36a) and the eighth day (v. 36b) can only be explained by supposing that this chief feast of the year, following the older use of a seven-day feast-time (as still in Deut. 16.15), very probably modelled on the old traditional seven-day Feast of Unleavened Bread, was joined by an eighth feast-day, added later, appearing for the first time in Lev. 23, and perhaps introduced for the first time by the Holiness Code. And now there was transferred to it the special prominence given to the last feast-day (cf. v. 8b). Besides this, it is characterized by a special technical term, *ʿaṣeret*. This word is mostly rendered 'solemn assembly'; but neither the use of the word elsewhere nor its etymology points to this meaning. On the other hand, although followed by the command to rest from work, it obviously means something different from *miqrā' qodeš*; for this latter expression stands alongside in v. 36b, in the framework of a quite different phrasing. The verb '*ṣr* has the sense 'hold back, stop, shut in', which suggests that *ᵃṣeret* means something which in scientific religious language would be called a 'taboo day'—hence an attempted translation might be 'special feast-day'. That is to say, it was a day that required special abstinences, though unfortunately v. 36b tells us nothing concrete about them.

[37–38] The concluding passage vv. 37, 38 shows that the foregoing has only dealt with the great feasts of the year and the offerings to be presented at them. The absence of any mention of the sabbath and of other kinds of sacrifice does not in any way indicate that these were no longer to be observed and practised.

[39–43] Following from this concluding passage, the section vv. 39–43 cannot be taken for anything else than a literary addition, although it is close to vv. 9–21 in manner and content. Both these sections, in contrast to the remaining parts of the chapter, give detailed· directions for cultic festivals, and both bring the cultic celebrations into connection with the course of the natural harvest year and thus obviously continue the old three-feast cycle (see above). The supplement vv. 39–43 intends then to continue, or go back to, the old cultic customs for the autumn feast. Verse 39 adds to the dating a reference to the natural season, and calls the feast simply 'the feast of Yahweh', the real chief feast (cf. Ezek. 45.25), which, in fact, it probably was from the beginning. It is a seven-day feast, but here also (v. 39b) an eighth great feast day appears to have been added. The festival custom itself is again restricted to the original seven days, as mentioned in v. 40. The usage is only incompletely and allusively described: the Israelites are to 'take' all kinds of fruit and branches and 'rejoice before Yahweh'. The thought in mind is a happy processing in or round about the holy place, carrying and waving fruits and branches. That was no doubt an ancient custom, even though it is first mentioned in this supplementary section within the Holiness Code. It calculated the end of the harvest year according to the harvesting of the fruit from the fruit trees. The concluding sentence v. 41 is followed by a further addition in vv. 42, 43, prescribing the dwelling in 'booths' on the old seven days of the feast for all 'native' in Israel (not including the guests and strangers), and this requirement gives an 'historical' reason. The requirement itself rests no doubt on an ancient custom, the basis of the name 'feast of booths', already known to the Deuteronomic law (16.13). The custom goes back to the original natural situation of the feast, with its dwelling in 'booths' in the midst of the orchards and vineyards at the time of fruit- and grape-harvest. Leviticus 23 is probably already contemplating a transposal of this natural situation into the setting of the one sanctuary, or into the district surrounding it. The 'historical' reason is secondary compared with the custom itself. It lays down that each growing generation of Israelites shall be freshly 'taught' that Yahweh (first person in v. 43) led the Israelites out of Egypt by the one fundamental mighty deed. When they had left the settled land of Egypt he had 'caused them to dwell in booths'—so the 'booths' usual in settled conditions, made of branches of trees and matting, were to be a reminder of the tents improvised with staves and tent-cloth by the nomadic shepherds. This identification is not altogether irrelevant, for both cases provide a contrast to settled living in houses. The 'instruction' of the Israelites consisted then of a vivid 'reliving' of the one-time situation in the desert. It is remarkable that the ancient and original traits of the harvest-home should only be mentioned in the Old Testament in a late passage from the literary point of view. It is obviously intent on preserving the ancient festival customs on into later days.

(*h*) DETAILS OF THE REGULAR SERVICE OF THE SANCTUARY: 24.1–9

24 ¹The LORD said to Moses, ²'Command the people of Israel to bring you pure oil from beaten olives for the lamp, that a light may be kept burning continually. ³Outside the veil of the testimony, in the tent of meeting, Aaron shall keep it in order from evening to morning before the LORD continually; it shall be a statute for ever throughout your generations. ⁴He shall keep the lamps in order upon the lampstand of pure gold before the LORD continually.

5 'And you shall take fine flour, and bake twelve cakes of it; two tenths of an ephah shall be in each cake. ⁶And you shall set them in two rows, six in a row, upon the table of pure gold. ⁷And you shall put pure frankincense with each row, that it may go with the bread as a memorial portion to be offered by fire to the LORD. ⁸Every sabbath day Aaron shall set it in order before the LORD continually on behalf of the people of Israel as a covenant for ever. ⁹And it shall be for Aaron and his sons, and they shall eat it in a holy place, since it is for him a most holy portion out of the offerings by fire to the LORD, a perpetual due.'

This section is rather different from the other contents of the Holiness Code. It has to do with some daily or weekly obligations of the priest in the sanctuary. In this the internal arrangements of the sanctuary clearly incline from P towards Ex. 25ff., and Aaron is named as priest. Alongside him, however, Moses plays a part. According to the present text, he has to see to the oil for the lamp looked after by Aaron; also to take the bread for Aaron (and his sons) and lay it on the table as an offering. The subject of v. 8a is not clear. It is not very apparent what figure or group is here concealed beneath the person of Moses. If we take further into account the fact that the introductory formula in v. 2a appears in a form quite unusual for the Holiness Code, we are forced to the conclusion that we are dealing with a late addition to the Holiness Code. It presupposes— as is nowhere else the case in the Holiness Code—the P-narrative and its picture of the holy place, and is intent on laying down some ordinances apparently important for the Jerusalem cult after the exile.

[2–4] The first section (vv. 2–4) deals with the lamp, which is to burn all night on the lamp-stand in the 'holy place' before the veil in the sanctuary of P. Aaron is to look after it regularly, and the Israelites are to bring him the necessary oil. Verses 2, 3 are almost word for word identical with Ex. 27.20, 21, a passage which in its present position is without doubt secondary (cf. Noth, *Exodus*, p. 217). Verse 4 assimilates this passage with the P-section about the 'lamp-stand' in Ex. 25.31ff., without material change of substance, by putting instead of 'light' (*mā'ōr*) the word 'lamp-stand' (*menōrā*) and instead of one 'lamp' (*nēr*) an unspecified number of 'lamps'.

[5–9] Verses 5–9 deal with the 'bread of the Presence' (without using this technical term), the 'Shewbread' (cf. Noth, *Exodus*, p. 206). The person addressed as 'thou' can from the context only be Moses; and it is not really possible to abstract this phrasing from the present context and substitute a priest as the person originally addressed, for rules for priestly functions are customarily given not in the address form, but in the objective style. There remains then the question already noticed, who in this undoubted time after the exile was to fulfil the role of Moses at Sinai. The action of preparing and offering the 'cakes' is fairly fully described in vv. 5–7. Only here it is stated that there should be twelve loaves, and these of considerable size (the measure for the 'two-tenths'—which is not named—must be the ephah; cf. above p. 45). It is noteworthy that v. 7 requires a supplementary gift of incense. The phrasing of v. 7a, taken together with v. 6, makes it clear that the twelve flat bread-cakes were to be piled up in sixes, and that the incense was to be laid on each of these piles.

This incense was burnt at the offering, and thus became an *'azkārā*, a 'fire offering for Yahweh'. (For the technical term *'azkārā*, of uncertain translation, used to designate the part of the meal offering to be burnt, cf. above p. 27.) Verse 8, with the verb in the third person and unrelated in the present context, raises the question of a later addition; in any case this verse provides for the offering of the 'bread of the presence' not each day, but only each sabbath. It can at least be asked whether this is not a later regulation in comparison with the instructions in Ex. 25.30, where the indeterminate *tāmīd* would rather suggest a daily presentation (cf. Noth, *Exodus*, p. 206). The question of the original form is also raised by v. 9, where the feminine subject of the first verb ('the bread' must be understood) has no proper connection in v. 7 or v. 8, and is then, moreover, taken up illogically by the masculine suffix of the second verb. At all events this badly constructed sentence assigns the loaves, which had to be taken away each time new ones were offered, to the priests as their share (v. 9a names Aaron and his sons; v. 9b refers to Aaron alone). They were to be 'most holy' food.

### (i) A SAMPLE CASE ON THE VALIDITY FOR FOREIGNERS OF ISRAEL'S DIVINE LAW: 24.10–23

24 [10]Now an Israelite woman's son, whose father was an Egyptian, went out among the people of Israel; and the Israelite woman's son and a man of Israel* quarrelled in the camp, [11]and the Israelite woman's son blasphemed the Name, and cursed. And they brought him to Moses. His mother's name was Shelomith, the daughter of Dibri, of the tribe of Dan. [12]And they put him in custody, till the will of the LORD should be declared to them. [13]And the LORD said to Moses, [14]'Bring out of the camp him who cursed; and let all who heard him lay their hands upon his head, and let all the congregation stone him. [15]And say to the people of Israel, Whoever curses his God shall bear his sin. [16]He who blasphemes the name of the LORD shall be put to death; all the congregation shall stone him; the sojourner as well as the native, when he blasphemes the Name, shall be put to death. [17]He who kills a man shall be put to death. [18]He who kills a beast shall make it good, life for life. [19]When a man causes a disfigurement in his neighbour, as he has done it shall be done to him, [20]fracture for fracture, eye for eye, tooth for tooth; as he has disfigured a man, he shall be disfigured. [21]He who kills a beast shall make it good; and he who kills a man shall be put to death. [22]You shall have one law for the sojourner and for the native; for I am the LORD your God.' [23]So Moses spoke to the people of Israel; and they brought

*Cf. BH.

him who had cursed out of the camp, and stoned him with stones. Thus the people of Israel did as the LORD commanded Moses.

This piece consists of a 'narrative' framework, within which appear in vv. 15b–22 a series of legal statutes. In its narrative framework this piece appears to stand in the Holiness Code; yet this 'narrative' framework has a nearly related counterpart in Num. 15.32–36, showing correspondences—even verbal ones—with the present framework. Now, in both cases it is obviously not a question of genuine 'narratives', or even of scattered fragments of the P-narrative. For the narrative serves on each occasion only to arrive at a legal decision in a particular penal case. We are dealing then with 'legal' texts; the relevant legal sentence is simply given in the form of a 'narrated' precedent, which was to serve for future guidance. It is incidentally assumed that special cases are being handled, for which the collection of legal sentences handed down orally or in writing contained no instructions, so that *ad hoc* decisions had to be imported; and this decision was produced in both cases through a direct 'speaking' of Yahweh to Moses. This means that the early history of this piece is put back into the primitive Sinai-Moses period, although the relevant portions in Lev. 24 and Num. 15 date no doubt from very much later times. Then the question arises who in these later times could have represented the original Moses. As the context pictures Yahweh giving the word directly to Moses, it seems that only someone with 'charismatic' gifts can be intended. We are dealing then with 'charismatic' judgments by which a case could be decided, forming a precedent normative for all similar cases in the future. The special feature of the case in Lev. 24.10ff. consists in this: a 'foreigner' has cursed the name of God, and the decision goes forth that there is the same law for foreigners and natives, and that 'cursing the name of God' is for a foreigner, too, an 'offence worthy of death'. As far as there are any points of attachment, the phrasing of the section points to exilic or post-exilic times; it can no longer be said for certain whether it belonged to the basic form of the Holiness Code or whether it was subsequently incorporated.

[10–14] The 'son of an Egyptian' (v. 10a) remains a foreigner, even if he has an Israelite mother, who is simply the reason why he lives among the Israelites. During and after the exile there must have been plenty of comparable cases. The assumptions and circumstances of the previous history of the case are only shortly and inadequately implied in vv. 10b, 11aα, because it is solely a question of the matter of fact that a foreigner has vilified and cursed 'the Name'. The expression 'the Name' (cf. Deut. 28.58) means naturally the divine name, not to be mentioned here out of reverence (contrast the probably older phrasing of v. 16aα). The sequence of v. 11aβ and v. 12 shows that Moses first of all cannot arrive at a decision, but must wait for the divine decision of which he becomes the mouthpiece. (Verse 11b, interposing the name of the mother, the basis of which remains obscure, disturbs the connection and must be supposed to be a later addition.) The decision (v. 14) is for stoning, before which all those who heard the oath are to lay their hands on the head of the malefactor in order to transfer to him the 'objective' guilt in which their common hearing of the oath has involved them. The execution of the sentence is finally reported in v. 23. **[15–22]** In between come vv. 15–22, with a special introductory formula (v. 15a), a series of legal statutes, based obviously on inherited earlier material. It is quoted here for the sake of its first sentence (v. 16aα) which reckons the cursing of Yahweh's name among the 'offences worthy of death', and is couched in the original participial form (cf. Noth, *Exodus*, p. 179). This normative sentence is quoted because the 'charismatic' decision in the previous case brings to it the detailed definition that it, too, is applicable to foreigners, as v. 16b expressly states. (Verse 16aβ with its demand for stoning represents a perhaps traditional expansion of the old *mōt yūmat* sentence in v. 16aα). At the head of v. 15b is the general sentence that 'anyone' (including the foreigner) must bear the consequences of 'cursing God'. Verses 17–21 quote from the tradition from which v. 16aα stems a few further sentences, to show by analogy from these that not only 'natives' but also 'foreigners' come under their ruling, as v. 22 lays down in comprehensive fashion. It is a question of the *mōt yūmat* sentence about the slaying of a man (v. 17), here expressed with a preceding dependent clause (for the older form and on this subject cf. Ex. 21.12). Alongside of it v. 18a places a sentence about the duty of compensation in the case of the 'slaying' of an animal (that is, one belonging to another flock or household). This juxtaposition is all the more remarkable as the quotation of the first part of the *lex talionis* in v. 18b (cf. Ex. 21.23b–25; Deut. 19.21b and Noth, *Exodus*, p. 182) can only refer to v. 17, passing over v. 18a. Further portions of the *lex talionis* follow in v. 20a; they refer to bodily injuries received; vv. 19 and 20b surround them with general sentences which lay down the basic principle of the *talio* (for ʿāmīt in v. 19, cf. above pp. 48f.). Strangely enough, v. 21 repeats these sentences once more in shortened form: was this to bring out expressly once again the difference between the slaying of an animal and the slaying of a human being?

### (*k*) THE SABBATICAL YEAR AND THE YEAR OF JUBILEE: 25.1–26.2

25 ¹The LORD said to Moses on Mount Sinai, ²'Say to the people of Israel, When you come into the land which I give you, the land shall keep a sabbath to the LORD. ³Six years you shall sow your field, and six years you shall prune your vineyard, and gather in its fruits; ⁴but in the seventh year there shall be a sabbath of solemn rest for the land, a sabbath to the LORD; you shall not sow your field or prune your vineyard. ⁵What grows of itself in your harvest you shall not reap, and the grapes of your undressed vine you shall not gather; it shall be a year of solemn rest for the land. ⁶The sabbath of the land shall provide food for you, for yourself and for your male and female slaves and for your hired servant and the sojourner who lives with you; ⁷for your cattle also and for the beasts that are in your land all its yield shall be for food.

8 'And you shall count seven weeks* of years, seven times seven years, so that the time of the seven weeks of years shall be to you forty-nine years. ⁹Then you shall send abroad the loud trumpet on the tenth day of the seventh month; on the day of atonement you shall send abroad the trumpet throughout all your land. ¹⁰And you shall hallow the fiftieth year, and proclaim liberty throughout the land to all its inhabitants; it shall be a jubilee for you, when each of you shall return to his property and each of you shall return to his family. ¹¹A jubilee shall that fiftieth year be to you; in it you shall neither sow, nor reap what grows of itself, nor gather the grapes from the undressed vines. ¹²For it is a jubilee; it shall be holy to you; you shall eat what it yields out of the field.

13 'In this year of jubilee each of you shall return to his property. ¹⁴And if you sell to your neighbour or buy from your neighbour, you shall not wrong one another. ¹⁵According to the number of years after the jubilee, you shall buy from your neighbour, and according to the number of years for crops he shall sell to you. ¹⁶If the years are many you shall increase the price, and if the years are few you shall diminish the price, for it is the number of the crops that he is selling to you. ¹⁷You shall not wrong one another, but you shall fear your God; for I am the LORD your God. ¹⁸Therefore you shall do my statutes, and keep my ordinances and perform them; so you will dwell in the land securely. ¹⁹The land will yield its fruit, and you will eat your fill, and dwell in it securely. ²⁰And if you say, "What shall we eat in the seventh year, if we may not sow or gather in our crop?" ²¹I will command my blessing upon you in the sixth year, so that it will bring forth fruit for three

*Or 'sabbaths'.

years. ²²When you sow in the eighth year, you will be eating old produce; until [the ninth year, when] its produce comes in, you shall eat the old. ²³The land shall not be sold in perpetuity, for the land is mine; for you are strangers and sojourners with me.

24 'And in all the country you possess, you shall grant a redemption of the land. ²⁵If your brother becomes poor, and sells part of his property, then his next of kin shall come and redeem what his brother has sold. ²⁶If a man has no one to redeem it, and then himself becomes prosperous and finds sufficient means to redeem it, ²⁷let him reckon the years since he sold it and pay back the overpayment to the man to whom he sold it; and he shall return to his property. ²⁸But if he has not sufficient means to get it back for himself, then what he sold shall remain in the hand of him who bought it until the year of jubilee; in the jubilee it shall be released, and he shall return to his property. ²⁹If a man sells a dwelling house in a walled city, he may redeem it within a whole year after its sale; for a full year he shall have the right of redemption. ³⁰If it is not redeemed within a full year, then the house that is in the walled* city shall be made sure in perpetuity to him who bought it, throughout his generations; it shall not be released in the jubilee. ³¹But the houses of the villages which have no wall around them shall be reckoned with the fields of the country; they may be redeemed, and they shall be released in the jubilee. ³²Nevertheless the cities of the Levites, the houses in the cities of their possession, the Levites may redeem at any time. ³³And if one of the Levites does not exercise† his right of redemption, then the house that was sold in a city‡ of their possession shall be released in the jubilee; for the houses in the cities of the Levites are their possession among the people of Israel. ³⁴But the fields of common land belonging to their cities may not be sold; for that is their perpetual possession.

35 'And if your brother becomes poor, and cannot maintain himself with you, you shall maintain him; as a stranger and a sojourner he shall live with you. ³⁶Take no interest from him or increase, but fear your God; that your brother may live beside you. ³⁷You shall not lend him your money at interest, nor give him your food for profit. ³⁸I am the LORD your God, who brought you forth out of the land of Egypt to give you the land of Canaan, and to be your God.

39 'And if your brother becomes poor beside you, and sells himself to you, you shall not make him serve as a slave: ⁴⁰he shall be with you as a hired servant and as a sojourner. He shall serve with you until the year of the jubilee; ⁴¹then he shall go out from you, he and his children with him, and go back to his own family, and return to the possession of his fathers. ⁴²For they are my servants, whom I brought forth out of the land of Egypt; they shall not be sold as slaves. ⁴³You shall not rule over him with harshness, but shall fear your God. ⁴⁴As for your male and

*Cf. BH.
†Vulg.; Hebrew: 'exercises'.
‡Reading *bēt ʿîr* for *bayit weʿîr* (BH).

female slaves whom you may have: you may buy male and female slaves from among the nations that are round about you. ⁴⁵You may also buy from among the strangers who sojourn with you and their families that are with you, who have been born in your land; and they may be your property. ⁴⁶You may bequeath them to your sons after you, to inherit as a possession for ever; you may make slaves of them, but over your brethren the people of Israel you shall not rule, one over another, with harshness.

47 'If a stranger or sojourner with you becomes rich, and your brother beside him becomes poor and sells himself to the stranger or* sojourner with you, or to a member of the stranger's family, ⁴⁸then after he is sold he may be redeemed; one of his brothers may redeem him, ⁴⁹or his uncle, or his cousin may redeem him, or a kinsman belonging to his family may redeem him; or if he grows rich he may redeem himself. ⁵⁰He shall reckon with him who bought him from the year when he sold himself to him until the year of jubilee, and the price of his release shall be according to the number of years; the time he was with his owner shall be rated as the time of a hired servant. ⁵¹If there are still many years, according to them he shall refund out of the price paid for him the price for his redemption. ⁵²If there remain but a few years until the year of jubilee, he shall make a reckoning with him; according to the years of service due from him he shall refund the money for his redemption. ⁵³As a servant hired year by year shall he be with him; he shall not rule with harshness over him in your sight. ⁵⁴And if he is not redeemed by these means, then he shall be released in the year of jubilee, he and his children with him. ⁵⁵For to me the people of Israel are servants, they are my servants whom I brought forth out of the land of Egypt: I am the LORD your God.

26 ¹'You shall make for yourselves no idols and erect no graven image or pillar, and you shall not set up a figured stone in your land, to bow down to them; for I am the LORD your God. ²You shall keep my sabbaths and reverence my sanctuary: I am the LORD.'

The Sabbatical Year and the Year of Jubilee have each in a special way the same theme—the *restitutio in integrum* or restoration to an original state. The holding of every seventh year as a sabbatical year is already required in Ex. 23.10f., with a measure laying it down that the crops of the land should not be harvested during this year (cf. Noth, *Exodus*, pp. 189f.); and Neh. 10.31 (cf. I Macc. 6.49, 53) tells us that after the exile this requirement was obeyed. The regulations in Lev. 25.2aβ–7 are to the same effect; v. 5b makes express mention of the term 'sabbatical year' (šᵉnat šabbātōn). This is lacking in the other Old Testament passages, which only mention the 'seventh year'. It is otherwise with the year of jubilee, which is dealt with only in Lev. 25, though it is briefly mentioned in Num. 36.4. As it was at

*'ō (or wᵉ) appears to have been omitted.

the same time a 'sabbath year', the regulations for this applied to it as well; but beyond this came in the requirement for the restoration of property, whether it was property in land or in human beings (slaves). This is something special and unique; yet there are a few portions of the Old Testament 'law' which have a distant or rather obscure subject-matter connection with this requirement of restoration in the jubilee-year regulations, namely the 'law of slavery' in Ex. 21.1–11 (and its newer form in Deut. 15.12–18). There, the 'Hebrew slave' was to be liberated every seventh year. Also the 'law of remission' in Deut. 15.1–11, where there was to be a remission (Heb. $\check{s}^e mi\underline{t}\underline{t}\bar{a}$) of all outstanding debts. The jubilee-year section in Lev. 25 deals likewise with slaves and—indirectly—debts; but above all it deals—and there is no other really comparable passage in the Old Testament—with the restoration of rights of ownership in the land. The name 'jubilee year' has really nothing to do with the content of these regulations. It obviously refers to the announcement of the beginning of this year by loud and solemn horn-blowing (cf. v. 9). For the word $y\bar{o}b\bar{e}l$ means originally the ram (so still in Josh. 6.5, in the compound $qeren\ hay$-$y\bar{o}b\bar{e}l$), and then the ram's horn as a wind instrument (so Ex. 19.13 and Josh. 6.4ff.). But the technical use of $\check{s}^e nat\ hay$-$y\bar{o}b\bar{e}l$ in Lev. 25 cannot be separated from this. If v. 9 uses, for the wind instrument employed for the blowing of horns to usher in the year, not $y\bar{o}b\bar{e}l$ but $\check{s}\bar{o}p\bar{a}r$ (likewise = ram's horn), this is only a sign that the name 'jubilee year' comes from a time and a tradition older than the present formulation of the ordinances for the year of jubilee—a time when it was still customary to use the word $y\bar{o}b\bar{e}l$ for ram's horn, and not the word current later, $\check{s}\bar{o}p\bar{a}r$.

In Lev. 25 the disproportion between the short section about the sabbath year (vv. 2a$\beta$–7) and the very extensive section about the jubilee year (vv. 8–55) is striking. The reason underlying this is that the complicated jubilee year arrangements needed more detailed directions; it is also because from v. 35 onwards especially it contains all kinds of accretions, in part very loosely connected with the subject of the jubilee year. The usual mixture of styles shows that the whole has undergone a process of growth. The element of instructions with direct address predominates, but the intermingling of singular and plural address points to a gradual development whose separate stages can, however, no longer be distinguished. The dating, too, is very difficult. For the first question raised is at what stage of development this chapter can be dated. We can only work from the end-product—

in essentials the present form of the chapter. This will mean on the one hand taking account of later literary additions; on the other hand it must be assumed from the start as at least probable that older material, not only directly on the subject but perhaps also in already fixed form, has contributed to the whole. The latter point is illustrated by what was said above on the probable derivation of the term 'jubilee year', although v. 9 no longer speaks of *yōbēl*, but of *šōpār*. The chief content of the directions for the year of jubilee, the restoration of 'original' land-ownership rights, presupposes an Israel already settled in civilized conditions on the land, but only assumes this to have already taken place, and might go back into the early period of Israel's settlement. We come further down in time, however, with the side-by-side mention of dwelling in walled cities and dwelling in unwalled 'villages' (vv. 29–31), which supports the idea that Israel also possessed houses in walled cities. As these walled cities surely mean in the first place the ancient Canaanite cities of the land, this must imply an already complete balance between the Canaanite and Israelite way of life, hardly to be put earlier than the early days of the kings. These considerations only concern the subject-matter. As far as the present form of the chapter is concerned, the dating in v. 9 by spring years and numbered months does not allow us to go back further than late pre-exilic times. On the other hand, v. 9 gives the beginning of the year—not merely the jubilee year—as the tenth day of the seventh month. This would indicate an earlier fixing of the beginning of the year than in 23.24b, 25 (cf. above pp. 172f.). The only parallel for this placing is the explanatory remark in Ezek. 40.1. This material reference might well be the sole concrete point of attachment for dating the main material of the chapter. It takes us into the time of the exile, to be sure at a somewhat earlier stage than can be posited for Lev. 23. At that time, accordingly, considerably older ordinances for the year of jubilee were formulated anew.

[25.1–7] Joined immediately to the introduction (vv. 1, 2aα), where the naming of the mountain of Sinai is unusual and remarkable, and indicates the fundamental quality of the following ordinances, are vv. 2aβ–7, which give the regulations for the sabbath year. The singular-phrased instruction sentences, vv. 3–5a, form its kernel. In material, it completely agrees with Ex. 23.10f.; for there, too, as in the wording of v. 10, not only harvesting but also sowing is forbidden. The more detailed instructions in Lev. 25 forbid not only the cultivation of the ploughland and attention to the vineyards (cf. Ex. 23.11b), but also the harvesting of any corn that has grown wild from the ears left lying after the previous year's harvest, and the gathering of wild grapes (*nāzīr*, occurring elsewhere in the sense of 'dedicated', originally means anything 'withdrawn' from ordinary use, and means here the uncultivated and unpruned vine-stem). All this is but a more detailed exposition of what is intended in Ex. 23.10f. Only in the underlying reasons is there a difference. Ex. 23 at once gives a 'social' reason for the regulations in v. 11aβ, namely that the wild growth of the fallow year is to be at the disposal of 'the poor', that is, those who have no stake in the soil, and further, of the 'wild beasts', i.e. those not in the ownership and service of human beings, so that they are not restricted to what men give them or leave over from their crops. In Lev. 25, however, the corresponding reason is not given till the end of vv. 6, 7, in a combination of sentences first plural and then singular in address, which probably represents the latest element in this whole section. Previously, however, the reason is given that the land should have a 'time of rest', a 'sabbath for Yahweh'. This is equally true of the heart of the section (v. 4a) as of the inclusive remark in v. 5b and the plural introductory sentence in v. 2aβb, which assumes the likely-looking derivation of the word 'sabbath' from *šbt* = 'to rest'. This sacral reason (cf. especially the apparently set form 'sabbath for Yahweh' in vv. 2bβ, 4aβ), might well be the more original one, as a matter of fact, in point of content. It rests on the understanding that Yahweh is the true owner of the land (cf. v. 23aβ) and that the direct-ness of this relationship ought to be restored every seventh year, without the land having its 'rest' disturbed by the intervention of men to whom it has passed and who use it for their own purposes. The sabbath year was certainly a year beginning from the autumn, according to the old Israelite calendar, that is, a full agricultural year, from ploughing and sowing to harvest.

[8–12] The section on the year of jubilee (vv. 8–55) begins in vv. 8–12 with a kind of introductory programme, in which the essentials are shortly comprised. Verses 8, 9 deal with the exact dating, laying down that every seventh sabbath year—that is every forty-ninth year—should be a jubilee year. It was to be announced and introduced by loud blasts on the horn throughout Israel: the noise of horns was to be 'sent abroad' through the whole country (*heʿabīr*) on the tenth day of the seventh month, here assumed to be New Year's Day (see above). The plural sentence v. 9b, joined on to the singular sentences vv. 8, 9a, is a later addition restoring the connection with 23.27ff. If vv. 10, 11 designate the jubilee year as 'the year of the fifty-year period' (the position of the article shows that 'fifty-year' is here a fixed self-contained idea), this is not a different regulation; it is rather another method of calculation, by which the starting- and ending-point are reckoned in at the same time. Verse 10 says that in this year, declared to be 'holy', that is, set apart from the run of ordinary years, a d<sup>e</sup>rōr, a 'liberation' is to be proclaimed; d<sup>e</sup>rōr is a loan word from the Accadian (an)durāru = 'freeing from burdens', as was arranged from time to time by the kings of Mesopotamia. Leviticus 25 announces that such a d<sup>e</sup>rōr should regularly and automatically take place in the year of jubilee at the command of Yahweh, the owner of the land (cf. v. 23aβ); and it was to be in force for all the 'inhabitants' of the land, meaning here in a precise sense all those who were settled on and had a stake in the land, in practice the heads of families, who were to return in this year to their 'property' and their 'family', in so far as they had had to separate from them in the intervening period. The context shows that the legal concept of 'property' (Heb. '<sup>a</sup>ḥuzzā, really 'occupation'), cropping up for the first time in this later language, means a stake in the soil, signifying at the same time a bond with the large unit of kindred, and with families settled in enclosed groups. As the separation between 'property' and 'family' was wont to arise from indebtedness, a 'freeing from burdens' was the prerequisite for the 'return' and thus for the restoration of the order of things as originally constituted. Each jubilee year being also a sabbath year, vv. 11, 12 (here with plural address) repeat the sabbath-year regulations from vv. 4b, 5a (somewhat shortened), but with this difference, that the wild crops of this fallow year are allowed to the 'inhabitants' of the land themselves; thus the 'social' reason for the sabbath year (vv. 6, 7) is given up, and we find preserved a probably older stage of the sabbath-year regulations which forbade only a regular and systematic 'harvesting' and 'gathering', but not the use of the crops.

[13–16] In vv. 13–16 the leading theme, 'the return to property' (v. 13), with its assumptions and consequences, is looked at more precisely. As the separation from the 'property' was caused by a sale of the stake in the soil—made necessary as a rule by debt—this section deals with the sale of land. First of all v. 14—phrased in a very defective manner and doubtless with secondary enlargements—prohibits the 'oppression' of others in buying or selling land. There is to be no use of superior advantages, no exploitation of another's plight. Then vv. 15, 16 (now in the singular) open up the question of purchase-or-sale-price in view of the 'liberation' in the year of jubilee. The 'liberation' did not permit of an outright purchase or sale: it was rather a case (as v. 16b expressly recognizes) of the sale or purchase of the yearly produce (cf. also the phrasing in v. 15b). Thus in calculating the price—apart from the area and quality of the land —it was a question of taking into account the number of years to the next jubilee year. Verse 15a speaks of the 'number of years after the (last) jubilee' because this was the only fixed and conclusive method of reckoning the number of years to the next 'liberation'.

[17-23] The parenetic sentence v. 17 first repeats the prohibition against oppressing 'one another' (here, as in vv. 14, 15, *'āmīt*; cf. above p. 48), then moves on to the stereotyped singular sentence about 'fear of God' (cf. 19.14, 32 and 25.36, 43), and finally passes over into first person for Yahweh in the reminder clause. In vv. 18-23 further parenetic details have been drawn in, all constructed with Yahweh as the speaking subject. Verses 18, 19 promise in return for keeping these commandments a 'secure dwelling' in the land and a plentiful yield from it. In vv. 20-22 there follows in a 'legal' setting a very unusual discussion between Yahweh the law-giver and the person addressed by the law, reminiscent of occasional explanations by prophets to their audience (cf. e.g. Mal. 1.6ff.). To the objection that there might be nothing to eat (v. 20) in the fallow year, Yahweh answers with the promise of his 'blessing', which will produce a double yield in the previous year. This is the obvious meaning of the 'three years' in v. 21, for a usual 'normal' crop had to suffice for 'two (harvest) years'—the remainder of the year of harvest and the first part of the following year, until the in-gathering of the new harvest. Verse 22 disturbs the sense by the mention of the 'ninth year'; but this must be an addition, as is shown by the piling up of phrases with 'until'. It probably came in through a secondary reckoning by spring years, in which the produce from the sowing of the 'eighth' year (v. 22a) would not come in till the 'ninth' year. A very remarkable concluding sentence (v. 23) brings together and expresses the principle behind the jubilee-year regulations. It shows that the land was in general and in principle not to be sold, because it was Yahweh's property, which men might not dispose of as of private property. For men—in this case the Israelites—were (in a probably supplementary explanation, v. 23b) merely in the position of foreign guests or 'squatters', who could be entrusted with the use of something without

establishing a claim to ownership. But as land was in fact bought and sold in Israel, v. 23aα is so phrased that a purchase or sale might not take place to the exclusion of a claim of ownership (*s̆emîtût*, from *s̆mt*, really 'pledge to silence', that is, prohibition of a claim). Yahweh, as owner, exercised this claim through the law of reversion in the year of jubilee.

[24–55] The general introductory sentence in v. 24 begins the new theme of 'redemption', Hebrew *ge'ullā*. It is dealt with in a series of subdivisions, all beginning with the conditional clause 'if thy brother becomes poor' (vv. 25aα, 35aα, 39aα, 47aβ). This redemption, not in general tied down to any particular time, was something quite different from the jubilee-year provision for the reversion of land every forty-ninth year, which automatically involved a redemption. On the other hand the law of redemption, especially when it was a question of land, had material contacts with the year of jubilee; and so it was natural for Lev. 25 to deal also with the law of redemption. At all events this context raises points which have scarcely anything or nothing at all to do with the year of jubilee. It can therefore be assumed that the second half of Lev. 25 has as its basis an originally independent corpus of *ge'ullā* regulations, not in the first place directed to the jubilee year, and perhaps originally containing reference to the jubilee year only in its first and last sections. Its other sections were only brought into relationship with the year of jubilee in part and as occasion served, on the basis of the present context.

[25–30] In a case where an Israelite, through poverty (and in-debtedness) was compelled to sell land (throughout this section the word *āḥ* = 'brother', in the sense of member of the same family group, tribe, or race), the 'redeemer' (Heb. *gō'ēl*) had to step in, that is, a near relation who had to preserve the solidarity of the family group or kindred by paying the purchase-price to the buyer on his own account and thus getting back the piece of land that had been sold. This was not in order to retain it himself, but only to return it to the original owner. In the case of no redeemer being at hand, or the redeemer not being in a position to purchase, the seller himself, according to vv. 26, 27, could aspire to buy it back if—probably as a daily wage-earner—he could raise the necessary sum. This sum gradually diminished in any case, for, as v. 27 tells us—and here there is obvious agreement between the law of redemption and the jubilee-year law—it was not really the land that was sold, but only the yearly crops, whose value was to be deducted from the redemption-price. If, as seems probable, the reversion in the jubilee year provided for in v. 28 in the case of an inability to redeem land belongs to the original material of this section, then the sale price had simply to be spread over the years between then and the next jubilee year in order to arrive at the price of redemption. Behind the special regulations for house-ownership in walled cities (vv. 29–34) there already stands the contrast between ancient ('Canaanite') city-law and Israelite land-law. The distinction between walled cities and unwalled cities seems very simplistic, and must go back to the beginnings of Israelite settlement in the promised land. In the present context it is at all events assumed that Israelites were already dwelling in former Canaanite cities, had their own houses, and thus also had certain newly founded walled towns of their own where they lived side by side and farmed the land. According to Lev. 25 the old Canaanite city-law seems to have survived in the latter. Verse 31 shows that the Israelite land-law with the possibility of redemption and reversion in the jubilee year was only valid for the houses in open 'villages'. For houses in walled cities, on the other hand, there was 'normal' definitive buying and selling (v. 30aβ), with express exclusion of reversion in the jubilee year (v. 30b). The possibility of redemption was restricted to the short space of one year, leaving some doubt whether this meant the rest of the calendar year of sale (so apparently v. 29aβ), or a full year after the point of sale (so apparently v. 30aα). This delayed power of redemption looks like a small concession of the ancient city-law to Israelite custom. [32–34] Particularly to be noted is the passage appended to the special regulations in vv. 29–31, dealing with the laws of possession for the Levites, for it gives us some information on their special position, though it certainly does not explain the special character of the Levitical body, which is assumed to be common knowledge. The Levites had as their 'possession' (*'aḥuzzā*) only cities, but no stake in the soil of the country. The wording suggests that these were special 'Levite cities', occupied exclusively by Levites, though in practice it can only have been a matter of dwelling-rights in cities occupied by other kinds of people (cf. also Josh. 21.1–42). The Levites' house-ownership in the cities, according to v. 32, was an exception to the usual city-law (vv. 29, 30), in so far as there was no question of a redemption in the year of jubilee of a possession that had been sold (at any rate it is not mentioned). But probably a power of redemption without delay was assured, which according to the present wording extended beyond a jubilee year; and v. 34 forbids altogether any sale of the share belonging to the city-house-owning Levites in the *migrāš* (perhaps 'pastureland') apparently reckoned in with the city territory. The regulations are obviously in the interest of the maintenance of the Levites' 'possession'. Verse 33 is very hard to understand. To correct the transmitted text, apart from a negligible trifle, would seem a doubtful procedure in view of the difficulty of understanding it. It appears to posit the case of Levites who have bought something—a city house—from some other Israelites. Then someone else, on the grounds of the *geʾullā* law, redeems the object of sale (*gʾl* with *min* elsewhere only covered by the extended use of *gʾl*). In this case the 'liberation' of the jubilee year was to be valid, but with reversion not to the original owner but to the Levites, who in the meanwhile had entered by purchase into the possession. This must have been a quite unusual and exceptional ruling in the interests of the Levites.

[35–38] In vv. 35–38 there follows a section covering neither the jubilee year nor the *geʾullā*. Yet, as its introductory conditional clause shows (v. 35aα), it was taken up—even if secondarily—into the *geʾullā* sequences and so came into the jubilee-year regulations. It was linked in subject-matter to the *geʾullā* sequence by the case for the 'brother who has become poor'. This specifically meant—according to the present, but perhaps not the original, wording of vv. 35bβ— the 'stranger and sojourner'. Interest was forbidden on any gifts by way of loan; and here two separate words are used for 'interest . . . increase', the one (*nešek*), as v. 37 tells us, referring to the lending of money, the other (*marbīt*) to means of nourishment.

[39–46] The section vv. 39–46 also did not, it seems probable, originally concern the year of jubilee or in any way the *geʾullā*; but v. 39aα shows that it was taken up into the sequence of the regulations in favour of the 'brother who has become poor' and has come along with them into the present context. It deals with the case of an Israelite (*āḥ*) having to sell himself (not just his property) on account of debt. This made him in principle the property of his buyer—a slave. But—so the section lays down—he is not to be treated as such (v. 39b), but in the manner of a 'hired servant' or 'sojourner' (v. 40a), whose power to work was taken into account, but whose person was not in any way at one's disposal. The parenetic explanation in v. 42 announces that Yahweh himself claims these men as his 'slaves'; therefore other men might not regard them as their property. 'Normal' slavery is designated in v. 43a (cf. v. 46b) as 'ruling with harshness' and characterized by the word *perek* whose precise sense can no longer be defined. It can well be rendered 'forced labour' (following Ex. 1.13f., where it also occurs), and apparently means something like 'torture'. Israelites were only allowed to buy real slaves from foreign peoples (v. 44b passes to plural address) and (according to v. 45) from the descendants of the 'sojourners' living among the Israelites, who would thus mostly belong to foreign peoples working among the Israelites as merchants or artisans. It is here assumed that they did not sell themselves as slaves, but might in a given case (perhaps because of economic depression) offer their children for sale as slaves. In this whole context dealing with the treatment of slaves the passage vv. 40b, 41, treating of the manumission of the Israelite 'slaves' (and it might be their families) in the jubilee year and their return to their original circumstances (including the remission of their debts), looks out of place; and it is at least questionable whether it did not come in by the connection of the series on 'the brother who has become poor' with the jubilee-year regulations. In content, there is considerable tension between it and the 'slavery laws' of Ex. 21.1–11 and Deut. 15.12–18, by which a 'Hebrew' slave was to be set free after six years of service. A general freeing of slaves in the jubilee year might indicate progress beyond this older law of slavery in conjunction with the tendency, observable in the Old Testament, to ease the lot of the Israelite slave; but only in the cases where less than six years of slavery were outstanding till the next jubilee year. In many cases this can have had little essential value. It might be that the original form of vv. 39ff. (without vv. 40b, 41) tacitly assumed the validity of these slave-laws, and therefore did not deal with *geʾullā* and the jubilee year, but only with the treatment of slaves. Then, as a later addition, there came into the context of Lev. 25, rather mechanically, the reference to the jubilee year, which appears to ignore the older slave-laws.

[47–55] Verses 47–55 are different. Here, we are dealing with the practically certain case of an Israelite who has become poor selling himself to a foreigner of some substance living in the midst of Israel. Perhaps it was not possible to impose on such a person the requirement for manumission of slaves after six years' service. But one could still keep in mind the possibility of 'redemption' (*geʾullā*), which was indeed a 'business' matter, and one could put it as an obligation of the nearest relative of the victim (vv. 48b, 49a) to undertake the redemption; and one could encourage the victim himself in case of need to procure for himself in some way or other the means of effecting his own liberation (v. 49b). In what follows, in the case of manumission not being effected, the freeing of the slave in question is required in the year of jubilee (v. 54). In theory at any rate this aims at the goal of demanding freedom of the foreigner living among the Israelites, if not by observance of the older law of slavery, then by obedience to the jubilee-year regulations. With this assumption vv. 50–52, by analogy to the land-purchase regulations in vv. 16, 17 and 27, from the viewpoint of the jubilee year, deal with the assessment of the redemption-price for slaves by the yardstick of the number of years outstanding before the next jubilee year. Verse 50b shows incidentally that the value of the slaves' work was apparently to be reckoned according to the usual payment for a daily labourer, a regulation which would point to an agreement with the foreign purchaser. The phrasing in vv. 51b, 52b probably rests on the fact that in any case the redemption-price must have been lower than the purchase-price, since the work done in the interval by the man to be freed was to be taken into account. Furthermore, v. 53 requires even in this case that the slave should be humanely dealt with (by analogy with the 'day-labourer'), and 'oppression' and 'torture' (cf. vv. 40a, 43a, 46b) are forbidden. This last is with the reflection that ill-treatment of an Israelite slave by a foreigner would take place in front of the Israelites, and would therefore have a particularly damaging effect. The parenetic sentence v. 55 may be compared with v. 42.

[26.1, 2] The appendix prohibiting the worship of idols and the making of idols, and the sharpening of the sabbath commands (26.1, 2) is of a quite general nature and has no special relationship to what has gone before.

## (*l*) THE ANNOUNCEMENT OF REWARDS AND PUNISHMENTS: 26.3–46

26 ³'If you walk in my statutes and observe my commandments and do them, ⁴then I will give you your rains in their season, and the land shall yield its increase, and the trees of the field shall yield their fruit. ⁵And your threshing shall last to the time of vintage, and the vintage shall last to the time for sowing; and you shall eat your bread to the full, and dwell in your land securely. ⁶And I will give peace in the land, and you shall lie down, and none shall make you afraid; and I will remove evil beasts from the land, and the sword shall not go through your land. ⁷And you shall chase your enemies, and they shall

L.–N

fall before you by the sword. ⁸Five of you shall chase a hundred, and a hundred of you shall chase ten thousand; and your enemies shall fall before you by the sword. ⁹And I will have regard for you and make you fruitful and multiply you, and will confirm my covenant with you. ¹⁰And you shall eat old store long kept, and you shall clear out the old to make way for the new. ¹¹And I will make my abode among you, and my soul shall not abhor you. ¹²And I will walk among you, and will be your God, and you shall be my people. ¹³I am the Lord your God, who brought you forth out of the land of Egypt, that you should not be their slaves; and I have broken the bars of your yoke and made you walk erect.

14 'But if you will not hearken to me, and will not do all these commandments, ¹⁵if you spurn my statutes, and if your soul abhors my ordinances, so that you will not do all my commandments, but break my covenant, ¹⁶I will do this to you: I will appoint over you sudden terror, consumption, and fever that waste the eyes and cause life to pine away. And you shall sow your seed in vain, for your enemies shall eat it; ¹⁷I will set my face against you, and you shall be smitten before your enemies; those who hate you shall rule over you, and you shall flee when none pursues you. ¹⁸And if in spite of this you will not hearken to me, then I will chastise you again sevenfold for your sins, ¹⁹and I will break the pride of your power, and I will make your heavens like iron and your earth like brass; ²⁰and your strength shall be spent in vain, for your land shall not yield its increase, and the trees of the land shall not yield their fruit.

21 'Then if you walk contrary to me, and will not hearken to me, I will bring more plagues upon you, sevenfold as many as your sins. ²²And I will let loose the wild beasts among you, which shall rob you of your children, and destroy your cattle, and make you few in number, so that your ways shall become desolate.

23 'And if by this discipline you are not turned to me, but walk contrary to me, ²⁴then I also will walk contrary to you, and I myself will smite you sevenfold for your sins. ²⁵And I will bring a sword upon you, that shall execute vengeance for the covenant; and if you gather within your cities I will send pestilence among you, and you shall be delivered into the hand of the enemy. ²⁶When I break your staff of bread, ten women shall bake your bread in one oven, and shall deliver your bread again by weight; and you shall eat, and not be satisfied.

27 'And if in spite of this you will not hearken to me, but walk contrary to me, ²⁸then I will walk contrary to you in fury, and chastise you myself sevenfold for your sins. ²⁹You shall eat the flesh of your sons, and you shall eat the flesh of your daughters. ³⁰And I will destroy your high places, and cut down your incense altars, and cast your dead bodies upon the dead bodies of your idols; and my soul will abhor you. ³¹And I will lay your cities waste, and will make your sanctuaries desolate, and I will not smell your pleasing odours. ³²And I will devastate the land, so that your enemies who settle in it shall be astonished at it. ³³And I will scatter you among the nations, and I will unsheathe the sword after you

and your land shall be a desolation, and your cities shall be a waste. [34]Then the land shall enjoy* its sabbaths as long as it lies desolate, while you are in your enemies' land; then the land shall rest, and enjoy* its sabbaths. [35]As long as it lies desolate it shall have rest, the rest which it had not in your sabbaths when you dwelt upon it.

36 'And as for those of you that are left, I will send faintness into their hearts in the lands of their enemies; the sound of a driven leaf shall put them to flight, and they shall flee as one flees from the sword, and they shall fall when none pursues. [37]They shall stumble over one another, as if to escape a sword, though none pursues; and you shall have no power to stand before your enemies. [38]And you shall perish among the nations, and the land of your enemies shall eat you up.[39]And those of you that are left shall pine away in your enemies' lands because of their iniquity; and also because of the iniquities of their fathers they shall pine away like them.

40 'But if they confess their iniquity and the iniquity of their fathers in their treachery which they committed against me, and also in walking contrary to me, [41]so that I walked contrary to them and brought them into the land of their enemies; if then their uncircumcised heart is humbled and they make amends for their iniquity; [42]then I will remember [my covenant with] Jacob, and I will remember [my covenant with] Isaac and [my covenant with] Abraham, and I will remember the land. [43]But the land shall be left by them, and enjoy* its sabbaths while it lies desolate without them; and they shall make amends for their iniquity, because they spurned my ordinances, and their soul abhorred my statutes. [44]Yet for all that, when they are in the land of their enemies, I will not spurn them, neither will I abhor them so as to destroy them utterly and break my covenant with them; for I am the LORD their God; [45]but I will for their sake remember the covenant with their forefathers, whom I brought forth out of the land of Egypt in the sight of the nations, that I might be their God: I am the LORD.'

46 These are the statutes and ordinances and laws which the LORD made between him and the people of Israel on Mount Sinai by Moses.

With the great announcement of reward or punishment for obedience or disobedience respectively this book of laws, the Holiness Code, closes, just as the Deuteronomic law does with the 'blessing' and 'cursing' chapter, Deut. 28. These two pieces are nearly related in function, structure and content. All the same, in spite of occasional verbal correspondence, no literary dependence is to be assumed, in one direction or in the other. They go too much their own ways within the common framework for this to be possible, quite apart from some more formal differences in the use (Deut. 28) or absence (Lev. 26) of the terms 'blessing' or 'cursing', or in singular (basically

*Or 'pay for'.

Deut. 28) or plural (Lev. 26) address. This circumstance shows that both pieces are following an older tradition which they each stamp with their own special character. Several different traditional elements have, in fact, entered into both of them, no longer clearly separable from one another, yet still clearly recognizable. It was customary in the Ancient East to close the text of contracts with express maledictions directed against anyone breaking the agreement, by which these agreements were put under the protection of the deities specified for the carrying out of the curse and for the efficiency of the maledictory sentences themselves. This use of conditional cursing was not foreign to the Old Testament either, as shown especially by the perhaps fairly ancient series of twelve maledictions in Deut. 27.15–26. There, each potential offender against a particular prohibition is put under the power of a generally expressed curse. The special weight of the cursing in this context can be gathered from the fact that the section on the announcement of punishments, both in Deut. 28 and Lev. 26, and thus in the presumably older tradition, is notably more extensive than the leading section of blessings and rewards. This disproportion can scarcely be traced back only to secondary accretions to the former, even when reckoning with the fact that in times of growing danger and irrupting catastrophe in the history of Israel the theme of God's curse was one likely to invite secondary expansion. Now the longer negative portion is preceded by a shorter and positive portion. It must have suggested itself to set an announcement of rewards over against an announcement of punishments, even if neither covenants nor laws needed any such incentive for their coming into or remaining in force. They could claim obedience and observance independently of any proffered reward. Even the famous ancient Babylonian law-book of Hammurabi prefaces its far-reaching announcement of curses against any future scorners of the law with a short announcement of blessings on those who in the future will obey the law. In the Old Testament the passage Deut. 27.11–13, unfortunately of somewhat uncertain origin, refers to a blessing and cursing ceremony (also Josh. 8.30–35) to be performed at Shechem, in which the 'two ways' of blessing or of cursing for Israel were clearly put forward. These, moreover, were set before the assembled 'people' as 'blessing' or 'cursing' for obedience or disobedience to their God, in specific announcements made by public proclamation. In this process use was probably made of definite fixed phraseology, usable again and again; and Deut. 28 and Lev.

26 contain a deposit of sentences that give the impression of ancient traditional fixed formulae. It must be admitted that this juxtaposition of blessings and cursings is in some tension with the Old Testament saying that God's blessing was freely vouchsafed to Israel, quite independently of Israel's prior obedience. The gift of the land, for example, which, along with its produce, plays a considerable part in the blessings and cursings announcement, was the fulfilment of a divine promise made without preconditions: it did not need to be earnt by Israel as a 'reward', and could only be forfeited by unfaithfulness. The prominence given by this stress to this blessing and cursing section gives full weight to this matter. There appears as a further traditional element in this section—giving it thereby additional importance—a schematic enumeration of plagues (cf. the formal new starts in vv. 18, 21, 23–24a, 27–28; also vv. 36aα, 39aα). This schedule appears in the Old Testament in a variety of contexts. First it is the 'plagues of Egypt' in Ex. 7–11, recounted in the framework of an historical narrative. Then secondly, prophets, looking back on the history of Israel, have from time to time spoken of a series of divinely sent plagues calculated to bring Israel back into obedience, yet not taken by them as an occasion for repentance (Amos 4.6ff.; Isa. 9.7ff. and 5.25ff.). In Lev. 26 the list of plagues occurs in the context of the punishment threats for the future (cf. Ezek. 5.10–17, with verbal correspondence in parts, and elsewhere). Such a list of plagues, from whatever viewpoint it arose, must contemplate a progressive stepping-up in the severity of the plagues; and such a stepping-up is recognizable each time towards the end of the list. Yet it is remarkable that in all the instances mentioned the stepping-up does not seem to be carried through consistently from the beginning.

Leviticus 26 is not quite a unity in form. Particularly, the end of second person plural address and the transition to the third plural for 'the remnant' marks off the section vv. 40–45—which in point of content passes to a new theme—from what has gone before. In the main part of the chapter, however, sentences occur between the personal address portions (Yahweh first person, Israel second person plural) couched in impersonal form. Their subject is something which is effective or ineffective towards the 'cursing' or 'blessing' (e.g. v. 4b with its negative counterpart v. 20b, where the second plural address intrudes with the help of a suffix). It is very probable that these impersonal sentences contain the oldest elements from the tradition, fixed 'blessing' and 'cursing' formulae. All these disparities cannot indeed give cause for an attempt to divide the material into different 'layers' or 'sources' from a literary-critical point of view. Rather, we are confronted—apart from odd items—with a relative unity, though one that has been somewhat unsystematically built up out of a variety of traditional fragments.

[3–13] The announcements of reward (vv. 4–13) first of all deal with the fruitfulness and 'security' of life in the promised land. Whilst v. 4 promises the regular 'normal' crop from the land, v. 5a appears to go beyond this (cf. Amos 9.13) and promises an alteration in 'nature' bordering on the miraculous. Probably, however, as the adjoining and summary sentence v. 5bα shows, it only means such a rich yield that the threshing of the corn will last on till grape-gathering begins. This in its turn, with the pressing and making of oil and wine, will go on so long that it will soon be time to think once more of sowing the new crops. 'Securely' and 'peace' (vv. 5bβ, 6a) refer to internal conditions and mean presumably the absence of evil men and dangerous wild beasts (this last specifically in v. 6bα). The passage vv. 6bβ–8 deals quite generally with external enemies; they will not enter the land at all (v. 6bβ); and if—perhaps on the borders —warlike affrays should arise, vv. 7, 8 promise that Israel shall be speedily and decisively victorious (cf.—with different figures— Deut. 32.30; Josh. 23.10—and—with reversed 'signs'—Isa. 30.17). In vv. 9, 11, 12 God promises Israel, in the event of their obedience, to 'turn his face' to them, with consequences rich in blessing, the maintenance of his covenant (this word in its basic meaning occurs in Leviticus only here, in ch. 26), the presence of his 'dwelling', i.e. his sanctuary, in the midst of Israel, and the continuance of the relationship between God and his people—in short, the enduring presence of Israel's true ground of existence. Verse 10 seems an intruder in between these sentences, with its reversion to the overflowing richness of the corn-yield; and one might take it for a later addition if one felt bound to make more or less strict demands of logical sequence in the structure of this 'blessing' section. The unusually detailed reference to Israel's liberation from the bondage in Egypt (v. 13), with its reminder of God's grace and might, makes a powerful ending to the whole section.

[14–17] After extensively linked conditional clauses in vv. 14, 15, the announcement of punishments (vv. 14ff.) begins, with the pro-clamation of a group of plagues (v. 16aβ) which was obviously traditional (cf. the occurrence of the rare words for 'consumption' and 'fever', here only and in Deut. 28.22, where they occur in the course of a longer list of similar words). There then follow in the first division the threats of sowing in vain and complete collapse before the attacks of enemies. Verse 16bα, with its 'sowing in vain', at first seems to suggest that the land would become unfruitful; but vv. 16bβ, 17 at once explain that the victorious enemies would appropriate the entire produce of the land. [18–20] Verse 18, with a new beginning, introduces the next division. The announced chastisement goes back perhaps to a traditional 'seven-plague-scheme' in the framework of a 'plague-series' that has been handed down (cf. above p. 197). Here, the number seven simply expresses the extensiveness and completeness of the divine chastisement. For the rest, this division deals in vv. 19b, 20 with the unfruitfulness of the land. [21–22] Verses 21, 22 threaten that wild beasts will get the upper hand, destroying the children, the domestic animals and the herds, and finally decimating the grown-up population, thus reducing the land to a wilderness. [23–26] Verses 23–26 are concerned again with enemy attacks compelling the population to withdraw to the fortified cities, where pestilence will break out and famine in, so that they will have to capitulate before their enemies. The 'breaking of the staff of bread' (v. 26; the same expression in Ezek. 4.16; 5.16; 14.13; Ps. 105.16) is probably a metaphorical expression, meaning that food is like a staff to lean upon in order to walk more securely; cf. the expression 'to support oneself with a morsel of bread' = 'to fortify oneself (with a meal)' in Gen. 18.5; Judg. 19.5, 8; I Kings 13.7. If ten women will only need one oven for their daily baking (v. 26aβ), although normally each family had its own oven, that means that only a tenth of the normal needs would be baked and that it will therefore only be worth while to heat one oven. [27–35] Verses 27ff. take up once more the distress of a siege, which may lead to the desperation of cannibalism (cf. II Kings 6.28f.; Jer. 19.9; Ezek. 5.10, etc.). In connection with this the theme of destructive defeat is taken up in broader detail. This and the foregoing do not produce anything indicating a specific historical situation belonging to one particular moment; rather do they express experiences that Israel must have undergone again and again from the beginning of her history, or at least since the Syrian wars of the ninth century BC. Yet the present concentration on this subject and especially the focusing on the element of deportation points to the end of the period of monarchy in Judah as a likely historical background. The complete devastation of the land will destroy according to vv. 30, 31 the 'high places' (= local cultic shrines) and furnishings (*hammān* perhaps = 'small altar of incense'; again in Ezek. 6.4, etc.) of the forbidden foreign cults (*peger*, really 'bodies', perhaps with a double meaning = 'corpses' and 'memorial pillars'; hence the idols' 'corpses'). The depopulation of the country through deportation (v. 23) is represented as so complete that the land is thought of as going completely out of cultivation in the future—in contrast to the historical reality—so that it will have no 'sabbath-years' (vv. 34, 35), of which it had clearly (in contradiction to 25.2b–7) been deprived for a long while. Thus the land will be compensated for its loss of the sabbath-years (so v. 34a), and will accordingly be able to compensate Yahweh for what it has also owed him for all the sabbath-years that were missing (so presumably v. 34bβ, following 25.2b, 4aβ). [36–45] 'Those who are left' from the catastrophe and are now deported, as vv. 36, 37 describe in most lively and vivid fashion, will be haunted by anxiety and the imaginary fear of pursuit in the foreign land, and shall perish (v. 38). Those who yet remain will gradually decline, as v. 39a tells us. Verse 39b—obviously an addition—says that even the following generations will have to share this fate. These following generations, some of whom will remain in spite of all this, now form the subject of vv. 40–45. Their future acknowledgment of guilt and their self-abasement (v. 41b) will be able to bring about a change. This behaviour will be accounted by Yahweh as 'amendment' for their 'iniquity' (v. 41bβ), so that he will once more 'remember' for good the patriarchs. The threefold repetition of 'my covenant' in v. 42 does not fit in at all with the syntax and is probably a secondary addition. Yahweh will also 'remember' the land (v. 42bβ). This reference to the patriarchs to whom once upon a time the promises of descendants and land had been given, and the mention of the land that was once put at the disposal of Israel, means that a new giving of land in the future and a gathering together and return of that which had been scattered is contemplated, although this is not stated in unequivocal terms. There is thus only an indication of quite indefinite possibilities in the future; and it is expressly added (v. 43) that its realization will still have to wait until the land has fulfilled over an indefinitely long time the 'sabbath-years' that had been denied to it. Only one thing is firmly stated in regard to the future return of the 'remnant': Yahweh will not break his covenant and will not destroy Israel completely; and furthermore he will remain her God, even as he has been since the exodus from Egypt. This must for the moment be sufficient for Israel. This glimpse of the future, as it appears from v. 30, might be best explained by the still direct impact of the catastrophes leading to the end of Judah as a state and depopulating the land for a long time to come, and by the deportations which took parts of the population into 'the land of their enemies'; that is to say, by a time in which definite expectations of return might be no longer entertained (as in Jer. 28.2–4), and when it was too soon to raise them afresh.

# VII

## AN APPENDIX ON DEDICATORY GIFTS

### Lev. 27.1–34

27 ¹The LORD said to Moses, ²'Say to the people of Israel, When a man makes a special vow of persons to the LORD at your valuation, ³then your valuation of a male from twenty years old up to sixty years old shall be fifty shekels of silver, according to the shekel of the sanctuary. ⁴If the person is a female, your valuation shall be thirty shekels. ⁵If the person is from five years old up to twenty years old, your valuation shall be for a male twenty shekels, and for a female ten shekels. ⁶If the person is from a month old up to five years old, your valuation shall be for a male five shekels of silver, and for a female your valuation shall be three shekels of silver. ⁷And if the person is sixty years old and upward, then your valuation for a male shall be fifteen shekels, and for a female ten shekels. ⁸And if a man is too poor to pay your valuation, then he shall bring the person before the priest, and the priest shall value him; according to the ability of him who vowed the priest shall value him.

9 'If it is an animal such as men offer as an offering to the LORD, all of such that any man gives to the LORD is holy. ¹⁰He shall not substitute anything for it or exchange it, a good for a bad, or a bad for a good; and if he makes any exchange of beast for beast, then both it and that for which it is exchanged shall be holy. ¹¹And if it is an unclean animal such as is not offered as an offering to the LORD, then the man shall bring the animal before the priest, ¹²and the priest shall value it as either good or bad; as you, the priest, value it, so it shall be. ¹³But if he wishes to redeem it, he shall add a fifth to the valuation.

14 'When a man dedicates his house to be holy to the LORD, the priest shall value it as either good or bad; as the priest values it, so it shall stand. ¹⁵And if he who dedicates it wishes to redeem his house, he shall add a fifth of the valuation in money to it, and it shall be his. ¹⁶If a man dedicates to the LORD part of the land which is his by inheritance, then your valuation shall be according to the seed for it; a sowing of a homer of barley shall be valued at fifty shekels of silver. ¹⁷If he dedicates his field from the year of jubilee, it shall stand at your

full valuation; ¹⁸but if he dedicates his field after the jubilee, then the priest shall compute the money-value for it according to the years that remain until the year of jubilee, and a deduction shall be made from your valuation. ¹⁹And if he who dedicates the field wishes to redeem it, then he shall add a fifth of the valuation in money to it, and it shall remain his. ²⁰But if he does not wish to redeem the field, or if he has sold the field to another man, it shall not be redeemed any more; ²¹but the field, when it is released in the jubilee, shall be holy to the LORD, as a field that has been devoted; the priest shall be in possession of it. ²²If he dedicates to the LORD a field which he has bought, which is not a part of his possession by inheritance, ²³then the priest shall compute the valuation for it up to the year of jubilee, and the man shall give the amount of the valuation on that day as a holy thing to the LORD. ²⁴In the year of jubilee the field shall return to him from whom it was bought, to whom the land belongs as a possession by inheritance. ²⁵Every valuation shall be according to the shekel of the sanctuary: twenty gerahs shall make a shekel.

26 'But a firstling of animals, which as a firstling belongs to the LORD, no man may dedicate; whether ox or sheep, it is the LORD's. ²⁷And if it is an unclean animal, then he shall buy it back at your valuation, and add a fifth to it; or, if it is not redeemed, it shall be sold at its valuation. ²⁸But no devoted thing that a man devotes to the LORD, of anything that he has, whether of man or beast, or of his inherited field, shall be sold or redeemed; every devoted thing is most holy to the LORD. ²⁹No one devoted, who is to be utterly destroyed from among men, shall be ransomed; he shall be put to death.

30 'All the tithe of the land, whether of the seed of the land or of the fruit of the trees, is the LORD's; it is holy to the LORD. ³¹If a man wishes to redeem any of his tithe, he shall add a fifth to it. ³²And all the tithe of herds and flocks, every tenth animal of all that pass under the herdsman's staff, shall be holy to the LORD. ³³A man shall not inquire whether it is good or bad, neither shall he exchange it; and if he exchanges it, then both it and that for which it is exchanged shall be holy; it shall not be redeemed.'

34 These are the commandments which the LORD commanded Moses for the people of Israel on Mount Sinai.

THIS CHAPTER, COMING after the great reward and punishment announcement of ch. 26, is clearly a later supplement. It refers to the Holiness Code, and particularly to jubilee-year regulations, but has no special connections in content. It was probably not added to the legal collection of the Holiness Code when it was still separate, but may have come in secondarily to the larger combined complex of the cultic regulations in Leviticus, especially as some connections exist beyond the Holiness Code with other portions of Leviticus. Moreover, it is a piece more or less self-contained in subject-matter, at one time probably a separate unit, before incorporation into its present context, and should be examined as such. Its introductory and concluding formulae (vv. 1, 2a and 34) link it in stereotyped manner on to the Law-giving at Sinai; but its contents have no reference to this situation and equally little to any particular historical or cultic situation, apart from the fact that Israel is assumed to be settled in the land. Throughout there is quite general mention of 'the priest'.

The subject dealt with is freewill gifts of various kinds 'to Yahweh'. Particularly striking here is the big part played by the money-valuation of such gifts. One might think that 'accounts' were to be kept at the sanctuary in money-value for the freewill offerers; but it is much more likely that the freewill dedicatory gifts were no longer bestowed in kind but in money-equivalent. This had obviously, as a matter of fact, taken place at least in some of the gifts provided. Here, there is a noteworthy connection with the *'āšām* regulations in 5.14–6.7, and it is not by chance that the technical expression met with there, (*b^e*)*'erk^ekā*, also recurs frequently in Lev. 27 (cf. above pp. 46f.). With this, however, we have reached a stage of considerably advanced 'secularization' (cf. II Kings 12.5) of the cultic apparatus. It is true that Lev. 27 does not seem to envisage a wholesale and consistent conversion of dedicatory gifts into their corresponding money-values. The original dedication of gifts in kind is still at work here, concurrently with the money-reckoning; and in places it is not clear what is really intended. Perhaps in practice there was provision for gifts both in money and in kind. But there is a clearly recognizable tendency to convert dedicatory gifts into money on an extensive scale.

[2–8] Verses 2aβb–8 deal with the dedication of 'persons' to Yahweh, i.e. to a sanctuary or to the sanctuary, by reason of a vow (cf. I Sam. 1.11). Such persons were originally set apart for the performance of auxiliary cultic services. Leviticus 27 now clearly provides for release from the fulfilment of such a vow through a money-payment. For the regulation in v. 8, in reference to the 'impoverishment' of an Israelite who has made such a vow, allowing the priest to assess the fulfilment of the vow at a level consistent with the offerer's means, that is, 'more cheaply', was only applied in the case of money-payment. Besides, this regulation reckons with current —perhaps yearly—payments in fulfilment of the vow. The latter is also assumed in the accurately differentiated scale of money-values for people dedicated by vows (vv. 3–7). This is calculated according to age and sex. For females, the value is set at half of that for males, the fractions counting as the next whole number above. The essential basis of this assessment lies apparently in the valuation of the person's worth in terms of work at the moment in question. For this valuation only makes sense in respect to regular payments. Once-and-for-all payments would have required the highest value to be set on children, with their longer expectation of life. It is not very clear how in the case of people over 60 years old (v. 7) the fulfilment of a vow concerning them could still be due; it must much more have concerned people previously dedicated by reason of a vow and still requiring payment on the part of their family.

[9–13] Verses 9–13 deal with the intended gift of an animal to the sanctuary, for any reason, but not expressly in fulfilment of a vow. Here a natural distinction is made between offerable (v. 9a), i.e. 'clean', and 'unclean', and therefore non-offerable, animals (v. 11a). For the latter, not being cultically usable, a money-payment provided on the basis of a balanced valuation by the priest (v. 12a) 'between high and low', literally 'between good and evil'. This was to be final (v. 12b). The animal was then to be taken before the priest, who performed over it a symbolic act of offering (v. 11b). As 'clean' animals did not need any such valuation, the intention here must be a dedicatory gift in kind. For this the only requirement is the complete handing over into the sphere of the 'holy', that is, into possession of the sanctuary (v. 9b). Verse 10a forbids any subsequent exchange of the dedicated animal for another one. In case of infringement, both animals could be forfeited to the sanctuary as a punishment for attempted dishonesty (v. 10b). The 'redemption' provided in v. 13 can also only apply to an actually brought and therefore 'clean' animal. In this case a money-valuation was required; and as a compensation for the subsequent recall of the dedication a supplement to the money-valuation had to be paid.

[14–24] This section on the dedication of houses and plots of land (vv. 14–24) is particularly difficult. Actual gifts and payment in money-value seem to run side by side. On the dedication of a house into the possession of the sanctuary an absolute valuation on average worth ('between high and low') [RSV: 'either good or bad'] is to be made by the priest (v. 14). This appears to contemplate a substitute for the dedicatory gift in terms of money-value, unless from the start—as v. 15 expressly states—a later 'redemption' was contemplated which could only occur in the case of an actual gift, requiring a supplementary payment on top of the assessed value. Even more complicated is the case of dedicated plots of land. Here, the jubilee-year regulations on the reversion of landed possessions had to be taken into account, which strangely enough were to be equally valid for dedications to the sanctuary, for in principle no one could dispose of his land beyond the next jubilee year. Verse 16 first fixes as the standard for land-valuation its seed-capacity and its yield-capacity. The unit of measurement is the *homer* of seed-barley (in dry measure about 11 bushels). Verses 17, 18 indicate that the money-value was to be reckoned by the number of cropping years to the next jubilee. The wording suggests that the money-value given in v. 16b$\beta$ should be valid for the full jubilee period and must in given cases be reduced (v. 18b). However, it appears remarkably low; and v. 23b envisages that in any case the money substitute for dedicated pieces of land would be paid yearly. All this appears to indicate that v. 16 is dealing with dedications in money-value and yearly payments till the year of jubilee. Regard for the closeness or distance of the jubilee year had then no effect on fixing the money-value. It was only of importance for the case foreseen in v. 19 of an actual gift involving a possible 'redemption' before the next jubilee year, for which the punitive supplement of a fifth of the value had to be paid. Verses 20, 21 are also presumably dealing with actual gifts; and they pose the case of someone dishonestly selling to someone else his piece of land which he has brought as a dedicatory gift, without having redeemed it and therefore without being in a position to dispose of it. Nevertheless he pockets the purchase-price. In this case, by way of punishment, he was to lose his right of redemption (v. 20b) and likewise the jubilee-year reversion (v. 21a$\alpha$). This meant that the land in question reverted in perpetuity to the sanctuary, or to the priest, and remained its property, as was the case with goods under a 'ban' (v. 21a$\beta$). There is no further reference to the swindled purchaser. Verses 22-24 are concerned with someone who offers a piece of land purchased by him to the sanctuary, as a dedicatory gift. Here, it is a question of money-value, and the priest had to assess this with regard to the number of years outstanding till the next jubilee year. Strangely enough, this sum of money had to be paid at once to its full amount (v. 23b), because such a dedicatory gift ran on in principle to the next jubilee year, though exposed to the right of redemption by the seller and real owner, realizable at any time before the jubilee year. It is implied at the same time that with dedicatory gifts from a man's own possessions, the money-payments, if instead of the actual dedication, would customarily be paid at regular intervals. Appropriately, then, in the jubilee year, the land in question reverted not to the dedicator, but to the real and original owner.

[25] To all the preceding v. 25 adds the observation that for all reckonings of money-value the cultic shekel-weight at 20 *gera* (the smallest recognized unit of weight) should be the basis (cf. Ex. 30.13; Ezek. 45.12); and alongside of these there was a secular shekel-weight for all ordinary commercial use (cf. Gen. 23.16).

[26–33] In vv. 26–33 are appended further observations on what could not be presented as dedicatory gifts because it belonged in any case to God. This was true of the first-born of domestic animals or animals from the herd, who in the case of 'clean' ones were to be presented without qualification (cf. Num. 18.17, 18, etc.). If 'unclean', they did not by the present regulations come under the ruling of Ex. 13.1, 2, 12, 13; 34.19, 20a, but were to be 'released' by a money-payment; or, as v. 27b adds in what is probably a supplement, if not 'redeemed' they were to be handed over to the sanctuary for sale. Verses 28, 29 give the same ruling for every 'devoted thing', the inalienable and unredeemable property of Yahweh, i.e. of the sanctuary. Originally all money-booty captured in the 'holy war' was reckoned as 'devoted'. Here, where an individual appears as the dedicating subject of devoted goods and land is also named as a possible 'devoted' possession, it can no longer be a question of 'holy war'; it must signify rather that someone could be sentenced to surrender his property or parts of it as 'devoted' possessions. Verse 29 implies as an echo of the ancient rigorous commandment (cf. I Sam. 15) that men belonging to this 'devoted' property had to be put to death without any possibility of redemption. Even the 'tithe' which belonged in any case to Yahweh could not, according to vv. 30–33, be offered as a freewill dedicatory gift. Verses 30, 31 provide—at all events for the tithe of the field-crops and orchards—that it could be redeemed by a money-payment, plus a supplement over and above the real value. (Contrast the regulations in Deut. 14.22–26 and Num. 18.20–32.) This does not apply to the tithe of domestic and herd animals (vv. 32, 33); these verses contemplate a gift in kind, to be effected by an automatic selection—not made very clear—of every tenth animal, for presentation to the sanctuary. It can no longer be made out with any certainty whether the observation in v. 32aβ refers to the selection procedure, meaning that the shepherd let the animals pass by in some narrow passage-way 'under his staff' and simply picked out each tenth one in some fashion; or whether this observation refers to all animals in general grazing under the supervision of a shepherd. At all events v. 33 forbids any later exchange of animals picked out for surrender as tithe in order to serve some private ends. In this case, following the ruling of v. 10b, both animals—the one picked out and the one exchanged for it—became the property of the sanctuary without possibility of redemption. The viewpoint governing the whole is that the animals marked off for the tithe could in no case be considered for freewill dedicatory giving.